Strategy for Political Stability

By

Uchenna Nwankwo

Centrist Books

i

Published by

Centrist Books – An Imprint of Centrist Productions Limited
19, Labande Street, Ikeja, Lagos, Nigeria
centristbooks@yahoo.com
WhatsApp (Tel): +234 8118195950

ISBN: 9781694103574

ALSO BY UCHENNA NWANKWO

Economic Agenda for Nigeria (1992)
Overcoming Our Poverty (1995)
Anatomy of Politics in Igboland (1999)
On National Reconciliation and Development (2002)
Way Forward for Ndigbo (2003)
Zik, Ndi-igbo and their Southern Neighbours (2013)
Shadows of Biafra (2018)
Pro-Biafra Movements, Ohanaeze & the Future of Nigeria (2018)
The Centrist Manifesto (2019)

"Only he who attempts the absurd is capable of achieving
the impossible."
— *Miguel de Unamuno (Sept. 29, 1864 to Dec. 31, 1936)*

DEDICATION

To all men of goodwill and candour

PREFACE

Today's world is scorched with civil strife, political insurgencies, organised crime, injustice, want, and above all international tension and terrorism. The spate of mass killings, liquidations, arrests, persecutions and tortures is appalling. The plight of man everywhere is in fact chaotic.

At issue are the old and basic questions of relations of production, socio-economic, socio-political, cultural and international relationships. These problems together constitute a potential source for the destruction of mankind. They have already brought about the demise of nations and the instability of many political entities while promoting the general insecurity and suppression of the individual.

This book is concerned with the above issues, with particular reference to the Nigerian question.

Indeed, it has to be observed that developments since the first publication of this book or the collapse of Soviet communism thirty years ago, have been even more debilitating and in fact appalling. In this revised edition therefore, we reflect on some of these developments as well as seek deeper solutions and avenues for enhanced management and containment of the problems.

UN   **18 December 2019**

TABLE OF CONTENTS

PART I
GENERAL FORMAT

CHAPTER I

THE VEXED QUESTION OF SOCIAL EGALITARIANISM

One of the central issues that has given rise to the development of various ideologies in the recent history of mankind is the concept of egalitarianism. This concept seeks to define the conditions that ensure an equitable or fair distribution of social wealth amongst members of a society. It is portrayed as the guiding principle in all existing modes of socio-economic and political organisations.

Pervasive as the concept has been rendered in sociocultural and political analysis, it is ironical that no concept is as controversial. It neither has any universally accepted definition nor mode of measurement. Most interpretations of the concept are based on emotional or subjective traits; thus making objective discussion of the subject difficult. Even more disturbing is the fact that there is disagreement as to what should be truly construed as the social wealth or social goods for whose distribution men are apt to clamour for. One is therefore, faced with a threesome question, namely:

(a) What indeed are the social goods?

(b) What constitutes a fair distribution of these goods? and (c) How can the fair distribution be achieved in society today?

For a meaningful examination of the above questions, it is pertinent to look back at the ways mankind tried over the centuries to resolve the questions.

First, we shall give a quick review of the major ideological theories of yesteryears. Subsequently, we will examine their exploits and applicability to the realities of today.

COMMUNISM

Communism arose as a direct challenge of the prevailing economic and political order in the 19th century Europe. During this period, the plight of the working class was to say the least, horrible, while the nobility and owners of industrial plants and other means of production and exchange lived in immense affluence and leisure.

Karl Marx (1818 - 1883) is generally regarded as the father of this movement having written the treatise upon which the movement was founded. Marx was dissatisfied with the status quo; the existence of widely separated social classes and was irked that the worker was not getting adequate returns for his labour. He had noted the rise to power of the middle class starting from the Magna Carta[1] through Cromwell,[2] and above all, that the 18th century French revolution had automatically "transferred social dominance from the nobility and the clergy to the industrial and commercial middle-class; it had created the state as a typical organ of middle-class repression and exploitations; and its philosophy the system of natural rights in politics and economics the ideal justification and rationalization of the middle-class' right to exploit the worker".[3]

Marx felt that these revolutions signalled the beginning of a process which would ultimately transfer economic power to the people, the masses or the lower classes.[4] In other words, he thought that just as political power had moved from the monarchs to the aristocrats and then down

---

1. Magna Carte – In 1215, rebellious English nobles forced King John to sign a document – the Magna Carta. This brought about curtailment of the King's power and led to decline of absolute Monarchy.
2. Cromwell, Oliver – the 17th Century English General who led the resistance that defeated King Charles I of England, culminating in the establishment of the structure of individual liberties and eventually to democratic self-government in Britain.
3. George H. Sabine and Thomas L. Thorson, *A History of Political Theory*, Dryden Press, Hinsdale Illinois, 4th Edition, 1973. Pg. 683
4. Ibid. Page 452; 682—684.

to the people, so would economic power move down the line until a state of classlessness appears. Thus he felt that just as some philosophy guided the realisation of the earlier political revolutions so would the people need a philosophy with which to pursue the realisation of the latter goal. He therefore set himself the task of producing this philosophy. The theory of Communism so produced is known as the 'Marxist theory'.

THE MARXIST THEORY:

The essential principles of the Marxist Theory as may be found in *The Communist Manifesto*[5] are as follows:

i) THE ECONOMIC INTERPRETATION OF HISTORY:

The mode of production in material life is the greatest determinant of the general character of the political, social and spiritual processes of life. The economic conditions of a society are deemed to constitute the real foundation upon which is erected the superstructure of culture, law and government, and to which other forms of social consciousness correspond.

Closely associated with the above are the notions of class war and the theory of surplus value. Marx was of the opinion that the establishment of private property divided society into two hostile economic classes: the capitalistic class and the proletariat. The interest of the capitalistic

5. Karl Marx & Friedrich Engels, *The Communist Manifesto*, Ed. by D. Ryazanoff, New York, Russell & Russell, 1963.

class which derives its income mainly from the ownership of property is antagonistic to that of the proletariat which derives its own income from labour-power.

To explain this antagonism, Karl Marx puts forward a theory of surplus value. The surplus value is deemed to arise because labour power produces values above the cost of tools, raw materials and the cost of its subsistence. According to the surplus value theory, the capitalistic class through its ownership and control of the means of production, appropriates the "surplus value".

ii) **REVOLUTION AND THE DICTATORSHIP OF THE PROLETARIAT**

Marx predicted that a social revolution was inevitable as long as capital or wealth continued to be concentrated in few hands a condition assured by the Capitalist System. According to Marx, such a situation would necessitate a conscious organisation of Labour or the proletariat, which would culminate in an overthrow of the capitalist class. Marx did not expect the capitalist class – at least in most countries of the world – to give up their position without a struggle. Hence, he argued that a violent and concerted struggle was necessary to dislodge capitalism. To Marx, this rigorous process of overthrowing capitalism would of necessity entail a dictatorship of the proletariat.

The dictatorship was however meant to be transient – a temporary stage in the march towards socialism. Since the capitalist class would not want to give up power nor property voluntarily, the proletariat would have to confiscate all private property, organise labour and compel all to work for the state by way of consolidating and perpetuating the results of the revolution.

iii) **THE NEW SOCIETY:**

The dictatorship of the proletariat is supposed to be a means for the highest possible intensification of the state and the realisation of socialism. As such, once it brings about the required results, the need for its own further existence and use would disappear. The dictatorship and the state would wither away because there would not be any more private property to confiscate. At this point, Marx assumes, the new or emergent society could be organised on the principle of "from each according to his capacity, to each according to his needs": Each man was to contribute to the social wealth according to his capability and take from it according to his needs.

These fundamental principles of Communism have been criticised by men from all walks of life from different standpoints since the publication of *The Communist Manifesto* in 1848, and still remains a source of great controversy not only among intellectuals but also among different peoples of the world. Even now, therefore, taking a hard and critical look at the theory cannot be considered outmoded.

On the materialistic interpretation of history, one must not fail to acknowledge Marx's brilliance in pointing out such a latent but strong factor in interpreting mankind's history. It is to Marx's credit that today, economic conditions of any society are regarded as very important factors in accounting for or interpreting her life processes. Before Marx, economic conditions were hardly reckoned with in this regard.

Whether this factor is the most important one is, of course, quite a different and difficult question. That any of such other factors like religion, politics, great men, etc., may take the upper hand or have a more pronounced or far-reaching effect on societal structure than economics is not in doubt. Therefore, while rejecting the notion that under all conditions, economic forces or conditions play the most important part in societal processes, we must accept the fact that they constitute a very important factor which could under certain conditions become crucial.

Marx's prescription of violent social revolution as a means to overthrowing the existing order and establishing Socialism stemmed from his conviction that the rich class would not give up its position willingly. In his view, members of the rich class were blinded by the dominant and prevailing conservative philosophy and so took the status quo as natural and therefore justifiable. Perhaps, if he had attached less weight to economic determinism, he would have realised that a possible emergence of new ideas could have weakened the prevailing philosophy thereby paving the way for a change of attitude on the part of the propertied class. In which case, it could have become possible to persuade them to accept change peacefully.

In fact, the passage in 1832 of the Reform Act in England and the Jacksonian revolution in the United States about the same time, which brought about power-sharing between the middle class and the aristocrats underlined this possibility.[6] However, since Marx viewed the world mainly from economic perspective he gave those revolutions only a fleeting and grudging consideration.[7] Since his thesis was anchored on the notion that the superstructure of society is built upon its economic foundations, accepting the view that the political gains made by the middle class in these revolutions could lead, in the long run, to a significant redistribution of economic power in favour of the lower-classes, would have run counter to his entire thesis and

6. William Ebenstein and Edwin Fogelman, *Today's –Isms*, Prentice-Hall. Inc. Englewood Cliffs, New Jersey, 8th Edition, 1980. pages 7—9.
7. In 1872, Marx admitted at a public meeting in Amsterdam that workers can attain Socialist objectives by peaceful means in certain countries, namely: England, USA and "perhaps" Holland.

belief. In other words, this would have given an apparent leverage to political determinism over economic determinism; hence, Marx's stubborn insistence on violent revolution.

It is therefore clear that Marx was guilty of blindly clinging to a pessimistic view. Surely, a class war or violent revolution cannot be the only means of change, as indeed the Jacksonian revolution and the 1832 English Reform Act, before Marxism, had indicated. Peaceful electoral process must be seen as an equally possible way of eliminating Capitalism or any other system for that matter. Reference is made here to the victory of the Nazi Party in Germany (1933) which ushered in Fascism, and the now commonplace victories of 'Socialist' parties in many countries of the world.

Furthermore, if Marx had given cultural, political, religious and other factors of social change their due regards, he would not have prescribed a dictatorship of the proletariat for the transitional stage of the envisaged revolution. He, for instance, discounted the political factor so much so that he failed to give sufficient consideration to the mode of power distribution that would follow the revolution. His dictatorship of the proletariat without a clear-cut leadership is akin to throwing political power unto a motley crowd and to chance. His hope or prediction that the dictatorship would crumble as soon as the new revolution took root points to shallow thinking and naivety. Even the injunction that in the new society each man would contribute to the social wealth according to his capacity, is to say the least, ludicrous. Who was to define what? If Marx believed that each and every man was going to willingly and honestly abide by such injunction without some form of coercive prodding, then he must have been an ignorant dreamer and a blind optimist. Ignorant in the sense that he failed to take a cue from the life of the social insects and blind in the sense that he expected a sudden and far-reaching change in what we may, for want of better expression describe as human nature, namely; the acquisitive and competitive tendencies in man. As Appadorai rightly pointed out, "a social ideal which assumes such fundamental change in human nature and habit is by the nature of things incapable of realization".[8]

As it turned out, these oversights were to stymie or delay the implementation or application of the Marxist theory until revised by Lenin.[9]

MARXISM-LENINISM:

"Lenin's most important contribution to the theory of Communism is to be found in his pamphlet, 'What is to be done?'"[10] published in 1902. Lenin unlike Marx, was more practical in his approach to Communism. Whereas Marx assumed that the working class would spontaneously develop its class consciousness in the daily struggle for economic existence and that its leadership would come largely from its own ranks, Lenin felt that communist activity is to be carried on along two lines. First, workers are to form labour unions and if possible a communist party. And secondly, there are to be small groups of professional revolutionaries, patterned after the army and the police, highly select and entirely secret.[11] This organisation is to constantly guide and supervise, much like the soldiers in a beehive, other communist-led economic and political organisations in the march against capitalism.

8. A. Appadorai, *The substance of Politics*, New Delhi, Oxford University Press, 11th Edition, 1975. Page 120
9. Lenin, Vladimir 1, (1870 -1924) – Leader of the Communist (Bolshevik) revolution which overthrew the democratic government of Alexander Kerensky in Russia to establish the first communist state in 1917
10.   William Ebenstein & Edwin Fogelman, *Today's - Isms*, Op. cit., Page 24
11.   Ibid

Lenin's position, therefore, amounted to a reliance on a perpetual dictatorship of the party as against Marx's hope for a temporary dictatorship of the proletariat. He did not delude himself into believing that once capitalism is overthrown, socialism would be sustained by the goodwill of all concerned. With Lenin therefore, the Communist Theory developed to a point of sacrificing individual liberty for perpetual one-party dictatorship. Having got this far, communism became ripe for application and export. It is now part of history that the first communist revolution occurred in 1917 in Russia and did spread to many other countries of the world.

Lenin's philosophy and contribution is no doubt more radical and assuming than the position adopted by Marx himself. Whereas Marx was ambivalent about the place of political power or its effect on societal structure, Lenin assigned little relevance to it. In other words, he failed to perceive or make use of the possible and detrimental effects that concentration of political power could have on the individual or society at large. Had he sincerely addressed himself to this problem, it is doubtful whether he would have opted for the permanent Vanguard of Communism which he created.

It must, however, be mentioned that in 1904, Leon Trotsky – then an orthodox Marxist critical of Lenin – predicted that the dictatorship of the party would be replaced by the rule of the central committee, and eventually a single individual would take the place of the central committee. This, according to Trotsky, was an inevitable consequence of Leninist concepts and organisational practices. The Stalin era proved him right. The brutality of the Stalinist era and the wave of purges which later characterised most communist states have proved a liability both to the world and the spread of Communism itself. They also did cast doubts as to the efficacy of the revolutionary method whereby these communist governments came into power. As such, there arose a movement and belief amongst some communists that a peaceful electoral process is a better method of pursuing power. Since this movement was mainly based in Europe, it is often referred to as Euro-Communism.

EURO-COMMUNISM

The basic principle which differentiates Euro-Communism from Marxist-Leninism is that Euro-Communism pledged to use constitutional or democratic means in the pursuit of political power. European communists (comprising communists mainly from France, Italy and Spain) declared that "all the liberties which are the result of great bourgeois democratic revolutions[12] including the traditional rights of free speech, assembly and religion, would be incorporated into the communist ideology. The declaration also supported "democratic institutions fully representative of popular sovereignty".[13] It approved "a plurality of political parties including the right of opposition parties to existence and activity"[14] According to this declaration, the final arbiter is "the verdict of Universal Suffrage".

Those assertions were further strengthened in 1977 by Marchais, the French communist leader, when he explicitly repudiated the doctrine of the dictatorship of the proletariat. He disagreed with the Soviet Communist Party about socialist democracy, emphasising that the dictatorship of the proletariat "does not correspond to the realities of our policy[15] and that "the word 'dictatorship' does not correspond to the realities of our goals and theses".[16] He made it known that the French Communist Party wanted to rally the majority of the salaried workers as

12.-16. Ibid., pp. 104

well as the working class on their road to political power. Accordingly, the word 'Proletariat' has been dropped from the statutes of the French Communist Party. The idea of a 'Social Revolution' is, therefore, to the true Euro-Communist, no longer fashionable.

Furthermore, the Euro-Communists have abandoned their earlier insistence of socializing all forms of capital. To this end, they have declared that small and medium peasant property, handicrafts, and small and medium industrial and commercial enterprises will be assigned a specific role in the construction of socialism.[17] This implies that large-scale business and heavy industries would be nationalized by a Euro-Communist government. However, the idea of paying any form of compensation to owners of properties so-nationalized is not accepted by the Euro-Communists.

The philosophical basis for this insistence on confiscation without compensation is unclear. Perhaps it comes from the doctrine of 'Surplus Value', which according to Marx is undeservedly appropriated by the owners of means of production and exchange. Perhaps also the Euro-Communists think that since "behind every great fortune there is a crime" *(Balzac)*,[18] owners of large-scale properties and businesses should be treated like criminals. If it were so, then the situation is grave. Perhaps, they need be told that even the not-so-great fortunes cannot be totally absolved from crimes. In which case, the question may be asked: why must the rich be singled out for punishment? Such isolated attack on only a section of the propertied class could, to say the least, be likened to a situation where winners in a long-distance race (usually in the minority) are deprived of their trophies or medals, not so much because

17. Ibid. Pg., 106.
18. Balzac, Honoré de, Author of *Pere Goriot*, et al, cited by Mario Puzo in *Godfather*, Pan Books, New York, 1970.

they did not abide by the rules of the game or competition, but because they were considered to have run too fast.

Now, it is not that there is anything basically wrong about changing the rules in a certain game or competition, especially when the prevailing rules are no longer capable of serving the ideals for which they were originally intended. But it is rather unfair and indeed retrogressive to formulate new laws which seek to destroy the gains of yesterday. The new laws must allow the winners of earlier competitions to keep their medals or trophies while ensuring adherence of all to the new rules in future competitions. It is when the earlier winners are denied those medals or trophies won in earlier competitions as Euro-Communism demands, that bitterness, rancour and hatred which are essential ingredients for counter-reaction, violence and civil disorder are given vent. After all, the rich could claim self-righteously that they played the ball according to societally approved methods and happened to be winners.

Under such a condition, the Euro-Communist commitment to peaceful change may become illusory or unrealisable even when they are democratically elected into office. In other words, a partial attack on private business or capital could boomerang, thus impeding the setting up of a Euro-communist government in a peaceful atmosphere – which is the very nightmare the Euro-communists say they are trying to run away from. Surely, it is doubtful whether freedom, liberty and progress can be built on the type of foundation on which Euro-communism is working.

COMMUNISM IN PRACTICE

The exploits of Communism started with the Bolshevik revolution of 1917 in Russia. Right from that date and even as the civil war was still raging, the Communists passed many decrees that had far-reaching effects on the Soviet people. For instance, Alexander Solzhenitsyn[19] who was an insider, in his many works especially, *The Gulag Archipelago*, has revealed a lot of what life was like or what happened within the Soviet Union since the revolution.

Generally, the Communists introduced many policies that brought the citizens of that country at loggerheads with the new regime. This was heralded by Lenin's demand, at the end of 1917, of the "merciless suppression of attempts at anarchy on the part of drunkards, hooligans, counterrevolutionaries, and other persons".[20] This was to include not only class enemies but also "workers malingering at their work" as Lenin put it, and peasants who refused to surrender their food and crops to the Central Rationing Committee.[21] These people were promptly shot, arrested or imprisoned. Millions were killed and many languished in concentration camps. The trend continued well into the twenties when Stalin[22] increased the terror many folds in his determination to see his collectivization programme through. It is estimated that between 1937 and 1938, Stalin executed 40,000 people per month —over 1,000 a day — for two full years.[23]

Collectivization of Soviet agriculture started in 1928 after the death of Lenin. Lenin had deliberately delayed this stage of the Socialist programme because the ravages of World War I and the devastations caused by the civil war

19. Alexander Solzhenitsyn was a Soviet Nobel Laureate, author and dissident who served long prison sentences in the USSR and was later expelled from that country

20. Alexander Solzhenitsyn, *The Gulag Archipelago I*, 6th impression, 1979 page 27

21. Ibid Chapter 2

22. Stalin, Josif Vissarionovich (1879-1953) was Lenin's successor who was named General Secretary of the Soviet Communist Party in 1922. After Lenin's death in 1924 he eliminated his political rivals to become a dictator.

23. Alexander Solzhenitsyn, Op. Cit. page 438-439

(1917-1921) had made immediate social reform impracticable. Hence in his *New Economic Policy* of 1921, Lenin had allowed limited private ownership of means of production. That Policy was meant to sustain production in the farms, workshops and factories while the new leaders consolidated their position. But after seven years of its operation and the consequent improvement of the economy, Stalin felt that it was time to enforce collectivization on the peasants. It is also possible that the Communist rulers felt that since mechanization was necessary to increase agricultural production, large-scale collective farms would go well with their plans to mechanise agriculture. In any case, the continued existence of private farms was a negation of Communist goals and served, Stalin must have reasoned, as both a challenge and a direct political and psychological threat to the acceptance of coercive political direction from the centre.

It is now part of Soviet history that about seven million peasants lost their lives between 1928 and 1933 while resisting the process of collectivization of Soviet agriculture.[24] Many died as a result of the famine that came with collectivization, others perished in slave labour camps in Siberia and the Arctic to which they were sentenced, while many were shot on the spot for their opposition to the collectivization programme. Certainly, there was marked resistance to collectivization from the very peasants whom communism was seeking to protect. Drives to nationalise other forms of productive enterprise in the Soviet Union were also resisted leading to purges and suppression. Forced labour became the order of the day while the nation turned into a Police State.

---

24   Ebenstein & E. Fogelman, *Today's –Isms*, Op. Cit., Pg. 30.

With collectivization, bureaucratization rose in the country. The effect of food rationing and centralised system of distribution became intolerable. Long queues of shoppers became commonplace in all parts of the USSR, causing an unquantifiable loss of man-hours.

However, even with all these sacrifices, it soon became clear that total collectivization was not the answer. It was adversely affecting the economy as well as the liberties and morale of the people. Furthermore, it became apparent that even the well-equipped security forces could never win the battle against isolated and, sometimes, mass civil disobedience. Thus, after some time, the government was forced to relax some of the policies. For instance, members of collective farms were allowed to devote part of their time to small plots of land for private purposes and management. Under this arrangement, an individual was allowed to sell his own products on the open market. Interestingly, although these private farms constituted only about one to three per cent of all Soviet farmlands, they were said to have accounted for as much as one-half of available Soviet meat, potatoes, eggs and vegetables.[25] Similarly, the inherent problems of over-centralisation did force reforms in industry, management, and so on, in order to accommodate, even if in part, the demands of individuality.

These revisions notwithstanding, there were still complaints bordering on the apparent neglect of the service sector and such other areas of life and industry where large-scale organisation is apt to be unsuitable. These include the repair industry, housing, catering, tailoring, and certain areas of transportation. It was to prove that revisionism was going to become an integral part of the socialist programme.

25. (a) Ibid. p. 32

    (b) *Time Magazine*, November 22, 1982, p. 22

Developments within the Communist world are full of such divergent and conflicting interests between the rulers and the ruled. And closely associated with these conflicts of interests is a long history of purges and suppression in all communist countries. These happenings go a long way to underline the inadequacy of the communist theory, which in turn has led many communist regimes to apply 'reforms' in an attempt to meet with the yearnings of their citizenry.

Mass action against communist rule was to become a recurrent feature in many communist countries especially in eastern Europe, where the actions of the Polish Solidarity Movement seemed the most dramatic. The first of such explosions occurred in East Germany in 1953 amid general feelings of hopelessness and disillusionment. Living conditions especially with regards to food, had steadily deteriorated under the East German communist management. The spark which finally ignited the smouldering resentment of the populace in this country was a government announcement in May 1953 that workers' wages would be cut further unless production rose by at least ten per cent. With this announcement, most workers came to the conclusion that a more direct action was necessary to get the ruling party to give them more consideration and voice in the scheme of things. As such, they quickly organised themselves and took to the streets in what was to be the first strike and direct challenge of the ruling communist masters. The demonstration was nationwide. In many towns and villages workers occupied police offices, released political prisoners and set government and communist party buildings on fire. While many policemen adopted the wait-and-see attitude, some even crossed over to the 'rebels'. The demonstrators demanded amongst other things free elections, free labour unions and an end to Soviet domination.

However, the government would not budge. But as it was losing grip on the control of the security forces, it had to seek external military aid. It took a direct Soviet military action to save the then East German Communist regime from collapse.

Three years later a similar revolt took place in Poland. The striking workers carried the old Polish Flag, occupied the communist party headquarters as well as the radio station and set some prison buildings on fire after freeing the prisoners. Again, the populace was suppressed but not with-out some key government concessions to the people. Collective farms were dissolved and private farming granted to the people. In industry, harsh control over workers were relaxed. Limited private enterprise in business and trade was permitted on a 'moderate' scale such as in the case of bakers, tailors, plumbers, repairmen, and skilled craftsmen in the building and tourist trades.

However, from the mid-sixties, the Polish government under Gomulka, gradually curtailed these concessions and in 1970, it announced steep increase in prices of some essential commodities. Again, demonstrating workers poured into the streets. It took a combined contingent of army and police forces to quell the strike with hundreds of casualties on both sides. Thus, it could be seen that even in a communist country a situation akin to Marx's class war could develop.

Such episode occurred in many other communist countries like Hungary and Czechoslovakia. Also the 1980s witnessed a very determined and protracted struggle between the peoples and workers of the Polish State on one hand and the ruling Communist Party on the other. It was described as the bluntest opposition to communist rule. And it culminated in the formation of a 'free trade' union (*Solidarity*), which demanded free elections and the outright abrogation of the one-party system, among others. The demonstrations of '*Solidarity*' were so intense that the party was forced to change its leader. And despite subsequent measures taken by the succeeding regime to stop the protestations of the Polish workers, 'Solidarity', still waxed strong. The Polish situation attracted world-wide attention.

That most peoples in communist ruled nations were dissatisfied with the communist dictatorship was not in doubt. The way and manner different peoples showed their resentment to the staggering abuses of their liberties which communist dictatorships in these countries brought about may have differed but their effects and presence were manifested in one way or another. Where the government approach to the problem was not the kind of purges and suppressions of 'counter-revolutionary' tendencies reminiscent of the Stalinist and/or Maoist era, it was the more sophisticated methods of Brezhnev's Russia or an enhanced revisionist approach of some the then contemporary communist leaders.

The Hungarian government, it would be remembered did set the pace in economic 'reforms' in the whole of communist Eastern Europe. Under their revisionist laws, private enterprises of up to 12 employees were allowed to exist and compete in the production and supply of consumer goods and services. Hungarian entrepreneurs were said to have been quick in seizing the new opportunity. Hence, private business rose rapidly.[26] In other words, capitalism gradually crept back into the national life of those communist nations. Even one-time Soviet leader, Yuri Andropov, now late, fell for this model, signalling that the USSR could be on the verge of adopting the said Hungarian model.[27]

Indeed, the above prediction came to pass when shortly afterwards the then Presidium of the Supreme Soviet

26. America's *Newsweek Magazine*. Feb. 14, 1983, Pages 29-30.
27. Ibid.

approved of a new law scheduled to be operative as from May 1987. According to Lagos' *Times International magazine* of December 8, 1986, the new law gave individual Russian families the right to embark on 29 different types of small scale businesses including land-cultivation for crops rearing, cloth-making, souvenirs production, car-repairs, taxi services, etc. In proposing the law, Karanzki, the then Labour Minister confessed that the State had realised that it was not producing enough consumer goods in quantity and quality. The Minister also agreed that many Soviet citizens had jobs outside official hours, and claimed that the "new law itself would simply help legalise such illegalities". Of course, Karanzki insisted, according to the report, that the shift "does not mean nor signify any intent to return to free wheeling and dealing in private enterprises in the Soviet Union".

Furthermore, there were indications then that the shifts in Soviet policy could also take on a political dimension. Shortly afterwards, according to Nigeria's *Newswatch magazine* of March 2, 1987, Soviet leader, Mikhail Gorbachev, "called for an adoption of a multi-candidacy for elections for regional party posts conducted via secret ballots...". His strategy of overcoming the intransigence of the bureaucracy was epitomised by his policy of 'glasnost' which called for openness, candour and publicity, and public debate of vital issues as well as government policies and plans. "We don't have an opposition. How can we monitor ourselves?" he asked. According to the report, Gorbachev "spelt out his far-reaching policies for the democratisation of the country".

Such tendency was not restricted to Europe or the USSR. Other communist regimes the world over were caught up by such changes or pressure to change. According to a report,[28] about the same time China

28. John Woodruff, 'China to expand private economy', Lagos, Daily Times, Feb. 2, 1983

announced a mammoth expansion of its fledgling private economy, opening 40% of the country's retail business to co-operatives and even individuals while greatly increasing the freedom of its 800 million peasants to sell what they raised in the open market. The new commercial policy was also billed to expand the country's toe-in-the-water experiments with selling big-ticket consumer goods on instalment plans, sending more travelling salesmen into the countryside and increasing the mark-up between wholesale and retail prices.

The communique further asserted that the new commercial policy was due to the recognition by the Chinese leadership "that the centralised socialist distribution system it inherited from Mao-Tse-Tung was hopelessly clogged and would never be able to deal with the new consumer-oriented production policies.

In the three years since China began to relax its agricultural policies, peasants began to develop real purchasing power in some areas, but an inefficient distribution network failed to get the merchandise to the villages even while factories put more emphasis on consumer goods. The State Council, China's cabinet, acknowledged the problem in June 1982 and demanded reform. And the October/November (1982) conference was an attempt to fashion a policy detailed enough to give local areas freedom to meet their own needs. It was said that much of the new policy did not amount to 'new ideas' but to the enlargement of ideas tested in the past few years.

Whatever the official results of these 'tests', China was gradually sliding or shifting into free market economy. For instance, it was reported by observers of the China scene that free markets and department stores were springing up alongside side-walks and in small buildings.[29] It became obvious that if those trends continued, then Chinese rulers could soon be raced with the type of capitalist problems

29. Ibid.

which brought the communist revolution into being in the first place. It was already being reported that those experiments had reversed the trend that had given the state a strong-hold on commerce, reducing the number of outlets by more than 80% between 1957 and 1978, eliminating private shops and squeezing hundreds of thousands of co-operative shops out of business even as the population grew by several hundred million.

The *China Daily Commentary* described the result of state control thus: "The most common complaints of the consumer are the bureaucratic airs and bad service in state run shops and restaurants where the attendants are guaranteed their jobs and pay irrespective of their performance of duty".[30]

Reforms or demands for reform in China were not limited to the economic front. The prospects of combining economic and political liberalization took the centre stage in China's intellectual debates and discussions. The question was whether China could free its economy without loosening the political system and allowing more democracy. Since December 1986, this issue according to America's *Time magazine* of January 26, 1987, "has been taken into the streets. Thousands of students around the country demonstrated for more political freedom, often burning Communist Party papers and denouncing party leaders". This then suggests that strong undercurrents for western-style political pluralism were already at work.

From the foregoing, it became clear that the communist experiment was gradually but steadily manifesting its glaring limitations and was, therefore, shifting away from its avowed goals, although the leadership was very reluctant to admit this. That reluctance underlined a strong aversion to a full return to a capitalistic system. Most of the

30. Ibid

leading communist theoreticians and politicians were in dilemma. It was obvious that communism was on its death bed. It is no wonder that most communist governments around the world collapsed shortly afterwards, leaving what might be called pseudo-communist regimes in places like Cuba, North Korea, etc. Even China has bid communism goodbye; its economic system is decidedly capitalist even though its political system might still be totalitarian or anti-democratic.

FASCISM

Fascism made its debut in the first quarter of the twentieth century when Benito Mussolini (1883-1944) came to power in Italy in 1922. Its appearance was occasioned by two major factors: the increasing degree of social and economic stagnation that had crept into the capitalist world, and the rejection on the part of fascist adherents of communist and socialist principles as worthwhile alternatives to the capitalist system. German Nazism, for instance, was predicated on the Wall Street crash of October 1929 and the social misery, unemployment, inflation, and so on that followed.[31] Also it is probable that the events in the USSR where communism was already having problems did not offer any encouragement for the adoption of the communist ideology as an alternative system or antidote to the problems that gripped the capitalist world. It became inevitable, therefore, that a different and new method of social organisation would evolve. It did, and became known as fascism.

THEORY OF FASCISM

Fascism may be regarded as the second major twentieth century revolutionary totalitarian revolt against the prevailing established ways of life. But unlike communism, it does not have a rigidly stated philosophy or manifesto. It aims at establishing a social system, different from capitalism, communism and socialism, that would bring the 'good' life about. Much of what is known about fascism is based on Mussolini's own essay, 'The Political and Social

31.. (a) Thomas L. Jarman, *The Rise and Fall of Nazi Germany*, London, The Cresset Press, 1955, Pp., 125-9
(b) *Time Magazine*, Feb. 1, 1982. Pp. 14 - 17.

Doctrine of Fascism'. The theory of fascism is, therefore, basically an Italian product, evolved to justify the fascist movement in that country at the time of Mussolini.

Essentially, fascism is the "totalitarian organisation of government and society by a single-party dictatorship, intensely nationalistic, racist, militarist, and imperialistic".[32] The creation of a State imbued with the authority to dominate all other forces within the country and at the same time maintain constant contact with the masses in all areas of life, is the central theme of fascism. Fascist opposition to democracy stems from the notion that the majority is not necessarily more reasonable than the minority and that the democratic notion of equality of men is incorrect. It claims that democracy gives to the masses the power to decide innumerable issues about which they cannot possibly have the knowledge required to exercise sound judgement. Hence, the masses are often led by unscrupulous demagogues who use the masses to cover and carry out their own designs.

Furthermore, fascists claim that a popularly elected government is not necessarily the ablest. As such, they adhere to the principle that authority should be exercised for the sake of the society, but should not necessarily be derived from her. In other words, "the specific sanction of government is its power while its reasonableness is its ultimate sanction".[33] To the fascist therefore, the surest way of installing and maintaining an ideal government is not through the ballot box, parliamentary eloquence, formulating constitutions or any other such machinery but by finding and installing the ablest man in the country to the presidency, then leaving him to conduct the affairs of the country without opposition.

32. Ebenstein & E. Fogelman, Op. cit. P.111.
33. Appadorai, A., Op. Cit. P.128

Again, fascism is opposed to individualism because it does not believe that the conduct of life should be left to the individual. It is deemed that since the interest of the individual could differ from those of the state, the state must preside over and control all forms of national activity – political, economic or moral. Leaving individuals to control such activities would amount to encouraging opposition to the state, a situation counter to the fundamental principle of fascism.

Fascist opposition to socialism also stems from her attitude to family ties. Family ties are considered beneficial to fascist practice and should therefore be encouraged. Since the institution of private property strengthens these ties it becomes inevitable that fascism would be opposed to socialism and her doctrine of public ownership of productive property. In place of collectivism, therefore, the fascist promotes the corporate economy – a form of command economy which places the interest of the state well above those of her citizenry. The aim of this mode of economic organisation is often the preparation of a war economy because aggressive imperialism is the cornerstone of fascist foreign policy.

Fascism tends to be anti-rationalist, sentimental and stressing the uncontrollable elements in man. Instead of being reflective and open-minded the fascist is fanatical and dogmatic. This leads fascism to have taboo issues like race md inequality.

Whereas democrats see politics as a means to resolving group interests and differences peacefully and if possible permanently, the fascist's view is that politics or resolutions are temporary pending when he is strong enough to assert his might. Thus, he regards conquests as the inevitable end of social conflicts. Therefore, where a democrat would normally talk of opponents, the fascist would talk of enemies, stressing bitterness and lasting hatred which should, in his view, be totally annihilated.

The major weakness of fascism is its stress on authority instead of freedom; totalitarianism instead of liberalism. Instead of seeing the state as a means to developing individual personalities, fascism regards the state as an end in itself. It opposes the fundamental principle of human existence which assigns to the individual the freedom to think for himself, express his views, plan his life and grow to his natural height without dictation from the state or any other quarter provided he, in turn, respects the rights of others to enjoy such freedom.

Furthermore, the fascist idea of picking the ablest man to lead is naïve. How, for instance, is the ablest man in a society to be identified and selected without using the democratic method? What are the yard-sticks for measuring this ability? Is fascism not relying on a subjective value as a basis for its own realization and survival?

Lastly, fascists tend to lose sight of the time-tested maxim that absolute power corrupt absolutely and that the interests of the leadership may not always coincide with those of the society.

DEVELOPMENT AND PRACTICE

From historical records fascism seems to have found favour in relatively wealthy and technologically advanced countries. This is probably due to the fact that a fascist state with her nationalistic and expansionist policies needs to be self-reliant in the production of vital materials necessary for the realisation of these policies. It must be able to produce her own food, arms and ammunition and must also possess powerful media for the 'education' of her citizenry. Industrial, sophisticated societies, unlike traditional ones, create social and psychological tensions which could confound the people to the point of believing that only an authoritarian approach to these problems can curb such tensions. In the words of Richard Nixon, "when people feel panic, tyranny can look attractive if it promises order".[34]

Again, a short post-democratic environment seems to be a good ground for fascist development. When the democratic way of life takes root on a society it is very unlikely that her citizens would tolerate any curtailment of their liberties; whereas the citizens of a society with a young unrooted democracy may be tempted to see authoritarianism as a means of achieving 'quick' political results during periods of chaos and disillusionment. In countries without any democratic experience, a dictatorship is more likely to result from authoritarianism rather than the type of mass support which characterises fascism.

Adverse socio-economic conditions or structures constitute another fertile ground for the development of fascism. Unlike communism which is poverty-induced, fascism develops in a society bedevilled by social tension, economic problems and political instability which are usually followed by labour unrest, general social discontent, and ultimately, mass unrest with a craving for change. Under such conditions, the privileged citizens almost invariably, feel threatened and unsafe, and therefore, readily accept any proposition that promises immediate relief. An authoritarian regime would be handy in the circumstance: it would silence the labour unions and ensure the survival of the state or society. Besides, fear and frustration which poor economic climate brings about can also undermine faith in the democratic process amongst people. Unemployment rates go up, leaving the unemployed with a feeling of hopelessness, lack of sense of belonging, social rejection and lack of identity. Under such conditions, fascism gives this category of people a feeling of acceptance and comradeship by finding them something to do.

34. Nixon, Richard, *The Real War*, London, Sidgwick and Jackson, 1980, p. 46

With this background, it should not be surprising that fascism cuts across all social groups and classes. While the wealthy industrialists find that fascism could provide a check on their teeming and often rebellious workers, the middle class could find job security in the same system. As for the lower class there would be at least the sense of belonging, of comradeship, and so on, to excite their feeling of loyalty and interest. And, of course, there would be those who would support fascism merely because of its nationalistic, racist and chauvinistic appeal. These might explain why fascist programmes tend to contain contradictory promises – in its attempts to satisfy all and sundry.

The military is also an important social group that is particularly susceptible to fascism. Professional soldiers tend to over-estimate the virtues of discipline and unity even in a well-established democracy. Where democracy is weak, this professional bias within the military becomes a political menace.[35] This is exemplified by the attitude of the military in both Germany and Italy during the fascist era in those countries. The military would in the face of fascism either openly demonstrate its support for the system or maintain an attitude of benevolent neutrality.

But it must also be pointed out that the military could and do play a very leading part in removing fascist regimes where their level of performance is unacceptable. Indeed, once fascism or any form of dictatorship is established, the army remains the last bulwark of decency and legality with the force to challenge the establishment.[36] This explains why fascist leaders always keep a sharp eye on the military.

35. W. Ebenstein & E. Fogelman, Op. cit. p. 114

36. Ibid. p. 115

Italy was the first country to practice fascism (1922), followed in Europe by Germany in 1933. In Asia, Japan joined the fascist club in 1930 while Argentina went fascist following the overthrow of a landed oligarchy in 1943. This fascist dictatorship was built up under the leadership of Peron. Fascism in Germany, Italy and Japan collapsed with the defeat of these countries in the Second World War while that of Franco's Spain fizzled out later. As for the Peronist regime in Argentina, a military coup brought it to an end in 1955.

Hitler's Germany provides a typical example of fascist rule in practice, and will be examined briefly in this chapter.

Life in the Third Reich as Hitler's Germany was labelled was certainly a unique and intriguing experience for those who witnessed it according to most historical accounts. It was marked by regimentation and curtailment of individual or civil liberties. The terror of the Gestapo and fear of the Concentration Camps were rife. Communists, socialists, liberals, pacifists and Jews were endangered. By June 1939, there was a great purge of members of these 'enemies of national socialism'. It was a warning of the things to come.

Mass enthusiasm and support were imbued by an unprecedented and rapid build-up of the country both militarily, economically and industrially. It is recorded that by the autumn of 1936 the problem of unemployment had been largely eliminated.[37] Almost everybody had a job and people were generally happy and cheerful even though they got that far by being practically cowed or reduced to slavish unthinking animals. This enthusiasm and support from the

37. Shirer, William L., *The Rise and Fall of the Third Reich*, New York, Simon & Schuster, 1960

populace was not only as a result of the rapidity of Germany's economic recovery; the harsh treatment being meted out to the Jewish race was also a contributory factor.

Racial laws which amounted to exclusion of the Jews from the German Community was heralded by the so-called Nuremberg laws of September 15, 1935. It deprived the Jews of German citizenship confining them to the status of 'subjects". Marriage and extra-marital relations between Jews and Aryans were prohibited, and the Jews were prevented from employing female Aryan servants under the age of thirty-five years. With time, some thirteen new decrees supplementing the Nuremberg laws were introduced out-lawing the Jews completely.

Nazi terror against the Jews saw the complete exclusion of the Jews from societal life. The severity of measures against the Jews were to continue and by 1938 one could see signs like 'Jews strictly forbidden in this town' openly displayed in German towns. But that was only the beginning of the road that was to lead to the massacre of the Jews in Germany -- an episode about which much has been written.

The Nazi regime in Germany also saw to the blatant curtailment and deprivation of the rights of individuals to freedom of worship and membership of religious groups. Steps were taken to dissolve the Catholic Youth League. Thousands of Catholic priests, nuns and leaders were arrested while the leader of the Catholic Action was murdered during the June 30, 1934 purge. What is more, scores of Catholic Publications were suppressed.

The story for the protestants is also a sorry one. By the time the regime matured, the church in Germany had been brutalised, disillusioned and cowed. About the end of 1937, Bishop Marahrens of Hanover was said to have been induced by the regime into declaring that, "The Nationalist Socialist Conception of life is the national and political teaching that determines and characterises German manhood. As such it is obligatory upon German Christians[38]. It was a complete humiliation!   The National Reich Church of German was formed with the exclusive right and power to control all churches within Germany.

Such embarrassment was not limited to the Church. Other facets of German culture were affected. In fact, there was a *nazification* of the German culture. Books which did not help the Nazi cause were destroyed. It was decided that all creative artists in all spheres be gathered into a unified organization under the leadership of the Reich. The Reich was to determine the lines of progress in the mental and spiritual spheres and also lead and organize the professions. Consequently, seven sub-chambers were established under the Reich to guide and control every sphere of cultural life.

These were the fine arts, music, theatre, literature, the press, radio and films. Persons in these fields were obliged to join their respective chambers and obey the rules set down by that chamber as guiding principle in their various works. Failure to toe these lines meant outright ostracism. Indeed, "political reliability" of individuals was a condition for admittance.

This meant that those who were even lukewarm about National Socialism were deprived of membership and hence their means of livelihood. The music of Mendelssohn, for instance, was banned because he was a Jew. The inevitable consequence of that 'bottleneck' was a rapid, appalling decline of cultural standards of the people.

Furthermore, there was massive suppression of freedom in manufacturing, industry and trade as well as a dictatorial control of German science, public schools, institutions of higher learning and the youth organizations.

The agricultural sector was not left out in this totalitarian control. In September 1933, a hereditary farm law was introduced as a move to increase farm production.

38. Ibid

All farms of up to 125 hectares were declared hereditary estates that could not be sold, divided, mortgaged or fore-closed for debts. Farmers were obliged to work their plots. Upon the death of a farmer, the estate was passed unto his eldest son or the nearest male relative who must work the estate providing food for his brothers and sisters until they came of age. Every aspect of the life of the farmer was strictly regulated by the Reich Food Estate: his convenience was not considered important. All that mattered was to 'feed the nation'. Only the Aryan Germans were exempted from this obligation. However, despite all Nazi efforts in the 'Battle of Production' only 83% self-sufficiency was achieved in agriculture.[39]

In sum, the Nazi regime was able to mobilize the people for the sake of building a militarily strong nation at the expense of the people's liberty and rights to self-determination. Hitler and his hench-men usurped the powers to make vital decisions for the people: a condition which led the German people into the Second World War, which they lost.

The story of the rise and fall of German fascism is similar to those of other fascist regimes in Italy and Japan which ended with the Second World War. And as already recounted, those of Spain and Argentina fizzled out in the post-World War II period. Today, the fascist philosophy itself seem outmoded or over-shadowed by other political ideologies. Although one hears of attempts by individuals to resuscitate the dying creed every now and then, little or no success has been recorded. The non-existence of any major fascist party in the politics of many nations of the World today underlines the fact that the fascist philosophy has come under serious disfavour.

39. Ibid.

CAPITALISM

This could well be referred to as the movement of individualism.

CLASSICAL CAPITALISM:

During the early period of man's recorded history when population was scant and resources abundant, each individual or family unit was able to produce almost all her material needs, obtaining very little materials service from neighbours. Even then, these requirements came in the form of exchange of goods and services among families in what is known as trade by barter, or outright gifts from one family to the other. At that period in man history, there was little or no specialization. Each individual was able to carry out a wide range of duties. Division of labour was not known and there was harmony between work and property. Also the type of occupation (if we could so refer to it) that a person held in this pre-capitalist era and the price he charged for his goods and services were pre-determined for him by custom and usage.

With growth in knowledge and techniques, as well as increase in population, the economy became less localized. The primitive method of barter or exchange became less effective necessitating a more pronounced market economy. Specialisation was introduced with each person supplying to the market part of the product of his labour and skill. The products were no longer designed exclusively for the producer's own household or that of his neighbour(s) but also for the market. The forces of supply and demand, instead of tradition and usage as in the pre-capitalist era, became the factors determining price. Consequently, competition became a very important aspect of classical capitalism. This competition was fuelled by the fact that virtually everybody or family was a producer of something and at least a little portion of everything thus making monopolistic conditions virtually impossible.

On the basis of the above, the prevalent view in the classical model was that there should be minimal interference of government with the economic life of the people. The government was meant to protect the individual from violence, fraud and external aggression. Such functions undertaken by the modern state like the provision of education, unemployment-insurance, the regulation of public health, and aid to agriculture and industry would have been considered improper.[40] The individual was expected to be independent of government as far as economic activities were concerned. Economic liberty was viewed primarily as the right of each individual to undertake private enterprise or earn his daily bread by marketing his labour-power without government interference.

The argument in support of the above was that individuals would, in the long run, discover and aim at their own interests better than a government could do for them.[41] On economic grounds, for instance, it was felt that an atmosphere of free competition was necessary because consumers seeking their own interests would create an effective demand for commodities and services while producers, seeking their own interests would meet this demand leading to a balance that would not allow for waste in the daily production of goods and services. It was also thought that competition between consumers and producers on one hand, and among producers on the other hand would keep prices at a reasonable level and ensure quality.

40. A. Appadorai, Op. cit., p. 97.
41. Ibid. p. 98.

From the biological standpoint, it was deemed that the fittest ought alone to survive. This was regarded as natural law. Since the health of the social and natural organism was supposed to depend on the observance of the law of specific function, everybody should perform that function for which he is intended by nature.[42]

Such was the psychological atmosphere which made private ownership of property or means of production and exchange the cornerstone of the capitalist system. This was complemented by the wage-system of remuneration for members of the labour-force and the democratic form of government in politics.

Laissez-faire, a term which means government abstention from interference with individual action, was popular in England between the middle of the eighteenth century and middle of the nineteenth century. This was due partly to the failure of mercantilism and partly to the industrial revolution. Mercantilism meant government control over industry, trade and commerce. But the adversity brought about by the loss of her American Colonies about 1780, couple with the introduction of mechanical power and factories made the protective measures of mercantilism unnecessary[43]. It was felt that leaders in industry could take advantage of the concept of laissez-faire to achieve increase in production.

As predicted, there was enormous expansion in trade and industry. But the social cost of this progress was later to outweigh the economic gains. The market economy was further developed as well as division of labour and specialisation. The advent of machines and industrialization brought craftsmanship into disfavour. People now had to work in factories as labourers remunerated by wages instead of profits obtained by

42 - 43. Ibid. p. 98.

producing and selling their own goods and services as before. As such, the number of producers or those who owned the means of production fell drastically.

This situation brought about the existence and use of monopolies, oligopolies and associations of dominant companies in particular businesses and industries in fixing prices of goods. The extent of free competition was drastically reduced. Besides, employers determined or fixed wages by using all forms of manipulations to force their wills. Monopolistic purchase of labour, for instance was rife. As a result, while the owners of the means of production and exchange prospered, the workers' plight deteriorated. Inadequate wages, long hours or work, insanitary arrangements and over-crowded factories and homes, etc., for the working class were in vogue. The modern form of capitalism had begun to take shape!

These anomalies led to a reaction against Laissez-faire. Critics pointed out that:

> "Free-competition can lead to the best social advantage only where there is approximate equality of bargaining power"[44] between labour and capital.

As was with Laissez-faire, "free competition" was free only in name; the employers in the long-run got their terms accepted by the starving workers. For the worker, freedom to reject the terms offered amounted to little more than freedom to perish. The argument was (and, I bet, still is) that society should moralise competition. While some people opined that social and religious organisations could provide the much-needed cure to ignorance and self-interest of individuals, others called for direct government interference in business and industry.[45]

44. Ibid. Pg.99.
45. Ibid. Pg. 99 — 100.

It was these periods and conditions that gave rise to enhanced socialistic notions of economic organisation. Note also that the ***Communist Manifesto*** was published about this period – 1848. However, all these calls and efforts to stem the suffering and hardships of the working class did not prevent the emergence of modem capitalism.

MODERN CAPITALISM

The major difference between the pre-capitalist era and classical capitalism is that while there was a high degree of harmony between work and property in the former, the latter brought with it the existence of a working class and a capitalist class. In the modern period, this disharmony has further developed from absolute ***Laissez-faire*** to a point where management and financial control of business are separable from ownership. This, in essence, means further alienation of work and property. The corporation may now be located thousands of kilometres away from the owners or shareholders.

This contrasts with the early period of modern capitalism when the owner or owners of business took direct personal involvement, financial and moral, in the management of their business. Partnerships involved very few persons, all of whom were involved in the running of the firm. Today, however, a managerial class of paid professionals see to the day-to-day management of many corporate businesses, making all the important policies, and even fixing their own salaries with little or no restraints or guidance from some other body or group of individuals.

The development enhanced the degree to which individuals can achieve unlimited wealth and also the trend towards big-business. The trend towards "bigness" can be shown if we compare the assets of manufacturing corporations for 1948 and 1976 in the United States.

According to available statistics,[46] in 1948, the two hundred largest manufacturing corporations held 48 per cent of all assets of the manufacturing corporations, while in 1976, their assets went up to 60 per cent. Besides, the five hundred largest industrial corporations accounted for 80 per cent of total United State industrial sales, 75 per cent of all profits in industry and 75 per cent of employment in all industrial corporations for the year 1976.[47]

Concentration of capital is shown by the percentage of people holding the highest stock. About 60 per cent of all corporate stock is said to belong to individuals but fewer than 0.1 per cent of the citizens own twenty per cent of all the individually held stock. In some major non-industrial sectors of the economy, such as banking, life insurance and public utilities, concentration of ownership and control is even greater than in industry.

With these developments, the classical model of competition has practically disappeared, since many markets have to be dominated by a few firms who often collude with one another on major policy decisions. This also implies that the number of employers of labour is steadily falling to the disadvantage of the labour force. One result of this, is a tendency on the part of labour to organise strong unions with the sole purpose of fighting for better conditions for their services. The emergent strong labour unions are daily at loggerheads with the employers of labour leading to strikes, lockouts and all manner of antagonistic relationships between the two classes – the employer and the employed.

On the other hand, where tacit or direct collusion is not worked out among the companies on important policy decisions, sabotage and violence become part of the daily

46.   William Ebenstein & Edwin Fogelman, Op. Cit., pg. 154.
47.   Ibid

struggle for supremacy among them. In this way, some inventions, research findings, etc., that would have served mankind are destroyed or suppressed in order to protect individual commercial interests.

Furthermore, because competition is localised, directed and forced, there is an ever-increasing rate of inflation. Since employers are daily exploring ways of maximising profit at the expense of labour the result is unemployment. In recent times, unemployment rates of up to fourteen per cent have been reported in some Western capitalist nations.[48] The extent and number of people affected by such rates of unemployment in rich industrialized societies with their overflowing resources or Gross National Product (GNP), or the fact that they are unable to accommodate all in the scheme of things, is the real pity of the capitalist system.

The effect of unemployment and lopsided distribution of national wealth cannot be over-emphasised. Generally, all forms of anti-social activities, notably crime, result. Men become susceptible to all forms of influences which frustration, abject poverty, etc., bring about. Drug addiction, alcoholism, etc., have become commonplace. In America, for instance statistics show a steady upward trend in crime rates as if in direct proportion to the increasing rate of concentration of economic power.

Statistics from the American department of Justice published in the *Newsweek magazine* of January 17, 1983 showed that whereas 8.6 murders for every 100,000 of the population were recorded in 1971, the figure shot-up to 10.2 in 1980. Robbery recorded 188 in 1971 for every 100,000 people but climbed to 243.5 in 1980. Cases of aggravated assault is said to have risen from 178.8 in 1971

---

48. *Newsweek Magazine*, Nov. 29, 1982, page 42

for every 100,000 of the population to 290.6 in 1980. Thus, it appears that as capitalism progresses, internal insecurity among the citizenry also increases. Man is turned against man and violence and brutality become rampant.

That strong links exist between socio-economic conditions and crime rates cannot be disputed. It is a fact of contemporary psychology that human behaviour is governed by both innate and 'environmental' characteristics.[49] As such, it is not enough to stress only the importance of individual virtues - self-reliance, endurance, patience, etc., - without regard to environmental or societal contribution or responsibility to create conditions conducive for individual upliftment. Now, this is no attempt to glorify human weakness or underplay individual responsibility to individual actions. Rather, one would like to be sure that we do not lose sight of the intricate and complementary roles which societal forces do have on individual attitudes. Even the strongest of men do waver under the intensity of societal or group pressure irrespective of whether the group or society is wrong or right regarding the issue or issues in contention.

49. Miller, George A., *Psychology – The Science of Mental Life*, Pelican Books, USA, 1962, Chapter, 14.

SOCIALISM

The origin of socialism is difficult to determine. There are claims and counter-claims on the subject, but suffice it to say that socialism as a major political force or movement is the product of the industrial revolution which led to the glaring social and economic inequality perpetrated by modern industrial capitalism. Socialism preaches the collective organisation of the community in the interest of the mass of the people through common ownership and collective control of the means of production and exchange as a means of solving the problems of inequality and social injustice inherent in the capitalistic mode of production. The point must be made, though, that unlike communism which sought to achieve similar aims by a radical violent revolution, socialism believes in the efficacy of the democratic process and so uses same in pursuing its objectives. Besides, socialists agree to the payment of compensation for nationalized property.

At the early period of the socialist movement, adherents talked of total collective control of all the means of production and exchange. However, this view has been progressively modified in recent years to exclude certain categories of property. Instead of total nationalization, the predominant view amongst socialists has become that public ownership is to be built-up gradually and by instalment. If one phase works, the next phase would be pursued. The feeling is that there is need to prove pragmatically, through accomplishment, the usefulness and practicability of public ownership in particular industries and services before moving to other industries. This line of thinking presumes that there may not be need for complete nationalization or collectivization of all means of production and exchange. This shift is mainly due to experiences from countries that are presently at different stages of socialism.

It is on this last model that some socialist parties the world over have taken over power from conservatives in a number of countries and at different times in the past few decades. In Britain, for instance, the Labour Party, Britain's socialist party achieved electoral victories in 1945, 1950, 1964, 1966, 1974 and 1997. It has remained in opposition from 2010 to date. The socialists have also presided over state affairs in West Germany, France and a few other nations particularly in Europe.

Because socialists generally agree that, "in places where small property has survived as a technologically efficient unit, as in agriculture, the arts and some areas of retail trading, services and manufacturing,"[50] collective ownership is unnecessary, "they have enjoyed long tenure in predominantly agrarian countries like Denmark and New Zealand".[51] This is mainly because farmers are sympathetic to the socialist programme which uses cheap credits and other such policies designed to protect the small farmer from the threat of domination by banks, insurance companies, wholesalers, etc. However, in industrialized countries socialism has not been that successful. This is exemplified by the history, achievements and perhaps, the future of socialism in a country like Great Britain.

SOCIALISM IN BRITAIN

The growth and development of socialism as a protest against the capitalist system is carried out in Britain under the flag of the Labour Party. Founded in 1900, the Party did not attain maturity until just before the 1945 general elections in that country, when it pledged to nationalize specifically-listed industries and services if elected into office, giving reasons why nationalization was necessary in these areas.

50. W. Ebenstein and E. Fogelman, Op. Cit. p. 210
51. Ibid. p. 211

With respect to water, gas and light, telephone and telegraph and other utilities, the reason for nationalization was the existence of a natural monopoly. The coal industry was to be nationalized on the ground of poor performance and inefficiency. Inland transportation by rail, road and air was listed on the ground that there was wasteful competition amongst private operators and that such waste could be avoided by a co-ordinated scheme and efficient public management. The National Health Service was suggested so that the best possible health and medical facilities might be available to every person regardless of ability to pay. As for the Bank of England, its purpose was obvious and the need for government ownership of the bank clear. The nationalization of the iron and steel industry was proposed on the ground that it was vital to the nation. In view of the strategic importance of the industry, its management could not be left to private individuals.

With the help of the above programme the labour party won the 1945 elections, and went ahead to implement the programmes although the nationalisation of the iron and steel industry was left out.

There has been further socialisation since 1945. A social security scheme was set up with the aim of providing protection against sickness, unemployment and old age. There are also maternity grants, widows' pensions and family allowances. In the years beginning from 1945 to 1956 further policies of the Labour government aimed at greater social equality and the enhancement of the basic institutions of the welfare state including the provision of educational opportunities for all were introduced: new colleges and universities were founded in an attempt to provide education for many rather than the selected few. The Labour Party tackled the problem of segregation in the education of different classes of people. The tendency toward academic education for a small minority of high class children, which led to college and vocational education for the mass of the people, was curbed.

Taxation was also used as an effective instrument of reducing inequalities in income. Through progressive taxation, the net income of the upper class was drastically reduced. Estate or inheritance taxes were raised as high as 80 percent. The effects of these measures were significant. Whereas in 1911, the top one per cent of the British population held about 69 per cent of the nation's wealth, the share was reduced to about 25 per cent by 1980.[52] Similarly, the share for the top 10 per cent is reported to have fallen from 92 per cent in 1911 to 50 per cent of the nation's wealth. It is also reported that there has been a sharp increase in the size of the middle income group.[53] Also, the proportion of national income paid in wages and salaries increased from 60 per cent in 1938 to 70 per cent in about 1980.[54]

That the Labour party did achieve much in terms of social justice and egalitarianism in the British society is not in doubt. But much remains to be done – and this at a period when even the party seems to have come to the inevitable decision that further socialization and nationalisation is no longer the best way of tackling the problems of inequality. The philosophy of pragmatic nationalisation and socialisation has therefore lost its impulse as a force for social-economic upliftment. As such, the trend towards a more equitable distribution of national wealth has lost its steam and would hover around the level already recounted or might even slide backwards unless, of course, drastic steps are taken to further correct the imbalance.

52. Ibid. p. 232.
53. Ibid.
54. Ibid.

PROBLEMS OF NATIONALIZATION

Socialist theory and practice have undergone marked changes on the issue of nationalisation in the past few decades. Faced with realities, the earlier socialist orthodox principles came into disfavour shifting to the doctrine of "limited and pragmatic nationalization".

The shift in emphasis and adherence to the orthodox principles are due primarily to the problems which arose from such practice. The first to come to mind is the issue of big government. In the parlance of early liberalism, the best government is that which governs least, that is a government which interferes least with the economic life of the people. Nationalisation of means of production and exchange implies increased state control and regulation in the economic life of the people. It brings about concentration of power in the hands of the rulers. And since individual freedom is inextricably linked to the diffusion of power (political as well as economic), we find that individual and political liberties are steadily eroded or sacrificed at the altar of increased nationalization.

Secondly, the case against nationalization is strong in industries that demand high adaptability to changing conditions. These include industries that produce largely for export or that operate with considerable elements of risk and competition. Because bureaucratically run enterprises tend to put security above adventure, risks and experimentation, publicly-run businesses tend to be incompatible with rapid industrial expansion or the rapidly changing mode of industrial production that characterizes our age. As such, it has been argued that limited public ownership and control does not necessarily lead to increased production (especially with respect to quality) or general improvement of a national economy. Rather, most people argue that on the contrary, collective ownership weakens, at least in the long run, the national economy by artificially propping up declining industries which should have been allowed to die. In the attempt to protect these industries, especially their workers, the health of the national economy is often neglected by socialist government.

On the other hand, limited public control of the means of production hardly produces the much desired reduction in economic inequality. Experience in most developing countries where governments own many industries testify to this. In Nigeria, for instance, most public-owned enterprises depend on government's grants for their continued survival, while well-placed individuals within such organisations amass stupendous fortunes (millions of naira) within a short period of time.

Furthermore, in competitive enterprises, where flexibility and innovation are essential nationalized industries find it more difficult to attract top-quality executives. This is because, as an enterprise is nationalized, it becomes monopolistic and routinized allowing less creativity and executive initiative. Also nationalized enterprises are generally regulated to the point of paying lower executive salaries thereby driving away abler executives to non-publicly-owned enterprises.

Lastly, high degree of nationalization brings about all forms of socio-political problems. A small political crisis – the type that would normally go unnoticed in less socialized nations –   tends to paralyse a whole national economy in predominantly socialist countries. In Portugal, for instance, where a petty feud in Parliament shattered the governing centre-right coalition in February 1983, the ripples were felt by nearly all facets of the national economy.[55]

55. *Newsweek Magazine*, Feb. 21, 1983; *Time Magazine*, Feb 14, 1983.

The minor crisis which erupted before Parliament could pass the 1983 budget paralysed the state enterprises which embraced close to 70% of the country's industries. They were left without funds and direction. The construction industry, said to be the country's biggest employer of labour, virtually collapsed because of lack of new jobs and materials.[56]

There is no gainsaying the fact that if these enterprises were not so centralised or nationalized, the entire nation would not have been subjected to such a high degree of economic paralysis. The 'political crisis would not have been much more than the politicians' headache!

Because of these complex problems, many leading socialists are increasingly reconciling themselves to virtually complete elimination of public ownership and control of means of production and exchange. But they still favour socialization in the service and welfare sectors of the economy. The general feeling is that governments are not efficient at producing goods but could play an effective role in the area redistribution of income and wealth.

PROBLEMS OF SOCIALIZATION AND WELFARE

Although the concept of socialization of services and welfare has enjoyed the most popular support and success of all socialist principles, it is not by any means devoid of defects. But the extent to which these defects are felt depend on what areas and to what degree the principle is applied within the society. Where welfare has concentrated on payment of unemployment benefits and the like instead of providing gainful employment to the unemployed, resentment against *welfarism* is pronounced. Generally, there seems to be a deep-seated psychological reaction against the dole. Normally, individuals regard living on the

56. Ibid.

dole or welfare as more disgraceful than poverty itself. Hence, some people accept such reliefs only in moments of extreme deprivation, while some would rather steal than accept government hand-outs.

Furthermore, such reliefs have the potential of creating and encouraging the existence of a class of loafers – people who would rather parasite on society than exploit available opportunities to channel their energies into useful ventures. Lazy adults find such conditions conducive to their inclinations to waltz through life: drinking and making merry at the expense of the employed labour force or society in general.

Also, where welfare amounts to indiscriminate provision of elaborate child-care schemes, free education and free health care, the tendency is for people, loafers as well as usefully employed citizens, to breed children at will trusting that government would come to their rescue when it comes to the children's training and upbringing. The result of course is a high rate of national population growth.

Too much governmental involvement in the up-bringing of children may rob the parents of their primary responsibility to their offspring leading to a progressive weakening of the very fabrics of the family institution. And since the family is the microcosm of society, this also implies weakening the entire societal structure. As such, too much state interference results in indiscipline and juvenile delinquency because such usurpation of parental duties reduces the chances of parental control and guidance over children – an aspect of child education which the state can hardly imbue in children.

Furthermore, many who advocate for increased socialization of services on the grounds of reducing inequality of wealth distribution between individuals and classes within a society often lose sight of the fact that the very concept or application of socialization could equally bring about increased inequality between sub-national groups and therefore, in the long run, negate the very reasons for which it was applied. This assertion is particularly applicable in a heterogeneous society made up of sub-national groups that are at varying levels of development. Because the disparity in development could give rise to a corresponding disparity in needs for certain services (or their socialization) amongst the various constituent groups, we find that socialization of given service might amount to society paying for a service that is enjoyed predominantly by only a group or segment of society. This could lead to a progressive exploitation of groups that have least need for that service since they are now forced to pay more (say, by way of taxation) than they normally would have paid for that service if it were not socialized.

A case in point is the socialization of education in a country where the different constituent groups or sections are not at the same level of educational advancement. By socialization here, we mean that the central government undertakes to pay the cost of education (at all levels) in the country. If that country consists of two sections that are equally populated but one section provides, say, eighty per cent of the pupils in the educational institutions while the other has only twenty per cent then the "free education" or full socialization of education would, in the final analysis, contribute towards a disproportionate distribution of societal wealth amongst the two segments of the society, unless, of course, there is another socialized service which is predominantly enjoyed by the disadvantaged group or section to the extent of offsetting the imbalance caused by the socialization of education.

These limitations are increasingly raising questions as to the soundness of continued government involvement or expansion of welfare programmes. While extremist opponents of welfare demand that the problems of poverty and unemployment be left to private and voluntary organisations, moderates opine that there should be limited government involvement designed to complement, not displace parental, family or other voluntary institutions.

The popular view is that avenues where government involvement produces the best social ends should be explored. But many do not delude themselves that such socialization would solve the increasing rates of social stagnation that is afflicting many countries today, and that it is hardly applicable in developing countries where fund and resources are scant. Not even the rich countries are entirely comfortable with paying the bills of socialization. The strain in many European economies over welfare bills is a case in point.[57]

57. *Newsweek Magazine*, July 25, 1983, pp. 8 - 14

OVERVIEW

We have in the preceding sections examined four political ideologies that have evolved in contemporary human history and how their applications affect or are likely to affect societies. From those sections also we can easily discern that the distinctions among these ideologies are based on: -

(a) whether the economy is predominantly in private hands or is publicly controlled; and
(b) whether the political system is based on one party dictatorship or multi-party democracy.

Capitalism, for instance, combines private ownership with the multi-party system while Communism combines public ownership with one party system. Unlike socialism which combines public ownership with multi-party system, fascism combines private ownership with one-party system.

These distinctions raise questions as to whether fascism tends more towards capitalism (because the means of production are in private hands) or towards communism because of its adherence to one-party dictatorship). Or whether socialism is nearer to capitalism (because of its commitment to the multi-party democratic tradition), or communism (because it subscribes to public ownership and control of the means of production).

Such discussions underline the fact that capitalism and communism are the dominant ideologies not only because of their enormous influence the world over but also because of their philological standpoints. Hence, the ideological spectrum is often conceived as a linear one with capitalism and communism at the two extreme and opposing ends, while socialism and fascism fall at different points along this line.

Because of the relative weakness of socialism and fascism, capitalism and communism constituted the two major ideological forces, that kind of divided the world into two major opposing blocks. So strong was commitment and adherence of different peoples and nations the world over to these blocks that the future and survival of mankind appeared largely dependent on the lure of the relationship between the two erstwhile blocks. These differences gave rise to international tension and intrigues as well as civil disorder and confusion in many countries of the world. This is not to say that our world has now become so unified as to go without tensions!

However, it does appear that everybody, every group is beginning to come to the realisation that neither of the four political ideologies we have been looking at is perfect, and that there is need for a genuine and sober reflection and re-examination of our socioeconomic organisational formats as well as a deepening of our socio-political thought processes especially as it pertains to international relations.

In searching for a more relaxed international relation, therefore, one must not lose sight of this important root cause of the severe tensions of the past and today. And considering the defects already enumerated for each of the four existing ideologies, one cannot but opine that mankind has come to a point where a new set of ideas or organisational format is required for better governance of peoples the world over, the achievement of global stability, unity and wellbeing included.

Of course, such a set of ideas must be capable of universal acceptance if it is to deflate international tension and also be able to reconcile the authority of the state with the liberty of the individuals within nations. Common-sense dictates that such a body of ideas must be at once socialistic and individualistic as well as globally conscious and encompassing.

THE CENTRIST IDEOLOGY

Arguably, the bi-polar world in which the forces of capitalism and those of communism were stacked against each other in a deadly contest that almost ruined earthly existence is on the wane. In the one and a half centuries since the publication of Karl Marx's *Communist Manifesto* events have developed in a manner that has imperceptibly narrowed the gulf between the capitalistic and communist ways of life. This though has not happened without a lot of tears, sweat and blood.

However, it appears that the old quarrel as to whether the means of production and exchange should be in private or public hands has given way to a theory or notion that what property should be publicly or privately owned should be a matter of pragmatic analysis of suitability, and must be a function of time and place. The dominant feeling today appears to be that it is not *who owns property* that matters but *how property* is *used*. Indeed, there has been a movement away from the extreme ends of the ideological spectrum, from the Far-Left and the Far-Right, and a convergence towards the Centre.

Laudable and refreshing as the above changes and tendencies may be, it has to be observed that the Centre itself has for too long remained a varied, vaguely defined and nebulous concept. This state of affair of course introduces its own strains and stress on the world order and the organisational formats and wellbeing of nations. Conversely, all references and talk about centrist governments, including the notions of centre-right and centre-left regimes and philosophy remain something which like loose talk is very much in the air.

Indeed, the strains generated by the status quo leave people and nations uncertain and disoriented, without an adequate and valid conception of events going on around them and in fact their place in the scheme of things. The disorientation and uncertainty of course create a dangerous and potentially explosive feeling of alienation in both man and nation. The situation therefore calls for more reflection, study and definition of this centrist ideology.

In the same vein, it is also germane that in dealing with issues of insecurity and peaceful coexistence in the world; in attending to issues about environmental safety and cleanliness, and other problems of common nature that affect mankind everywhere, no nation should be by-passed or left behind. In other words, problems of international nature should be handled by all concerned.

Policies to be pursued at the international arena should be democratically determined or sanctioned by all nations. The present system of leaving such discussion to a select few in the UN Security Council leaves much to be desired, more so since the composition of that council constitutes a stumbling block, a drag on the resolution of many disputes, with the veto used most often to frustrate democratic processes and to achieve stalemate.

What we have now is like a situation in which old-order leaders of the capitalist, communist, socialist and fascist parties in a country were brought together and asked to chart the political direction of the nation. Nothing useful is likely to come out of such a set-up, as such leaders are most unlikely to agree on anything. In contrast, a system in which *leading* nations of the world strive to canvass support for their respective viewpoints from the other nations of the world and have these participate in decision-making through democratic elections is workable.

Such consultations, we believe, will help stabilise the global community and would help eliminate certain misconceptions, ensure healthy development and revolution in our living standards as well as consolidate the emerging centrist ideology and the attractions and lure of multiple power centres and dispersed or diffused power in the world. No doubt, this goal is worth working at!

CHAPTER 2

THE EGALITARIAN SOCIETY

Most of the squabbles and conflicts that pervade our planet today are traceable to the inability on the part of societies to work out appropriate methods of sharing jointly-owned resources and commonly-earned incomes. In industry, there is the age-old problem of relations of production, of distribution of income. This partly results in disagreements between capital and labour over what proportion of the 'value-added' or fruits of a venture is appropriated and by whom. Among sub-national groups as well as other primary and secondary groups the same problem is noticeable in revenue allocations and power-sharing processes. Even international relations are not spared of this problem. In fact, they appear to be the arena where the contest is hottest given the claim of every nation to sovereignty and the freedom to act as it deems fit.

Over the centuries, lasting and permanent solutions to the above problems have been elusive for a number of reasons, one of which is the absence of a generally or universally accepted definition or identification of what items or goods (tangible or intangible) men are likely to clamour for. Even where these goods are identified, there are differing notions as to the degree of importance or relevance that ought to be attached to each one. A global survey readily shows that while one good is given prominence in one part of the world, it is undermined in some other part or region. It is, therefore, necessary to define at the onset what constitutes these items or goods that man naturally tends to clamour or fight for.

Secondly, we are going to tackle the age-old question of what constitutes a fair distribution of these goods. And thirdly, the relative importance, if any, of each of these items or goods will be examined and related to the entire question of social harmony and stability.

SOCIAL GOODS

What societal goods do men clamour for? Do they end with economic wealth as certain writers tend to advocate or do they go beyond economics? To answer these questions, we need to delve a little into the elements of social stratification.

In every society it is common to find some men who are regarded as 'superior' while the others are regarded as 'inferior'. Very often, there are distinctions between higher and lower, richer and poorer, powerful and powerless individuals, etc. These categorizations together constitute the substance of social stratification. Except, perhaps, where everybody lives at a bare subsistence level, some people are always better-off than others. And from the fact that different individuals possess different abilities, desires and drives, it appears that even if all men were reduced to the same level economically, socially and otherwise, some form of differential development is bound to set in with time.

Social stratification is so complex and multi-faceted that categorization is mainly a tool for analytic studies rather than concrete domains in themselves. Although different people view stratification from different angles, three broad categories are generally discernible and widely accepted. These are known as CLASS, POWER, and STATUS. Although these arose from different sources, phenomena and criteria, they are usually closely related "and one of the central problems in the study of social stratification is the nature and extent of their relationships".[1]

1. El Chinoy, *Society, An Introduction to Sociology*, 2nd Edition, Random House, New York, 1967, p. 168.

CLASS

Class is usually associated with groups of people occupying the same economic position in society and may be defined "as a number of persons sharing a common position in the economic order".[2]

The existence and history of class is an old one, dating back probably to the earliest period of man's civilization. Aristotle, for instance, noted that there are "three elements" in all states: one class is very rich, another very poor and the third is average.[3] Marx defined classes in terms of their relationship to property, distinguishing; among those whose sources of income are from wage-labour, those from capital and those from land.[4] In that analysis, the capitalists were supposed to represent the rich class while land-owners and wage-labourers represented the middle and poor classes respectively.

Although the validity of this analysis in the times of Marx may not be disputed, its application in modern times has been blurred for a number of reasons. First is the emergence of the managerial cadre in modern capitalist economy whose members may own little in terms of property but who are, all the same, powerful in terms of both the power they exercise and their earning capabilities.

Second is the modern form of ownership (of means of production) based on the widely dispersed medium of stock ownership which blurs the dividing line between the capitalist and the labourer by simultaneously making one man a capitalist and a wage-earner. And thirdly, are the modifications in land laws (lease-hold to free-hold, etc.) in

2. Ibid. Pg. 171
3. Ibid pg. 169
4. Kari Marx, Capital, III, translated from the 1st German Ed, by Ernest Untermann, Kerr, Chicago, 1909.

different countries over the years which have *underplayed* the concept of land ownership and land-rent as criteria for defining a social class. Hence, it is now widely accepted that being self-employed (i.e. owning some form of productive property) does not necessarily qualify an individual for the rich class. Skilled labourers, managers, etc., who though may own little or no means of production, might well be found very high in the economic order by virtue of their earning power.

One lesson one learns from a close study of classes, is that men who occupy similar positions in the economic scale are very likely to face identical problems and experiences, and therefore, develop similar interests and attitudes especially in societal or group affairs. As such, in the daily struggle for existence and influence, members of one class, in the course of defending or protecting their class interests, are likely to coalesce. Even when a class remains only a social category, lacking group consciousness or organised structure, the fact that its members may act in roughly the same way, like in voting together and exhibiting similar social attitude, makes class – its nature and study very important in the societal process, and therefore, in figuring the true meaning or nature of equitability.

The relevance of class to the benefits derivable by an individual in a society is immense and variegated. Class position determines not only what one may wear or eat but also what type of house one can live in, what type of transportation facilities are available to him and generally what degree of leisure he can hope to enjoy. It partly determines the type of persons he would associate with and the reciprocation he could reasonably expect from them.

Indeed, even his self-esteem is partly dependent on what class he belongs to. Thus, it is widely believed that the higher the class a man belongs to, the higher his chances of living the 'good life'. Put in another way, class position partly determines the degree of contentment a man can have on earth. And since every normal man seeks maximum contentment, it stands to reason that every person is likely to make every possible effort (legitimate and sometimes, illegitimate) to belong to the higher classes, i.e. to want to possess a lot of money and/ or economic power.

From the foregoing, we can easily deduce that the pursuit and acquisition of wealth is a natural and legitimate aspiration of each normal member of the society, and that the instinct, desire or propensity to struggle for economic advantage is one of the fundamental rights of man. In this sense, therefore, we can say that class-position may be regarded as a social good. For it represents something so dear to man that he has to work, scramble, clamour and if necessary, fight for it. However, for the sake of simplicity we shall continue to refer to this social good as CLASS.

POWER

Power may be defined as the capacity of one person to control the action of others as well as resist such control from others. There is also the frequently correlative phenomenon, authority, which applies to societally recognised right to command in specific areas. Although many roles and statuses carry with them some prescriptive authority or approved freedom to command in certain areas that may affect the actions or behaviours of others, our primary focus here is on political power because of its over-riding effect on almost all other forms of power. Public office holders possess the power and authority for enacting and/or enforcing laws that can affect all facets of societal activities, and also determine what individuals must do or must not do. Furthermore, the fact that the state possesses the legal monopoly of force in all modern societies, makes all other forms of power and authority presumably subject to political control.[5]

So encompassing is the influence of political power on society and the lives of its individual members that almost everyone desires some form of power not only to exert obedience on his fellows but also to forestall others influencing him. A successful politician, for instance, enjoys a unique opportunity to make or influence decisions that affect, directly or indirectly, the lives of others, as well as his own fate. As such, the struggle for power is a very keen aspect of all societies, whether totalitarian or democratic, and the higher the power attached to any particular role or office, the higher the intensity with which people are inclined to compete for such a position.

These luring aspects of power then underscore the desire to participate in the political process or to seek political office as a natural and legitimate aspiration of any man. In fact, this is what makes political liberty or the freedom to political participation part of a man's fundamental rights. In this sense, therefore, we may regard political power as yet another social good because, like class, it is something so relevant to the totality of a man's "life chance"[6] that he has to scramble, work, clamour and sometimes, fight for it.

As a result of the foregoing, the mode of power distribution in any society becomes one of the crucial factors influencing the health of that society. Put another way, the type of institutions set up by society to supervise the distribution of political power and the method of determining and changing what role an individual can perform in the political arena, become very important factors vis-a-vis equity and what degree of peace and unity is achievable.

---

5. El Chinoy, *Society*, Op. cit. p. 175.

6. Life Chance" – an expression used by El Chinoy to describe – in his words "the opportunity to secure the things valued by society – income, goods, power, prestige etc. See — *Society, An Introduction to Sociology*, El Chinoy. Random House, New York, 2nd Ed. 1967. Page 171.

STATUS

We are often reminded by sociologists that wealth and power are not the only criteria with which men assess one another. Such seemingly intangible criteria as family, life style, sex, age, etc., provide alternative or additional bases for social ranking. The system of status – the ranking of roles and their incumbents – constitutes, therefore, another dimension of social stratification. Roles, for instance, vary in the prestige they carry and the reward they provide depending on the authority they carry, their relative importance, the number of persons capable of performing the requisite tasks, and so on.

Although empirical studies of status-ranking often make use of occupation as the chief index of status, it is by no means the only attribute or even the most vital. The importance of any one aspect is a matter of circumstance. The family, for instance, provides the initial or immediate status rank for a child and often forms a very important basis for his future ranking.

However, no matter the empirical characteristics or accepted prerequisites of status, it normally must be ratified by behaviour.

Of the many statuses men may occupy, we may distinguish those based on ASCRIPTION and those based on ACHIEVEMENT. An ascribed status derives from those attributes over which a person has no control, e.g. sex, age, family, tribe, colour, etc. A female remains a female no matter whether she dislikes being one or not and there is nothing she can do to alter it. On the other hand, an achieved status is based "upon qualities or attributes that can be gained only by some direct action – or luck."[7] One must, for instance, pass through or graduate from law

7. Ibid. p. 172

school to be a lawyer or must marry to become a husband or wife.

In primitive societies, ascription is the main or major mode of status-ranking especially with respect to assignment of roles. Leadership is, for instance, by inheritance or succession with a father passing the throne to his own child or children. In the Indian-Caste structure for example, society practically determined what role and, therefore, reward a person must carry out depending on what caste he is born to. His abilities or capabilities are not considered. On the hand status-ranking by achievement is mainly an attribute of modem societies.

Again, the status that men carry or are identified with, provides another basis for the determination of the liberties and perquisites each man may enjoy. The higher the status occupied by an individual the higher his chances of enjoying more liberties, leisure and other societal perquisites. In other words, the occupation of higher statuses contributes positively to the realisation of the good life. And since we have already established that the pursuit of the good life is a natural and legitimate concern of the average man, it can also be said that the tendency on the part of each member of society to work towards improving his status (at least the non-*ascriptive* aspect) is also a fundamental right. In fact, it is part of his civic liberty. Thus, status becomes the third and final social good in our analysis.

ESSENTIAL PROPERTIES OF THE FAIR DISTRIBUTION

From the foregoing, three social goods, namely; Class (or economic power), Power and Status have been identified as the principal attributes of social stratification. We are also led to understand that these three social goods are what men are inclined to clamour or fight for, and that a man's 'life chance" is largely a function of what quantity or quality of each of these items he possesses. We are also led to believe that when men judge the totality of an individual's social worth, they make use of these three criteria. Hence, the man who scores high on all three criteria inevitably appears on the top of the social scale and is accordingly treated. Conversely, those who score low on these counts, of course, find themselves at the bottom of the social scale, and so have to face the unfortunate consequences. Thus, the drive to escape the unpleasant and dire consequences of lagging behind or remaining at the bottom of the social ladder gives men the added impetus to carry on the daily toil and struggle that characterise existence. In the parlance of the modern psychologist, the quest for respectability remains one of the motivating forces behind life.

However, because men differ from one another in their capacities for work, desires and drives, as we pointed out earlier, it follows that not every man will attain and stay at the top of the ladder. In other words, some people must be high on the social scale while some must occupy lowly positions. All these are ways of saying that stratification or gradation (of individuals) is natural to any group or society. If we accept this basic assumption, then we can get on with the real issue: the proper nature of that gradation.

Depending on the rules established by society for the competition implied above, the proportion of people that find themselves either on the high or on the low side of the social scale varies within the society. This, in turn, generates different reactions or responses from members of the society. Where the rules are such as to help place only a few individuals high up on the social scale and the majority at the bottom, we may then witness the incidence of widespread bitterness and contempt for that system by the majority of its members. This, in turn, could cause some members – acting individually or in groups – to side-step the established rules in their desperate bid to achieve success. Put in another way, these people may resort to criminal or illegitimate ways in their pursuit of the good life. Where a majority of the inhabitants of that society turns against the established rules or order in an organised fashion, then a social movement, rather than isolated deviant behaviours, would result. Ultimately, social change may result. That is, a change of the existing or earlier rules.

Needless to add, the change can come about peacefully or, where there is sufficient resistance to peaceful change, it can come through violent means or revolution. Thus, we can conclude that peace and social stability are partly dependent on how properly the social goods of a society are divided among its citizens. For it is the response of man to the facts of stratification that partly leads to patterned behaviour which goes on to determine social structure.[8]

We can see from the above that the perceived weakness in the distribution of social goods partly accounts for the incidence of strife and chaos in societies. This leads directly to the questions as to what constitutes a fair distribution of these social goods in a society? That is to say, when does the distribution of social goods best assure the realisation of healthy social ends?

Those who interpreted fair distribution of economic power in terms of equal pay or remunerations for everybody regardless of role or skill are often forced by the consequences of such a policy in real life to re-think their stand. They are confounded by the very fact that differential pay or remuneration constitutes the most lasting and effective method of inducing or creating incentives for acquisition of skills, increasing outputs, accepting authority and responsibility, etc.

8. Social Structure — Defined by El Chinoy as the organised system of roles and statuses that define relations among groups and individuals'. Ibid. Page 471.

On the other hand, where differential income or remunerations are pushed up to a position of virtual concentration of economic power or wealth in a few hands, the result has always been negative to social aesthetics and political order.

With respect to political power, it must be emphasised that those who favour absolute freedom of individuals from any form of control by others or a constituted authority are only preaching false equality and, hence, anarchy. On the other hand, the apostles of concentration of power have often found themselves confounded by the inevitable abuse of such powers by their custodians. What is more, the usual unwillingness to obey orders, coupled with violent efforts by the ruled in such circumstances and societies to overthrow the rulers, reminds one of the inherent weaknesses of concentration. Strictly speaking, power that rests on naked force or is concentrated on a few individuals is by nature of things, unstable and transient.

With these points in mind, one is led to conclude that since both extremes (concentration and absolute lack of it) are defective, the ideal must be a compromise position corresponding to the gradation or stratification that is most acceptable to the majority of the members of the society.

In order to appreciate the nature of this compromise, it is considered necessary to apply some statistical concepts known as *normal distribution* and *skewed distribution*.

Normal Distribution

Statisticians use the term "normal" to describe anything or event that exists or occurs in its natural or unbiased form. Thus, a normal distribution is that distribution which, for all practical purposes, appears natural and unbiased. By way of illustration, let us assume, for example, that we are dealing with a class of 56 (fifty-six) students. When these students take an examination, how do we expect their marks to be distributed? *Naturally*, we would expect a few students to score very low marks, perhaps less than 20% each; some students to score extremely high marks, perhaps above 80% each; while the rest of the students would score marks ranging between these extremes. The following list (Table I) shows an example of what the scores might look like:

61,	17,	23,	33,	39,	70,	53,	6 6 ,
	13,	41,	73,	9,	26,	26,	
75,	24;	49,	67,	50,	64,	52,	4 1 ,
	87,	30,	47,	52,	58,	69,	
30,	46,	78,	31,	37,	42	73,	5 0 ,
	55,	53,	77,	64,	28,	52,	
64,	40,	47,	53,	62,	64,	56,	6 1 ,
	44,	75,	67,	43,	37,	59.	

Table I: Distribution of Scores.

If we add these figures or scores together, we will obtain a total of 2803, which when divided by 56 gives us an average mark of 50.05. This average is called the *mean* by statisticians. We can also arrange the marks in ascending or descending order as shown in the Table II below:

9,	13,	17,	23,	24,	26,	28,	3 0 ,
	30,	31,	33,	37,	39,	40,	
41,	41,	42,	43,	44,	46,	47,	4 7 ,
	49,	50,	50,	52,	52,	52,	
53,	53,	53,	55,	56,	58,	59,	6 1 ,
	61,	62,	64,	54,	64,	66,	
67,	67,	69,	70,	73,	73,	75,	7 5 ,
	77,	78,	87.				

Table 2: Distribution of Scores in ascending order.

The purpose of this re-arrangement is to enable us know the middle score. Since we have 56 scores, there are two middle scores: the 28th and the 29th scores. These are 50 and 52 in the table. In order to find the actual middle figure, we need to find the average of these two scores, i.e. $(50 + 52) \div 2$. This gives 51. This middle figure is what statisticians refer to as the *median*. A count of the number of times that each score occurs will also reveal to us the most frequently occurring figure as 64; it occurs 4 (four) times. The most frequently occurring figure is known as the *mode*.

Another thing that we can do to analyse these scores is by grouping them. For example, we can group the marks in such a way as to know the number of students that score below 10 marks, those who score between 10 and 19 marks, and so on. Using this grouping, we would arrive at Table III below. This table is known in statistics as the frequency table, because it tells us how frequently each group of marks occurs. For example, the marks in the 10 — 19 group occur only twice, while those in the 60 — 69 group occur 11 times.

Marks%	0-9	10-19	20–29	30–39	40–49
Frequency (no. of students)	1	2	5	7	10

Marks%	50-59	60-69	70-79	80-89	90–99
Frequency (no. of students)	12	11	7	1	0

Table III: Frequency Table

We can construct the graph of these figures as statisticians normally do to further highlight the characteristics of these marks. The graph is shown in figure I below. the curve shown on this graph is known as the

Frequency Distribution Curve.

It will be noticed that the curve appears symmetrical about the 50 – 59 line. That is, it looks as if this line divides it into two equal halves, one to the left and the other to the right. This is only coincidental, for many frequency curves give frequently asymmetrical shapes. But this leads us to the ideal frequency curve, the one that is perfectly symmetrical. It is known as the normal distribution curve, an example of which is shown in figure 2.

The curve is symmetrical about its mean, it is tallest at the mean, and its mean, median and mode are equal to each other. For example, in the above frequency distribution curve, the distribution would have been a perfectly normal one if, like the median, the mean and the mode are each 51.

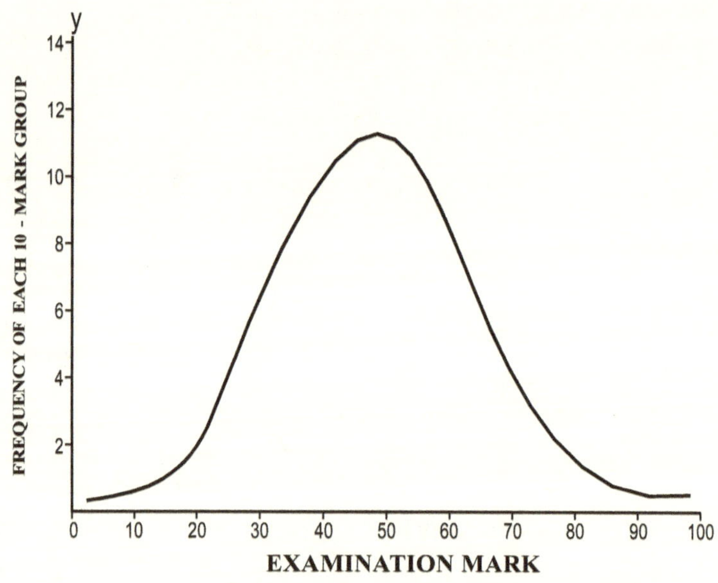

FIGURE 1: FREQUENCY DISTRIBUTION CURVE

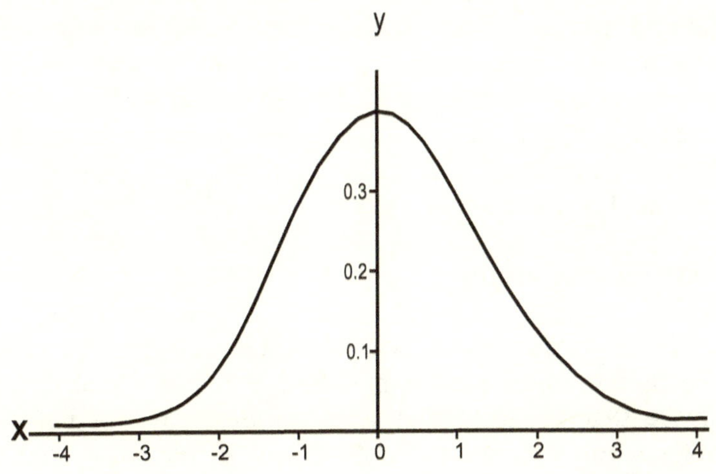

Fig. (2)   THE NORMAL DISTRIBUTION CURVE

$$y = \frac{1}{\sqrt{(2\pi)}}\, e^{-\frac{1}{2}x^2}$$

One major underlying condition for obtaining normal distribution curves is that the population (in this case, the students) being measured must be homogeneous. Homogeneity is obtained in the above example by the fact that all the students are from the same class, exposed to the same level of preparation for the examination, and hence, have equal opportunities to perform to their best. The results, therefore, reflect the natural pattern of performance that should be expected from any group of students, especially if their number is large enough.

Skewed Distribution

Now, let us imagine what would have happened in the most unlikely situation in which Forms III and V students are merged together to take an examination meant for Form V students only. Quite clearly, the Form III students would be placed in a position of disadvantage having not been prepared, like their Form V counterparts, for that level of examination. This will reflect in the results sheet through the recording of a large number of students with extremely low marks and a very small number of students with extremely high marks. This is said to be skewed on the positive side and may be represented by the curve shown in figure 3(a) below. It should be noticed that the curve is far from being symmetrical and hence from being normal.

The complement of this curve will occur if the examination had been set for Form III students with the Form V students as invitees to take part. Many with a large number of high marks and few with very low marks, a condition referred to as negatively skewed distribution, and depicted in figure 3(b), is likely to occur.

A skewed distribution curve should, therefore, be seen as a graphical representation of a distribution in which the set of conditions is biased or loaded against or in favour of some numbers of the population that is being observed. It is patently an abnormal type of distribution which relies on a method that fails to guarantee equality of opportunity.

Fig. 3a. POSITIVELY SKEWED DISTRIBUTION

Fig. 3b. NEGATIVELY SKEWED DISTRIBUTION

Significance of the Normal and Skewed Distribution Patterns

Because schools and colleges normally permit only the students of the same class to sit the same examination, the students usually produce results that follow the normal distribution pattern. And unless there are artificial attempts to manipulate results, every student would accept his or her result as a fair indication of his performance.

From the foregoing, it can be deduced that a normal distribution of any item (tangible or intangible) among the individual members of a society is least likely to bring about any serious opposition and disapproval. In other words, it is the fairest mode of distribution possible in this imperfect world. Furthermore, normal distribution shows a fluidity in ranking which abhors compact categorization. There is absence of rigid lines of separation from the various levels of stratification. This means that where a society is so stratified, there would be the least likelihood for people to develop undue class-consciousness – which is why we consider it the optimal point or the midway between concentration and absolute lack of it, and, therefore, a vital property (as far as distribution is concerned) of a true egalitarian society.

In summary, we would like to re-emphasise that for the distribution of economic power among individuals in a society to be deemed fair or equitable, such distribution must exhibit the following properties:

i) The frequency curve of the distribution must tend to normal. That is to say, that the averagely rich individuals or group must constitute the modal group with the number of richer and poorer individuals diminishing in relatively equal proportions from that point on either side of the modal group. That is, the eventual number of excessively rich or excessively poor individuals within the society is relatively small.

ii) That the income distribution among the various economic strata must reflect the properties of the normal distribution curve. *Also see chapter 3 for more characteristics.*

With respect to the distribution of political power, normalcy in distribution can hardly be expressed quantitatively as one does when handling more tangible items. However, a prudent qualitative analysis can readily give us a fair idea of what form of government is best suited in guaranteeing a semblance of normalcy in the distribution of power among individuals in a society. Such qualitative analysis is treated in chapter 6.

THE IMPORTANCE OF EACH SOCIAL GOOD AND ITS PROPER DISTRIBUTION IN SOCIETY

As already pointed out, the three principal attributes of social ranking or stratification — power, class and status are not mutually exclusive. They always hang together, reinforcing and promoting one another; the realisation of one often leads to the realisation of the rest. However, despite their inter-dependence and commonality, one notices that very often, societies tend to attach different degrees of importance to each of them and indeed, often rank or grade their principal attributes according to a socially perceived notion of importance and relevance.

Different societies stress different attributes of stratification. While one may emphasise power, the other may emphasise class or status. Emphasis on any of them as the dominant determinant of social worth is usually expressed by the degree to which society relies upon her in the determination of the social position of individuals. Thus, we find that in "any traditional societies with their little role-differentiation and primitive economics, stratification is usually anchored on STATUS position while money (which is often uniformly distributed anyway) and political power are often basically relegated to the background.

In contrast, modern associational societies often employ the CLASS and POWER indices as the chief determinants of social stratification. Amongst the communist countries, political power or the power attach to the different offices men occupy is the more dominant feature of stratification, while CLASS position remains, generally speaking, the crucial Index for measuring social worth or standing in the capitalistic societies.

A survey of societies and their stratification systems readily brings out the fact that the tendency to rank or to emphasise different attributes of social ranking is potentially dangerous. This is because it leads inevitably to the unfair use of the rest and consequently to the deterioration of the entire social order. To buttress this assertion, we are going to take a brief look at a few societies and the influence of their respective stratification systems on their various social orders.

The United States and the Soviet Union (now defunct) are typical examples of societies that are characterised by a relatively open stratification system. That is to say that the distribution of roles and statuses are largely dependent on achievement rather than ascription. Social mobility is also relatively high in these two countries. Notice the emphasis on relativity; it underlines a comparison with what obtains in the traditional societies where closeness and/or reliance on *ascriptive* principles is the order. It aims at bringing out the fact that while inheritance is a dominant feature of traditional and closed societies, the modem/associational and open societies tend to emphasise competition as an instrument of role and status allocation. Thus the USA, the USSR (and other modern societies) can be said to be leading the way towards the realisation and actualisation of one of the above-stated characteristics of a fair society, namely; the existence of the highest possible degree of achieved or achievable statuses and the lowest possible degree of ascribed statuses, buttressed by a high social mobility.

But there ends the similarity. When it comes to the distribution of class and power indices, these two countries are poles apart. While one emphasises class the other tends to lay more emphasis on power.

STRATIFICATION IN THE CAPITALIST COUNTRIES AS TYPIFIED BY THE USA

Comparatively, the commitment to 'political liberty' by the capitalist countries like the United States expressed in their democratic tradition, not only brings widespread political participation but also makes the occupation of any political office by any individual both temporary and transient. The electoral process, the existence of open and legalised opposition and pressure groups, etc., plus the relative diffusion of political power inherent in the democratic process all combine to weaken the awe that normally surrounds political office or office-holders. All these tend to make for fair distribution of power in capitalist countries, to the extent that inequality in wealth and status distributions would allow.

However, despite the constitutional provisions of "economic liberty" in these countries, the capitalist mode of production and distribution for which these societies are known make nonsense of fair distribution of economic power. (See Chapter 1.) The result is skewed distribution of wealth or economic power and an unequal opportunity for individuals to rise from low to high economic positions.

In the USA, concentration is shown by the fact that "fewer than 0.1 per cent of the citizens own 20 per cent of all individually held stock".[9] Difficulty for individuals to rise appreciably from low to high economic positions in America is succinctly expressed by El Chinoy in an ingenuous analysis. In his words, "Social mobility and equality of opportunity, however, have probably never been as widespread as Americans have believed ... Measured against a standard of equal opportunity for all, one might conclude that social mobility has been seriously

9. William Ebenstein & Edwin Fogelman, *Todays -Isms*, Op. Cit. P. 154.

limited. (It is only when) compared with a society in which social position is usually inherited, (that) America has always offered rich and unusual opportunity".[10]

Hence, rigid class structure has over the centuries become a common feature in the USA as well as many other capitalist countries. And as a result of the shameless exploits of the upper classes, membership of that class continues to elicit uninhibited awe, fear and respect. The rich are literally worshipped, while the poor is held in contempt, oppressed and often abused. Thus, the fundamental division in the USA and other capitalist countries is based on class lines. Whereas violent clashes between the rich individual or his class and the poorer individual or his class are a regular and persisting feature of most capitalist countries, while antagonism, violent movements and state repression based on political differences are less evident.[11]

So pervasive is the importance attached to monetary wealth and material acquisition in the USA that CLASS practically subsumes POWER and STATUS, becoming the principal index of stratification. Possession of strong economic power is so emphasised that even in the political arena it is more or less a definite pre-condition for aspiration to high political offices; overshadowing the other more important issues of personal integrity, fitness and sincerity of purpose.

To this end, many now view American political races or elections as more or less contests of 'money-bags'. According to A. Sero,[12]

---

10. El Chinoy, op. Cit. Pp. 201 – 202.

11. *Newsweek Magazine*, Jan. 17, 1983 page 18 – 29;
    Newsweek Magazine, Feb. 14, 1983 page 10 – 19

12. A. Sero, U.S. Election as 'A CONTEST' of moneybags', *National Concord*, August 8, 1984.

Money remains the main factor for ascending to power in the United States ... Leading Corporations provide the bulk of election funds. This is quite natural as elections in the United States boil down to replacing one henchman of the leading corporations with another.

In one instance, A. Sero pointed out that American millionaire, Joseph Kennedy, father of the late American President John F. Kennedy,

> paid some $200,000 for his son, John, to become a congressman. Six years later the parent spent nearly $500,000 to make his son a Senator. In 1958, he invested $1.5 million so that John would be nominated the Democratic Party candidate for the Presidential election. Two other sons of the millionaire, Robert and Edward became Senators in a similar way.

Furthermore, there is a persistent feeling that despite all the external impressions of noble resoluteness, inner strength and non-compromise that some American political leaders and elected officials or representatives exude, many of them are but mere pawns in the hands of over-rich and often ruthless individuals – the so-called political financiers and party well-wishers – who end up pulling the myriad strings ever hooked unto the politicians they sponsor or finance. Because many politicians are financially handicapped, they usually make behind-the-scene pledges and sign secret allegiances to some rich socialite cum political overlords in order to secure the much needed and all-important financial support necessary to run and win elections in that country.

Consequently, these often shady and sinister millionaires who stick to the background, assume the role of de facto rulers or decision takers as they are usually consulted at every turn by their puppets in public offices. Reference is made here to Charlie 'Lucky' Luciano's[13] own revelations of mafia control of New York politics as far back as the mid-twenties and their surprising involvement in the 1928 and 1932 American Presidential elections.[14] American famous novelist, James Hadley Chase, ingenuously portrayed the typical American saga and inner picture of the thriving financier-politician nexus and indeed the exploits of gangster politicians of America in his books entitled, *The Whiff of Money*, and, *Tiger by the Tail*.[15]

Thus, we can say that the over-reliance on CLASS as the chief instrument of social gradation or the existence of widely separated classes in America as well as other capitalist countries effectively pollutes their social scene. It encourages political corruption and economic crimes among others. It also encourages ultra-acquisitive tendencies, and makes monetary pursuits a life or death affair thereby making crime an everyday pastime. All these go to explain the myth surrounding the much publicised American notion that power flows from the dollar. Indeed, they tell us why "fulfilling the American dream" is just another phrase for amassing unlimited wealth.

13. Charlie 'Lucky' Luciano (1897 – 1962) — America's acclaimed most notorious gangster who supervised and organised the American Underworld. He was later imprisoned and subsequently expelled or exiled from USA. Till his death, he remained at least in name, the head of the American Mafia.

14. Martin Gosch and Richard Hammer, *The Luciano Testament*, Pan Books, 1976; pp. 88 – 89, 103 – 105, 159 – 170. See also, *Uncle Frank, The Biography of Frank Costello* by Leonard Katz, Pocket Book, New York 1975. Chapter 8.

15. James Hadley Chase, *The Whiff of Money*, Panther BK Ltd. '70, p. 12; *Tiger by the Tail*, Panther Book Ltd. 1966.

STRATIFICATION IN THE COMMUNIST COUNTRIES AS TYPIFIED BY THE USSR

Although differentials in wages for Soviet citizens may be comparable to wage distribution in the Western world or the rich capitalist societies, the distribution of wealth in the two worlds is quite another thing. Because of the institutionalised state ownership and control of productive properties in the Soviet Union and the communist world in general, individuals did not accumulate, and could not have easily accumulated (whether by covert or overt means) disproportionate amounts of wealth as we see in the West or the capitalist countries. As a result of this relative fairness in the distribution of wealth or economic power, there was little room for conspicuous consumption, subversion of justice by the use of monetary inducements or influences, existence of a large number of professional killers who murder solely for monetary rewards, and all those other sinister occurrences that characterise societies with lopsided distribution of wealth. As such, the tendency to estimate the social worth of individuals primarily in terms of financial standing or to underplay the import of personal integrity, behavioural traits, and sometimes the social impetus of political office, was relatively non-existent in the defunct Soviet Union.

On the other hand, the totalitarian nature of Soviet politics with its reliance on, and adherence to, the one-party system, caused an acute skewness in the distribution of political power. (See Chapter I) Looking at the effectiveness of each of the three basic attributes of social ranking in the Soviet Union, one is struck at the over-riding predominance of power. It is easily noticed that the fundamental division in Soviet life was based on power. Political power rested solely with the Communist Party members and especially the leadership of the party. This means that only a minor section of the populace monopolised the politics of the land, making all the decisions without recourse to the wishes or mandate of the people.

In 1961, the Soviet Communist Party had only 9 million members even though there were over 200 million people in the country.[16] Because political power was concentrated in few hands, party membership became extremely difficult to achieve. It was the privilege of a few who act like tin-gods, exuding awe, and keeping the ordinary man in a state of permanent servitude. The position of the individual on the political scale was, therefore, crucial: it practically determined an individual's social worth. Thus, politics not only determined salary or income differentials but also who got preferential access to state shops, reserved vacation resorts and other perquisites. Alexander Solzhenitsyn clearly brought out these deficiencies in his true to life accounts as recorded in his following books, *The First Circle;* and, *One Day in the Life of Ivan Denisovich.*[17] In fact the latter gives us an insight into the nightmare that could befall the powerless in the Soviet Union. Although these books were set in the form of novels, it is widely known that they are based on the author's personal experience and on-the-spot assessment.

We, of course, subscribe to the notion that the struggle for power exists in both democratic and authoritarian or totalitarian societies, but we would like to point out that the

16. El Chinoy, *Society*, Op. Cit. P.187.

17. Alexander Solzhenitsyn, 1. *The First Circle*, Fontana, 1970. 2. *One day in the Life of Ivan Denisovich,* Bantam Bks, 1963.

degree differs. In the Soviet Union as with every other totalitarian society, the struggle for power was more or less a matter of life and death.[18] A loser in that game is a doomed man. Thus, to ensure success, the participants were prepared to employ any means including, assassination, treachery, sabotage etc. to achieve their goals. In the words of Richard Nixon,

> Those who get to the top in the Soviet system [did] so by being more cunning, more brutal and more ruthless than their rivals. Leon Trotsky wrote that 'Lenin at every opportunity, emphasised the absolute necessity of terror!'[19]

In short, just as the American may be inclined to eliminate others because of economic-related differences or quarrel, so did men tend to eliminate others in the Soviet Union on the basis of politics-related differences or quarrels. Also, just as many Americans languish in jails or suffer because of 'economic crimes', so did many Soviet citizens suffer because of 'political crimes'.[20] Finally, just as we may say that political power flows from economic wealth in the USA, so we may say that economic advantages flowed from the possession of political power or influence in the defunct USSR.

18. William Ebenstein and Edwin Fogelman, *Today's -Isms*, Prentice-Hall, Inc., Englewood Cliffs, New Jersey, 1980. Page 43.

19. Richard Nixon, *The Real War*, Op. Cit. Page 254.

20. *Newsweek Magazine*, Feb. 14, 1983, 'The Forgotten', pp. 10 -19.

Newsweek Magazine, Jan. 17, 1983, 'Portrait of America', pp. 18 - 29

STRATIFICATION IN INDIA

The traditional Indian society presents a typical example of a closed society. Her rigid rank order, clear-cut hierarchical arrangement of the different social groups, reliance on ascription as the principal yardstick for role and status distribution, etc., have made that society the model of a closed society or what sociologists usually refer to as a Caste System. Within the traditional Indian society, life-chance is chiefly dependent on birth: social mobility is virtually non-existent. Men are born into a caste, grow up and eventually die as members of that particular caste. El Chinoy has given extensive description of the Indian caste system. And the brief outline given below is from that source.[21]

The traditional Indian society is usually divided into four main castes – the priests, warriors, merchants and the peasants or workers. A fifth group consists of those who have been expelled from their original castes mainly as punishment for violation of some group norm. These fall into a class of citizens known as outcasts or the untouchables. They may be allowed back into their original castes only after the fulfilment of certain laid down conditions or the performance of some cleansing rituals.

Membership of a caste is hereditary, depending on what family one is born into. Within each caste could be found many more sub castes with members assigned very distinct and unique positions. These members are expected to behave or act in styles that befit or are expected of those who belong to the particular social niche. The number and roles assigned to each of these sub castes are difficult to

21. El Chinoy, Society, Op. cit., pp. 179—184.

determine because of the large numerical and territorial size of India. The caste structures within the localities and provinces are different from one another both in form and character as few castes extend throughout the whole sub-continent. However, certain common characteristics can be discerned from all the various shades and colours of castes and sub castes existent in the country. Amongst these are:

1. Caste membership is hereditary and is fixed for life except for those who may lose membership for one reason or the other.
2. Members are expected to marry within their castes: hyper-gamy is very limited and often frowned at.
3. Individuals are expected to carry on the occupations of their fathers or more generally to cling onto the traditional callings of their castes.
4. There are strict rules and regulations on the relationships among members of different castes as well as members of the same caste. During communal rituals or festival, each caste is expected to perform certain laid-down functions, provide certain needed materials and generally behave or act in some prescribed ways.

Within the traditional Indian society, STATUS as distinguished from CLASS and POWER, has remained the chief index of social stratification. Despite all the modern industrial, economic and educational policies embarked upon in recent times by succeeding Indian governments, which have paved the way to a progressive dilution of the traditional emphasis on inherited statuses, family, racial, ethnic and religious backgrounds still play a crucial role in the determination of one's life-chance in India. Even when one may have, in some way, achieved better class and power positions in today's Indian society, one's social esteem might still be looked upon through the eyes of one's ancestral status.

And very often caste or ancestry plays a vital role as to how far an individual can move on the economic and political ladder. Thus, the problem over there is oppression of man by man based on atavistic chicanery.

In the light of the foregoing, it is evident that society must place all three social goods on the same pedestal when considering their distribution. As America's news magazine, *Time* put it while assessing the legacy of the late and great American Ex-President Franklin Delano Roosevelt (1882 – 1945),

> Government has a duty to promote a reasonably fair distribution not only of wealth but of power and status and what Roosevelt called simply 'the good things of life'.[22]

22. *Time Magazine*, Feb 1, 1982, p. 28

FURTHER ATTRIBUTES OF AN EGALITARIAN SOCIETY

The existence of society is based on the fact that the behaviour of one person is oriented, in innumerable ways, towards the behaviour of the other person or persons. Not only do we live together and share common values, beliefs, opinions and customs, we also continually interact, responding to one another and in the process shaping and reshaping our individual perceptions and attitudes in relation to the behaviours and expectations of those around us.[23]

Social expectations, the benefits derivable from conforming to societal demands or sanctions, therefore, partly cause human behaviour to show regular and recurrent patterns, and for each society to possess in the final analysis, what may be called its way of life – a culture that defines appropriate, acceptable or required modes of thinking, talking, acting, etc., in the society. It is upon this general framework that society's laws, customs, mores, folkways, and so on, which guide the ways men relate to one another, are built. It is also the fore-runner of social stratification. By establishing rules that govern behaviour and values upon which men estimate (or judge) themselves and those around them, culture inadvertently brings social ranking or gradation into the fore.

But so far as class, power and status or their realisation are dependent on some other cultural traits of a society, the issue of what constitutes proper social ranking cannot be exhausted without due reference or regard to the effects of some other factors which influence the ultimate social structure of the society. Among these factors are education, religion, the judiciary, technology, healthcare, and the like.

23. El Chinoy, *Society*, Op. Cit., p. 25

We shall examine some of these factors in order to keep their contributions at the back of our minds and bring out their relevance in the determination of the essential features or properties of an egalitarian society.

EDUCATION

Formal education is without question the product of modern times. Prior to the modern era, education – the process through which skills, knowledge, values, and perspectives needed or necessary for adult life are transmitted to the young – was largely an informal affair. This was so because during the early periods of man's known history, there was little or no role differentiation, and available knowledge was relatively limited or small. Hence by simply following the footsteps of their parents or elders, children were able to learn all the farming and hunting techniques there were, and the primitive methods of predicting the weather, while social norms, traditional beliefs, customs and moral standards were unconsciously absorbed in the course of daily life, interaction and seasonal rituals.

However, with the current and ever-increasing explosion in knowledge, and the prevailing complexity in cultural values and systems of social control, have come a system of education specifically designed to inculcate appropriate values and know-how because the old and casual system can no longer satisfy the needs of the moment. Today, formal education, as the new system is appropriately called, may start with nursery classes and end with post-graduate studies thus taking a considerable portion of an individual's life-span as well as demanding the expenditure of large capital that may be beyond the means of the individual.

Although formal education is only a part of the complex process of socialization that transforms an infant into a social being, it is very vital in determining the suitability of an individual to performing certain roles or occupying certain important positions or offices in modern, commercial, scientific, military, cultural and political endeavours. The acquisition of certain levels of education is linked to job placement, income, power as well as the prestige attached to the role the individual plays. Put in another way, education has become the cynosure of life-chance in all modern societies and the availability of adequate educational opportunity for all has become a primary indicator of social justice.

All these go to underline the social relevance of formal education vis-a-vis morality, social mobility, stratification and equalitarianism. Every society now places a lot of importance on education as an institution, and to the relative opportunities which the individuals in the society have for acquiring formal education. Thus, education has come to occupy a prominent position in many countries, and hence, is treated as a matter of considerable national interest which, if ignored, can lead to very serious and adverse political consequences.

Historically, the provision of educational facilities was considered the responsibility of religious organisations in many countries of the world. As a result of the recognition of education as a potent factor in national development, the involvement of the state became imperative. Ironically, however, religious bodies were not to willingly relinquish their role as the traditional custodians of education.

Consequently, they have put up stiff resistance which tended to undermine the sovereignty of the state in the matter of education. In Nigeria, for instance, where the various state governments systematically and progressively took over the control and administration of primary and secondary educational institutions from religious and voluntary organisations in the seventies, the latter put up a stiff resistance and in some cases, went as far as taking the government to court to challenge it for taking over educational institutions established by private, particularly, religious organisations. These organisations did not only believe that their provision of educational services was a right, but also that they were in a better position to provide the type of education best suited for the training of morally sound citizens. But as far as the state is concerned, its control of education was so necessary as to warrant the socialization of educational institutions.

Besides, this control is important if education must be accessible to as many citizens as possible. The state also believes that religious activities in schools sometimes jeopardise the process of national integration since different religious groups and denominations often espouse sentiments that create bitterness, hatred and antagonism among themselves thereby undermining the moral argument for their control of education The old religious related quarrels in Lebanon and Belfast (Northern Ireland) are often cited as examples of the destabilizing effects of the involvement of religious organisations in the control of education.

Whichever way the situation is viewed, there is no denying the fact that modern man has come to the point where some degree of socialisation of education or the educational institution is a sine qua non for the evolution of a viable and humane social order. Also it determines the chances of proper and effective distribution of social goods in the society.

RELIGION

The religious institution provides yet another strong influence over what modes of social relationship and interaction should develop within societies. Since religion is a unified system of beliefs and practices (relative to sacred things) which are capable of producing one single moral community,[24] it influences not only the process of

24. Ibid. Page 354.

mustering consensus and solidarity within the society but also the behavioural patterns of individuals and those unconscious and often subjective gradation of the statuses of individuals to which our minds are always vulnerable. In the final analysis, the influence of religion on the society is reflected in the prevailing social order. Because the religious institution or belief system provides a primary context of self-identification and social location, human beings, from time immemorial, not only take particular interest in knowing what religious group or denomination to which others belong or are born into but also often make extra efforts to discern the extent to which those around them are committed to their professed creed. They distinguish the fanatics from mere subscribers and those who merely follow for the sake of group identity. In the process, the degree of commitment, non-commitment or the extent of internalisation of a person's chosen faith is held either for or against him by others.

The impact of religion as a tool for social ranking is considerable in many modem societies where civilized conduct has made the co-existence of diverse religious groups possible within a single political entity. However, where individuals subscribe to the notion that Christians, Muslims, Jews, Buddhists or whatever religious group, behave in a certain peculiar way without paying due regards to personal relativity, individual differences and styles, or the age-old adage that "a thousand monks represent a thousand religion", a most dangerous and alarming state of affairs is created. The system of status or social ranking, that is the much contributed by religious colouration becomes grossly biased. Instead of normal ranking and fluid gradation, we have rigid compaction and skewness. But where individual relativity and differential commitment to creed is reckoned with by his fellows, a tendency towards normal ranking or gradation is enhanced, and the extent to which religion affects one's life-chance is mellowed thereby giving the prevailing social order a more humane colouration. At group level, such awareness and/or tolerance helps to prevent religion-based conflicts and schism.

JUDICIAL AND LEGAL INSTITUTIONS

Although every society provides positive rewards for conformity to group norms in the hope of forestalling deviancy, "there remains occasions when, for various reasons, men prefer or decide to disregard the dictates of their culture".[25] They act or behave in ways detrimental to group goals in order to satisfy their own individual yearnings. To check such inclinations, society invariably sets up various sanctions or penalties to which those who defy social norms must be subjected. Depending on the specific types of deviancy, the sanctions devised against non-conformists and the prevailing climate of opinions, some individuals are forced to obey certain cultural prescriptions. Thus, penalties and sanctions represent vital elements of social control and the bedrock of the judicial and legal institutions. They also give definite directions to the behavioural patterns of individuals thereby influencing the structure of societies and the freedom of the members of the society.

Sanctions come in various shades and forms, and are designed to check various degrees of deviance. For example, teasing and ridicule may be employed to check minor infringements especially within small close-knit communities, while ostracism or ex-communication may be applied in more serious circumstances.

25. Ibid, p. 457

In the large, more formal, impersonal social-setting however, law-breaking as deviancy is regarded, may lead to fines and imprisonment. In very extreme cases, like first-degree murder, the state or society may even impose or demand the death penalty.

Despite the drive towards exacting conformity to cultural and legal prescriptions and the maintenance of ordered relationships, society still recognises that there are certain human reactions or behaviours which though may amount to deviancy, nevertheless provide outlets for stress and tensions generated by social restraints, and by cultural and structural inconsistencies. Also there are certain individuals, who by nature, may possess certain basic but excessive drives which even the all-powerful forces of social and cultural pressure cannot effectively contain. Hence, it is widely recognised that to impose sanctions on some of these drives and on some of the categories of individuals may be unrealistic and counter-productive, either because of the large number of individuals likely to contravene such rules or because the commitment of such actions by some people provide satisfaction and psychological relief to others.

In order to contain these abnormalities therefore, without sacrificing or jeopardizing orderliness, society often makes rules aimed at the regulation of these critical behaviours rather than erecting permanent barriers against their performance. Thus, we have what sociologists usually refer to as institutionalised safety valves. Many jokes, games and sports, various rituals and regulated forms of conflict like boxing, wrestling, etc., come under this sphere. This may explain why a society which frowns at street fighting and brawls encourages and promotes or at least condones the enactment of vicious and murderous engagements within the roped square. No matter how one looks at the whole set-up, it is debatable whether the cancellation of these practices will do much to encourage or enhance social justice or whether it will bring about anarchy and social disequilibrium. Indeed, the American experience in the twenties to the early thirties provides a good example of the futility of legislating morality or enacting laws that are beyond the threshold of the acceptance of the majority of members of the society.

On January 16, 1919, "the eighteenth Amendment to the Constitution of the United States was ratified, to become the law of the land a year later. It banned the general manufacture, sale and transportation of intoxicating liquors and beers".[26] It was a failure right from inception. By December of 1933 when it was repealed, it had only succeeded in:

(a) producing a generation of Americans that saw nothing wrong with breaking an unpopular law;

(b) making alcohol distribution and sales the business of the underworld, turning small-time criminals into powerful millionaire gangsters, and the now renowned American Mafia, and

(c) Lionizing the bootleggers; giving a moral boost to the infamous and the deviant.

This experience notwithstanding, the judicial and legal institution is such a vital organ of social control and the sustenance of civilized behaviour that is often referred to as the last hope of the common man. It provides the only legitimate antidote against the oppression of the weak by the mighty, and serves as a unique tonic to social well-being and ordered collective life. Hence, judicial and legal

26. *The Luciano Testament*, by Martin Gosch arid Richard Hammer, Pan Books! Macmillan, London, 1976. Pages, 37-52, 73-74, 88, 103, 104, 112, 126 and 171

corruption, ineffectiveness or inefficiency are conceivably amongst the worst tragedies that can befall any civilization. As such, the sanctity of the judiciary must be seen as a pre-requisite for the evolution and sustenance of a humane and equitable social order.

SCIENCE AND TECHNOLOGY

"Technology – the tools, machines and implements men create, plus the knowledge and skill required for their utilization – is a vital component of a people's culture and is crucial in the transformation of available resources into the things men want or desire".[27] The relevance of practical skill, scientific principles and generalised knowledge to the state of a people's technological know-how is underlined by the fact that without the necessary technological base even a complex machine becomes more or less useless to any people. On the other hand, where the basic skill exists, a very simple or crude implement could produce extra-ordinary results.

For most of mankind's recorded history, available technology was scant or crude and technological progress was due mainly to trial and error methods based on on-the-spot practical experimentations. However, in more recent times, a marked change has occurred both in the volume of available technological know-how and in the ways technological innovation are pursued. The untrained inventor has given way to a class of professionally trained engineers and scientists who now utilize abstract scientific knowledge and research institutions to chart the progress of technology. Thus, modern technology, as today's technological know-how is christened, has become a far-cry from the crude technical know-how of a few centuries ago. This revolution in technology has created many

27. Chinoy, Society, Op. Cit. Page 5

outlandish innovations amongst which are nuclear power and spaceships.

Discussing technology from a universal standpoint as above, it must be pointed out, often creates a deceptive picture about the state of technological advancement in different regions of the world. It tends to eclipse the fact that all nations are not at par vis-a-vis technological know- how. That, in reality, the extent of differentiation in technological know-how for different nations is so high that it has given rise to the categorization of different countries into different "worlds". Thus, we have, at one extreme the "First World" which includes the technologically advanced countries of Europe, North America, Asia and Australia, and at the other end of the stratum, the "Third World" which is made up of the least technologically developed countries of Asia, Africa and South America.

Many reasons have been advanced for the existing disparity amongst nations in technological development. Among the most favoured is the concept of geographical determinism. According to this view, geography sets most of the important problems men must cope with and also provides the resources that can be utilized. Thus, it is argued that the propensity for technological development is higher in areas with harsh environmental conditions and in which the relevant resources exist, other factors being constant. However, no matter what reasons are adduced for the existing poor technological culture in some countries, one cannot question the increasing relevance of modern technology to the wellbeing of nations and the promotion of egalitarianism in all modern societies.

So widespread is the influence of technology that there has emerged a school of thought which more or less subscribes to a monistic technological interpretation of society and history. There is also the correlative tendency to equate technological progress to social progress. Technological determinism, as this monistic interpretation is referred to, is then the view that men's attitudes, interests, habits and thinking are inevitably determined by the prevailing technological climate. Thorstein Veblen, a prominent advocate of this view, went to a great length in explaining the subtle aspects of this view. He contrasted the different demands the machine industry makes, as compared to the erstwhile handicraft system, upon man and society, and then concluded that culture, social structure, etc., change according to the prevailing technological environment.

The technological interpretation of history, social change and social structure, despite the elaborate treatment given to it by men like Veblen, has been rightly criticised by many social analysts as only a one-sided approach to the issue. They argue that although technology does exert enormous pressure on such other institutions as religion, the family, education; military organisation, demography, and so on, as well as the way men look at these institutions particularly in the long run, it is not in itself insulated from counter-influences by these institutions. In other words, technological progress is itself largely determined by such variables as the value system, social structure and the demands of other social institutions erected by men. Hence, the adaptation of any given technological alternatives or innovations, depends on such criteria as efficiency, possible effects on employment levels and the expected effects of the alternatives on the workers, the environment and the society at large. It is also argued that in the final analysis, the impact of any technological innovation is conditioned to some extent by the social and cultural context.

However, while rejecting technological determinism or the correlative misconception that technological progress necessarily amounts to social progress, one must not lose sight of the immense contribution technology makes in shaping the society and the attitude of man to life. This assertion can be illustrated from many standpoints; firstly, it is a truism that the stability of any social or political entity is partly dependent on the ability of its members to provide themselves the basic material needs of life or that there is a minimum level of economic well-being required for the survival of any social unit. Thus, where the conditions of living are below the subsistence level, as may be found in societies with primitive technology, the chances are that the pre-occupation with the daily or seasonal food-gathering schemes, hardship and hunger would impede lasting civilised social relationships as men are more likely to think with their stomachs than with their heads. Conversely, where a certain degree of technological know-how and, therefore, economic well-being exist, men are freed from constant concern for immediate needs giving way to leisure, planning and a diversification of activities that are likely to usher in better cultural and social relationships.

Secondly, technology provides opportunities for the development of concrete ideas for the achievement or sustenance of sound economic and socio-political formats and/or serves as a vehicle for the transmission of these ideas to the individual. But apart from these, it can also provide the instruments for (coercive) social as well as political control. Within the technologically advanced countries, one finds that technology is being used for the enforcement of laws ranging from minor traffic offences to the more serious issue of state security. Sophisticated mass-communication equipment make possible the daily task of moulding public opinion and in forestalling the mutual suspicion and mistrust that characterise big countries in which ethnic and geographical distances serve as obstacles to national integration. The late and ex-Pakistani President, Ali Bhutto, was right when he asserted that, "what the developed countries control with their sophisticated technology, we (the Third World) fight with bare fists".[28]

The above then may explain – at least in part – the turmoil that today characterises the social, economic and political life of the emergent nations of the Third World. It goes to underline the importance of acquiring a measure of technological sophistication as a prelude to the evolution, sustenance and improvement of modes or patterns of social relationships. In this sense, it can hardly be disputed that the march towards true egalitarianism or an equitable social order must be accompanied by a commensurate increase in a people's productive capacity or technological know-how.

ABSENCE OF CULTURAL IMPERIALISM AND ETHNOCENTRICISM

For as long as the perception of what constitutes a society varies from one community to another and for as long as the belief is held that the freedom of man everywhere is partly dependent on the vagaries of international relations, for that long will the issue of cultural imperialism and ethnocentrism remain a central one in the definition and estimation of the fair society. Although the problem of cultural imperialism and ethnocentrism exists within small communities and nation-states, we intend here to focus on its international dimension, since nation-states are supposed to represent unified political entities.

28. Lagos, *Daily Times*, 1982

Ethnocentrism – "the tendency to regard as natural what is widespread or conventional in one's own society, the view that one's own group is the measure of man everywhere"[29] – constitutes a major obstacle to healthy intergroup or international relations and to scientific objectivity. Because ethnocentrism tends to judge people by the standard of other presumably superior culture as compared to moral relativity (which takes into consideration the diversity in the cultures of different peoples and so tries to judge each culture in its own context), it (ethnocentrism) tends to promote misunderstanding, suspicion and antagonism between peoples. It also encourages cultural imperialism.

This is inevitable when an individual is so fanatical about his own culture that he is unable to appreciate that some cultural traits in another's culture might be as good or even better than his and that no culture can lay claim to perfection. A living example is the antagonistic relationship that existed between communist countries and the capitalist countries. Certainly, if these groups of countries were inclined or disposed towards appreciating the possible good traits in each other's culture, the world would not have been the nightmare that it was, say during the cold war era.

Thus, we may conclude that for our society (the global community) to become a fair society, we (every nation) must eschew cultural absolutism. Instead, we should cultivate the doctrine of cultural relativity which teaches us that, "each society or nation, with its norms and values, is one of many, capable of change – in various directions – and is a product of man's effort to come to terms with the world around him and

29 El Chinoy, Society, Op. Cit. P.6

with the needs of an ongoing social order".[30] Indeed, selective acculturation should be the motto in the fair society because this helps or leads us to emulate the better traits in one another's culture while doing away with bad and unfavourable aspects of our own culture to produce a more refined and admirable society. Surely, when every nation on earth adopts this attitude, then they would all be helping the drive towards a fair society (global village).

30 Ibid. Page 55.

PART II
SOCIO-ECONOMIC FORMAT

CHAPTER 3

ELEMENTARY DISTRIBUTION OF ECONOMIC POWER

In any given period, a business organisation produces a certain total output. The value added gets divided or shared amongst the individuals who in one way or another contributed to the productive process. In the same way, every nation has its total output, the net returns of which must be shared among the citizens. This chapter is concerned with the problems of sharing, with particular interest on how best to share the society's goods such that a normal distribution of economic wealth is ensured or is attainable for the society as a whole.

FACTOR INCOMES

Classical economists tackled the problem of income distribution amongst what then were the three great social classes: workers, land owners and capitalists by defining three basic factors of production: labour, land and capital. But as already pointed out in the preceding chapter, the evolution of the modern form of ownership and developments in land laws have continued to de-emphasise the concept of land owners as a social class. Today anybody who wishes to establish a productive enterprise can get land either through governmental aid or intervention, or through direct purchase. In which case, land can be treated as an extension of capital in an enterprise. This leaves us with two main factors labour and capital – in the distribution tangle.

The members of the labour force and owners of capital in any business are PARTNERS in the production process. This symbiotic relationship produces a certain income. As such the logical thing is for LABOUR and CAPITAL to share this income at a definite ratio. There should be no arbitrary fixing of wages or salaries to the advantage of capital and disadvantage of labour. The reward for each should be related to the total INCOME, and therefore, to productivity or the total WORK-DONE.

The logic behind the above argument is not new nor is its practice novel. As a matter of fact, it implies for some of us a resuscitation of a system whose development and continued existence was gradually terminated or diluted by the movement of individualism which brought about the capitalist system. It will be recalled that in the olden days as in many surviving traditional societies, labour was never hired or employed for fixed salaries or wages in the productive process. Instead, labour price or income used to be a definite pre-determined percentage of the income derived from the co-operation of the labourer and owner of capital.

Examples of this practice may be found in records of ancient religions and history, or in some existing traditional societies where the impact of other foreign modes of socioeconomic organisations has been limited. Hence, we find that in the cattle-rearing cultures, shepherds are normally remunerated according to the number of off-springs produced by their flock. The off-springs here represent the income (while the original number of cattle represents the capital), and are normally shared between the shepherd (labourer) and his employer (capitalist) at a given customarily predetermined ratio.

In the traditional Igbo communal setting (as with many other traditional communes, we believe) it was the general practice and custom a few decades ago for the rich or well-to-do farmers who have over-stretched their own capabilities to further expand the sizes of their farms and barns by direct ploughing, to seek the co-operation of the younger or poorer farmers. The system was operated in such a way that the rich farmer provided the seedlings which constituted a major part of the capital, while the new hand or poor farmer (the labourer) did the cultivation, tendering and so on until harvest. The two parties then came together and shared the produce of this venture in the normal customarily pre-determined ratio.

This way, the investor increased the size of his barn while the venture provided for the new hand some capital in the form of seedlings, which he could, come the following planting season, use in his own farm while still providing service for the rich farmer – if the need still existed. With time and luck, the young farmer would accumulate enough capital to go it alone, working only his own farm, and as he got richer by possessing a lot of seedlings for his direct ploughing, he too, like his mentor, invites a poorer farmer to work as his junior business partner. Ultimately, as he gets older and weak for the difficult task of tilling the land he could turn all his seedlings to the management of younger fellows while he sat back reaping the fruits of his capital investment.

We hasten to add that this practice is fast dying out already. In many places, big-time farmers now pay wages to an impoverished class of labourers while keeping all the produce to themselves. It is only in the so-called backward areas of Igbo land, where the setting is still traditional (the people refusing to accept the modern associational pattern of relationships) that one may still notice the existence of this old culture.

In the commercial sector, a similar practice obtained and still obtains with respect to the relationship between the big-time rich traders and the younger ones that train under them. While undergoing the training, the apprentice provides the labour needed for the continued expansion and management of the enterprise. At the end of his apprenticeship (which lasts 5 to 7 years), he is given some independence to manage a particular level of capital while still being supervised closely by his mentor. After a period of about three years, he is allocated his own capital the amount of which is partly a function of his contribution to the growth of the business during his apprenticeship/ semi-apprentice period. With this capital, he is released completely to start his own independent business career.

Again one must observe that this practice is slowly but certainly giving way to the conventional employer-employee system of the capitalist nature. This means that the movement of individualism continues to gain ground in this part of the world, creating lopsided distribution of wealth and all the undesirable consequences of the capitalist mode of socio-economic organisation.

The traditional system of co-operation between labour and capital described above guaranteed for every (poor) young man the chances of changing from being a labourer to being a labourer/capitalist, and ultimately, becoming a rich capitalist at the evening of his life. Put in another way, the sources of income which were labour-based at the early part of life would later come from both capital investment and labour power; and ultimately, from capital alone. Unlike the capitalist system that condemns many to wage-labour till the last days of their lives, this system guarantees security and reasonable means of livelihood, within the society's context, to every member even at old age.

The system is therefore, more humane and reasonable than any of the dominant modes of socio-economic organisations that rule the world today. All that is needed is for us to elevate, develop or give this system a modern outlook in line with the realities of modern life. For only then can we truly have begun to counter the negative forces militating against man in the prevailing modes of societal organisations, and so restore the dignity of labour and of man in general. This would also bring about a semblance of harmony between work and property.

If we accept the above logic, then we can get on to the next question, which is, HOW and WHO determines the ratio at which LABOUR and CAPITAL should share incomes or the value-added to a business venture?

Economists recognise the existence of two categories of capitalists: the investor, who uses capital to set up productive properties in order to make profit; and the lender who loans out capital in order to earn interest. In the early days, these two categories of capitalists used to fight over interest rates and modes of debt payment. But today, with the intervention of government, such disagreement is hardly noticeable. Modern governments now determine interest rates or provide guidelines for their eventual determination by the banks; and review same from time to time in accordance with certain set down principles. They therefore play the part of umpires by presiding over two competing interests.

By so doing, governments infuse a sense of civility with regard to what may after all be referred to as income distribution between these two "factors" of production. So why can't governments play the same role with respect to income distribution between LABOUR and CAPITAL?

DETERMINATION OF FACTOR INCOMES

The duty of determining what fraction or percentage of income or value-added in a business organisation that goes to LABOUR and CAPITAL rests with governments who can carry out this function in much the same way as they handle interest rates. Usually, in determining interest rates or in formulating guidelines for their eventual determination by the banks, governments use such criteria as:

(a) relative profit between lenders and borrowers/investors;
(b) rates that would stimulate investments;
© achievement of fairer distribution of wealth nationwide;
(d) inflationary trends; etc.

These same conditions may be used in finding and adjusting the ratio, at which labour and capital share incomes.

And the ratio or percentage must be uniform for all profit-oriented organisations – for obvious reasons.

Now, let us suppose that an enterprise produces a certain income, I, in a given period after paying the running costs – raw materials, energy, etc. If the tax payable on this income is t then the net income is $(I - t)$. $(I - t)$ may be represented as I_t. If the established ratio or percentage for sharing this net income is P% to labour, then labour income

$$\text{labour income} = \frac{P(I_t)}{100},$$

and capital income

$$\text{capital income} = \frac{100 - P(I_T)}{100}$$

It should be noted that taxation is applied to the income or added-value before sharing it between labour and capital, instead of after paying labour price as is currently in fashion. The reasons for this are dealt with later in chapter five.

DISTRIBUTION WITHIN FACTORS

CAPITAL

The present system of sharing capital's income amongst members or individuals who own or contributed the capital for a business is an established practice. The age-old method of dividing up the income in the ratio of individual contributions cannot be faulted. The practice is therefore upheld.

LABOUR

Statistical measurements of distribution of abilities, physical or mental, for a large number of human beings show that these obey the normal distribution pattern. Similarly, one expects that for any company (employing a large number of workers), the amount of useful work done by the employees would assume the normal distribution pattern if measured and plotted into a frequency polygon or curve. In which case, the question may be asked: why shouldn't the distribution of labour income amongst these same individuals take the same form? That is, why should it not be normally distributed?

Common sense dictates that a fair distribution of labour income $\left(\frac{P1_t}{100}\right)$ amongst the members of the labour should indeed follow the normal distribution pattern, especially where there is a large number of workers with highly differentiated roles and duties. (Note that the labour force here means the sum total of all individuals who in one way or the other contributed the labour power needed for the day to day running of that enterprise, regardless of whether the individuals also own all or part of the capital used in setting up or running the enterprise).

The problem of evolving a normal distribution of labour income amongst the members of the labour force can be tackled by making use of an important quality of the normal distribution curve: the area of the normal distribution curve that has real practical relevance is between 'X' equal to plus and minus four (± 4). This statement is based on the fact that the area under the curve approximates unity between minus four and plus four. The above statement is shown diagrammatically in figure 4. The rectangles are such that the area under the curve is approximately unity. It can be proved mathematically that the area between minus one and plus one is 0.6827, area between ± 2 is 0.9073 and area between ± 3 is 0.9545. Hence the area between 4 is approximately one. The qualitative deduction from the above is that there are approximately nine levels of gradation of naturally gifted abilities; these being from —4 to +4. In other words, the most gifted ability is about nine times the size or strength of the least gifted.

However, the above are only approximations. Actually, the area under the normal distribution curve between minus infinity ($-\infty$) and plus infinity ($+\infty$) can be proved
mathematically to be exactly unity.

As such, we may assume that the most gifted ability in a frequency distribution (normal) approximates to ten (instead of nine) times the size or strength of the least gifted in the sample as long as the population is large. This last deduction is in cognizance of the fact that the former which was based on area between ± 4 neglects the area between minus infinity and minus four as well as the area between plus four and plus infinity even if these tend to zero. Hence, we can now say that under normal conditions the most gifted man, animal, tree, etc. in any large random but homogeneous sample would probably possess only about ten times the ability of the least gifted. The gift in this case may be height, intelligence, physical strength, etc.

On the basis of the above hypothesis, one may conclude that the labour income, $\left\{ \dfrac{P}{100}\ 1_t \right\}$ should be distributed amongst the members of the labour force in such a way that there are ten (or multiples of ten) income levels, but with the highest level or pay being only ten times the least. Hence, if there are only ten income levels and the first is N1.00 per time, t, then the highest should be N10.00 for the same period, t. Similarly, if there are twenty or forty income

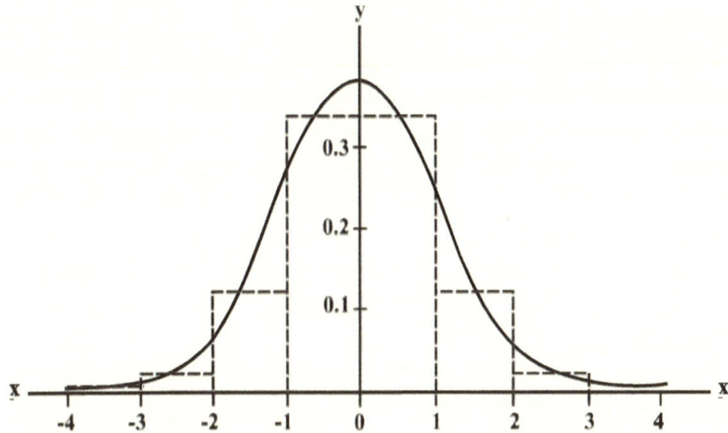

Fig. 4. Dotted rectangles used to show that the area under the normal distribution curve is approximately unity. Between x $= \pm \infty$, the area is exactly unity. Mathematically this is stated as:

$$\frac{1}{\sqrt{(2\pi)}} \int_{-\infty}^{\infty} e^{-\frac{1}{2}x^2} . dx = 1$$

levels the twentieth or fortieth, as the case may be, would still be N10.00 while the first is N1.00. The levels between these two should be worked out in such a way that there are equal intervals between succeeding levels. The present trend whereby the remunerations (basic salary plus sundry allowances) of some corporate executives represent sometimes as much as fifty to one hundred times the remuneration of the least paid worker in the same organisation or company is too arbitrary and must be discouraged. It smacks of that repulsive and counter-productive principle – winner-takes-all – that has practically become the rule in many modem societies.

Furthermore, the frequency of the number of workers in each income level should obey the normal distribution pattern as far as there is a large number of workers in the enterprise unless, of course, the enterprise is such that there is limited specialization or gradation of the tasks performed by each worker. For instance, where each worker is performing exactly the same task as the other, one would expect equal income for them all. But then we know that in reality this is hardly the case. Hence, we expect that normalcy would prevail in many large-scale enterprises. An ideal conformist enterprise can be regarded therefore as one whose income distribution is normal.

Now the value of 't', the time or period during which labour income $\left(\dfrac{P.\,I_t}{100}\right)$ is earned has not been defined. So let us consider the effect different values of 't' will have on the above distribution method. If 't' is one month, then labour income for one month is what should be distributed or shared by the workers for that month. But often, real or actual income for a company may not be known until the end of a year. To accommodate this lag, we need to introduce a form of living allowance payable to each labourer every month pending the time (end of the year or every half-year) when final audited account/income is ready.

The living allowance for each worker should bear a direct ratio to the income level (of the ten or multiples often advocated above) the worker belongs to, and the total living allowance paid out to the workforce should not exceed the anticipated annual labour income. Actually, it should be less than the anticipated income for reasons of precaution. Two-thirds of the total labour-income is a realistic figure. Hence, if we denote the total allowance by A, then the remaining labour income would be

$$\frac{P.\,I_t}{100} - A$$

This much then should be due to labour at the end of the year and should be shared accordingly. (Of course, it could be arranged in such a way that a part of labour income is retained by the company in order to boost the investment pool and enhance the relative competitiveness of the company. But then, this would amount to selling shares to members of the labour force with each worker being credited with what would have been his share of the income had it been divided up amongst them).

CHAPTER 4

SECONDARY AND TERTIARY DISTRIBUTION OF ECONOMIC POWER

Distribution of economic power amongst the various groups in a society is yet another facet of distribution that touches not only the state of individual well-being but also social harmony and survival. Whereas individual dissatisfaction with a system may lead to isolated deviant behaviour and takes a lot of time and number to be manifested on the social scale, group displeasure, dissatisfaction or protest against a societal attitude are important ingredients for social movements, disorganisation and social change. As such, the mode of distribution of societal or communally-owned wealth amongst the various constituent and often contending groups in a society becomes crucial vis-a-vis the stability and continual survival of that social and political unit.

SECONDARY DISTRIBUTION OF ECONOMIC POWER

Although many forms of social groups may be defined or identified within a society, our primary focus here is on ethnic groups. These are made up of persons who are united by virtue of the fact that they share a common cultural tradition or background. In a sense, "any society, with its distinctive culture constitutes an ethnic group. But within many of the politically unified societies of the modern world some groups are set off to some degree by their practices, beliefs, religion, or language – and in some cases by distinctive physical characteristics as well".[1] Since these

---

1.   El Chinoy, *Society*, Op. Cit. Page 45.

117

characteristics are often used as the basis for division of modern politically unified societies or countries into smaller constituent parts, or subnational groups (often referred to as states, regions, provinces, etc.) we may translate the ethnic groups into states.

Membership of an ethnic group is relatively closed or ascribed; made up of such criteria as family, clan, state or even nationality, over which the individual has little or no freedom to relinquish his membership. Movement from one group to the other is practically or relatively difficult. Hence, an ethnic Russian cannot easily become an Australian aborigine. Nor can an indigene of Ondo State (Nigeria) easily become a Sokoto State indigene. In contrast, open or formal groups such as sectors of the economy, trade unions, political parties, schools, etc., generally possess very loose criteria on which their memberships are drawn, complemented by a high rate at which those members may change from one group to another. Many of these groups – often referred. to as "secondary groups" – are associational; "made up of individuals who come together to seek some similar or common goal or goals, or in advocacy of common or like interests,"[2] and often dissolve when the criteria on which they were founded seize to exist.

With respect to distribution or division of societal wealth as in budgetary and revenue allocation, we find that the reaction of the open groups is less directed or less likely to tear a society apart as compared to the more closed ethnic groups. This is due primarily to the amorphous nature of this type of grouping and the ease with which members of an open group can migrate to other open groups. This means that society is hardly threatened by this type of groupings.

1.   El Chinoy, *Society*, Op. Cit. Page 44

Hence, uproars that often follow announcements of governmental budgets often take the form of academic disagreements and analysis of how different sectors of the economy would be affected. In contrast, revenue allocation formula, which not only deals with what fraction of the national revenue goes to what tier of government but also, and most importantly, what amount goes to what ethnic group (state), often generates lasting controversy about its equitability or fairness.

Deep-seated feelings resulting from unfair revenue allocation formula are capable of and often lead to separatist movements and instability in many modern nations. This becomes very apparent and crucial in large, heterogeneous countries with many ethnic groups at different levels of development and with wide population differentials. Yet, the controversies about fairness of these revenue allocation formulae and attempts at resolving them are often beclouded by the very fact that most formulae are based on rather doubtful criteria and are applied arbitrarily – which is why we intend to give the subject a more scientific treatment in this chapter.

REVENUE ALLOCATION FORMULA

Of all the criteria on which different revenue allocation formulae are based the world over, three essential ones are discernible. These are derivation, population, and "equality of states". Derivation is used to denote the amount or proportion of the total revenue that accrued to the centre from a given area or state. Population refers to the numerical strength of the given area or state. While 'equality of state' is derived from the liberal democratic notion of equality of every human being but in this case the notion is applied to states.

The case for derivation as a factor in the redistribution of national revenue to the states is obvious; it goes to reflect the importance attached or assignable to ability to contribute to the national wealth by each state. It underlines the principle that those who produce more or who contribute more to national economic prosperity, ought to appropriate more of the common wealth.[3] Thus a revenue allocation formula which neglects the derivation factor negates the principles of rewarding hard work, industry – or even luck – that gave rise in the first place, to a differential in the respective contributions (or revenues) that accrue to the centre from different states. In fact, doing away with this principle in a setting where the highest contributions or revenues come from relatively small populated states, would give the impression that the system encourages a tyranny of the majority, thereby weakening the oneness and unity of that political entity.

On the other hand, the introduction of the population and equality of states principles can be rationalised on the grounds that there is a crying need to redistribute national income in such a way as to help the economically disadvantaged or backward states or groups in keeping with that noble injunction which exhorts every man, every state to be his brother's keeper. Of course, it is a well-known fact that if allocations were to be based solely on derivation, they might perpetuate a meritocracy of inequality among the various states – a situation which runs counter to the very spirit of balanced group-life and co-existence.

On the basis of the above, it stands to reason that after the central government has deducted that percentage of the centrally collected revenue earmarked for its use and for carrying out those works and duties for which it is created, the remaining amount or the states-bound revenue must be

3. For detailed treatment of this subject, see, P. N. C. Okigbo, et al, Report of the Presidential Commission on Revenue Allocation (Federal Republic of Nigeria, 1980. Page 26, .90 -95

distributed among the states using the three basic factors of derivation, population and equality of states. This leaves us with the question; what fraction of the states-bound revenue should be shared out on the basis of what factor? And how do we justify same?

Ideally, an equal third of the States-bound revenue should be shared on the basis of each factor since one factor is as important as any other. That is, each third of the revenue should basically be shared according to the weight of each state in that regard, the third allocated to the equality of states principle being shared equally among the states, and allocations on the basis of population and derivation being shared according to the respective and proportionate value of each state on each count. But in a world bedevilled by inequalities and biased distribution of every available resource, society has to qualify the way and manner the distributions of allocations in the two later factors are carried out if she is to seriously tackle the problem of inequality between groups.

Since we have equated a fair distribution to normal distribution, we can again use this to formulate the modality for sharing each third of the states-bound revenue. Of course, the share allocated to the equality of states principle need it come under this treatment since equality in distribution is not necessarily against our concept of fair distribution. In fact, where the distribution of the population or derivation attributes among the states is found to be normal, equal or anywhere between absolute equality and normalcy, we should feel free to share out each third of the states-bound revenue in direct proportion to the values of those attributes.

However, where the above is not the case, that is, where distribution of the derivation and population attributes are non-normal, all we have to do is to apply a form of *normalization* technique (the mathematical details of which we cannot go into in a book of this nature)[4], and then proceed to use the resultant quantities in sharing the revenue.

COMPOSITION AND USAGE OF COMMUNAL FACILITIES AND INSTITUTIONS

There are in every society certain communally owned facilities or institutions whose composition and/or usage often generate a lot of interest, anxiety and sometimes tension among the various constituent ethnic groups because they are viewed once again as an extension of distribution or sharing of the communal wealth. These emotions are traceable to an atavistic fear of domination of one group over the other. Domination here may be military, political, economic, social, etc., and no matter from what angle it is viewed, the fear is a legitimate one and, therefore, must be reckoned with in the process of societal organisation and governance. This implies that in a pluralistic society there is a critical need for a careful and strategic balancing in appointments, enlistments or intakes of individuals into major areas of communally owned institutions in order to reflect the existence of diverse ethnic groups and take care of their interests.

The composition of a country's armed forces, for instance, can be used to illustrate the intrinsic negativity of lopsided recruitment. Where the armed forces personnel are predominantly drawn from one ethnic group, state or section of that country, there would exist a latent intimidation of the other groups or sections that make up that political entity. This deficiency which is an inherent weakness in the composition of the armed forces can be and would often be exploited to the disadvantage of the

---

4.This technique is a derivative of the standard mathematical process of a non-normal distribution using its mean and standard deviation.

latter groups. Latent but effective intimidation is often manifested in the latter's approach to social, political and even economic issues which is characterised by marked timidity, weakness and amazing indisposition to articulate or defend their rights and interests. This same state of affairs is applicable to the composition and usage of other strategic societal institutions and facilities, be they educational facilities, the civil service or any other.

In view of the above, the question may be asked as to what criteria should be used in formulating the mode of drawing individuals that make up the work force or that enjoy the services of societally-owned and financed institutions/facilities taking cognisance of the existence, within that society, of different and diverse ethnic groups. Then the question must also be asked as to what extent each of these criteria should be applied if we are to meaningfully allay the inherent mutual fears of the different groups, thereby accommodating the fact that different ethnic groups possess different and distinct social characteristics that impose limiting effects on individual drives and motivations.

Although one concedes that the traditional reliance on ability or merit as the sole yardstick for selection or drawing membership of the work-force of various strategic public institutions and agencies, or the recruitment of those who enjoy the use of certain public facilities and services promotes efficiency, one must equally point out that it should not be the only factor because efficiency is not the only issue at stake nor is it the most important. There are the issues of nation building, of peace and stability, as well as social aesthetics. If ability alone is allowed to operate it would establish and/or perpetuate inequality not only between individuals but also among social groups. As such the need for ethnic balancing must be considered because it adds equity and social stability to the principle of efficiency.

Common-sense dictates, therefore that a pragmatic distribution of intakes or enlistments should be based on these three criteria:

(a) Individual ability or merit;
(b) equality of states or of ethnic groups; and
© the actual physical demand of each state for enlistment or admission into the particular institution or facility under consideration.

The merit factor refers to the suitability of each willing individual or applicant for placement. This is based on the "credentials or qualification" of the individual which underline his relative ability to fit into the requisite tasks or cope with the demands that entry into the said institution would make of him. It has nothing to do with his state of origin or any such group characteristics or considerations.

The second criterion refers to the right to equal representation for each state. It is meant to assign to each state the same number of entrants because the states are considered to have equal status.

The third factor is a function of the actual number of individual from each state or ethnic group who possess the requisite credentials for placement or admission and are, indeed, gunning for same. The requisite credentials, it must be pointed out is as per the definition of the experts whose duty it is to lay down the lowest acceptable qualification for admission or enlistment.

As for the extent to which each of these factors should be used, common sense dictates that we follow the model already developed for revenue allocation since we are basically dealing with the same issue. Thus, merit and actual demand of each state for placement may be respectively treated as derivation and population.

Note that the different numbers assigned to each state in the final analysis at the central level could likewise be redistributed by the different states to their local government areas using the same method above and according to their respective, relative heterogeneity or distribution of demands for placement or usage of the facility under consideration. However, it must be pointed out that within each commune or group, the quotas must be filled by the brightest qualified candidates. Besides, no person who does not possess up to the minimum stipulated entry requirements must be offered a place. Quotas that cannot be filled by any state must be filled by the central commission or board, this time, on merit.

Note also that in the case of university admission, common sense dictates that a central admission/matriculation board should handle admission of students to universities owned and financed by the central government. Where a university is owned and financed by a state or local government, that government should have the right to choose how the facility is run. It may of course choose to set up a matriculation board (either as a department within the university where there is only one university or a Joint Admission and Matriculation Board where there are more than one university) to admit students into the universities. The state should also be allowed to determine the ratio of the intakes that comes from outside that state. This right is meant to compensate for the opportunity cost to both the government and peoples of that state for funding the said university or universities, in much the same way the central body determines the proportion of foreign students that are admitted into her own universities, but with the added injunction that non-indigenes who have resided in the said state for a given minimum period, say five years, should be treated as full-fledged indigenes.

SOCIALISED SERVICES, ITS FUNDING AND THE PRIMARY GROUPS

Despite all the arguments that may be adduced to the contrary, free services, public ownership, control or subsidy of certain ventures or services remains a fact and a necessary ingredient of modern life. The major areas where this is applicable are education, health services and provision of such basic facilities as water supply. Other services like subsidization of energy bills, e.g. gas and electricity, can be included in this definition because they may also be used as vehicles of progressive equalitarianism.

The *welfarist* nature of this programme suggests free service but because "free service" is often seen as total, we need stress here that there are degrees of freedom and that as already pointed out in chapter I while discussing "Problems of Socialization" absolute or total freedom may not always serve the best social ends. "Thus any service for which the consumer pays less than a hundred per cent of the cost of providing such service (to say nothing of the profit that normally would have accrued over and above the cost of production to the provider), can be said to be free to the degree (or percentage) by which part of the real cost is defrayed by the provider".[5] Which is what in fact subsidy is all about.

Having accepted the premise that partial rather than total socialization of services should be the watchword guiding socialization drives, we may go forward and examine or discuss what services should be subsidized, the optimal degree or extent of such socialization and who foots the bill for the socialized services. In this regard, we must accept the inevitability of a trilogy of responsibility involving the

5 Oladele O. Kale, 'Prospects at free health in Nigeria', *The Guardian*, June 20 & 21, 1984

individual (or family), the state (or ethnic group) and the central government or the total unified political entity, in the socialization tangle.

Basically, the areas and extent of public participation and, in a sense, who foots the bills for socialized services, would be a matter of place, people and circumstance. But arbitrariness should never be allowed to guide these quantities. It would not be sufficient for anyone to advocate 1%, 10%, 20% or even 99% subsidy for this or that service, without a sound basis for such opinion.

The three essential factors that should influence the choice of services to be provided free or subsidized by society or the government are:

(1) The healthiness or buoyancy of the economy or financial resources.[6]
(2) The nature of the particular service, and
(3) The relative need of the various ethnic groups (states) for the particular service or its socialization.

Number one above is obvious and needs no elaboration. The second criterion explores the intrinsic benefits derivable from socializing a particular service. Although socialization is generally advocated for the sake of better balancing of opportunities between individuals or groups of individuals (primary or secondary), it could go beyond these ends for certain services. In socializing preventive Medicare and treatment of infectious diseases for instance, society strives to ensure not just the safety of a few individuals or groups from poor health but the entire populace regardless of class, ethnicity, creed, etc. In this regard, we find that that aspect of public health-care delivery cannot be compromised no matter the state of the

6. Ibid

national or communal economy, or the group of people that are affected or are most likely to enjoy financial relief from the socialization of that aspect of health-care delivery

In this regard, it stands to reason that such special schemes as immunization programmes, solid and liquid waste disposal, screening for diseases, pest and vector control, etc., should be provided by the society free to all at all times.[7]

On the basis of the above, the aspect of medical health delivery that we need ponder about, that is whether it should be subsidized or not, would be the treatment of non-infectious diseases and illnesses, the treatment of other diseases being regarded as a fundamental necessity for the well-being of the larger society.

The third factor which refers to the relative needs of various ethnic groups for the particular service or its socialization is to ensure that no group is adversely disadvantaged because of societal participation in, or subsidization of, any service. This may be illustrated by citing the politics of free education (at all levels) in Nigeria. Because the northern part of the country provides a very small percentage of individuals who attend school relative to the southern part even though the two sections practically have the same or equal population and, about the same number of states as the statistics show[8] – a federally subsidized free education scheme for all levels of education in Nigeria would definitely be to the disadvantage of the North. This is because such a policy would imply using federally controlled common fund to pursue or finance a scheme that is predominantly enjoyed by the South. And unless there is another scheme that is so

7.   Ibid
8.   Statistical Abstracts, I9S2, Federal office of Statistics, Lagos.

financed but is predominantly enjoyed by the North, i.e. providing a countervailing effect against the imbalance created by the federally financed free education scheme, then a critical departure from the norm which requires the federal expenditure to be evenly distributed among the different states or sections of the country would have been introduced. Yet, this is as a result of a presumably genuine benevolent consideration.

The situation above is therefore capable of bringing two legitimate forces into conflict, i.e., the forces of progressive equalitarianism and that of pragmatic ethnicity. If the free education scheme is not introduced, the former would suffer, and if it is introduced the latter would suffer. Thus, rather than introduce a federally financed free education at all levels or restrain the introduction of free education at all, Nigeria could, for instance, assign the basic responsibility for different levels of education to different tiers of government while at the same time socializing education. The federal government could take care and control tertiary (higher) education, while the state governments take care of secondary education and the local governments take responsibility for primary education. In this way, the problem is largely localised, hence, the burden of socialization – to whatever degree – would be relatively borne by each group (not necessarily ethnic) to the degree of her needs.

Pursuant to this, the portion of the federal revenue allocated to states and local governments could be increased in order to enable these tiers of government subsidize secondary and primary education in their respective domains. Note that the above is not intended to frustrate the respective desires or the existing rights of states or local governments to own universities or secondary schools. Where a state government or local government owns a university or secondary school respectively, the government should bear the burden of its socialization and should be allowed to determine the distribution of intakes into the institution.

As for the extent or degree to which services should be socialized, two crucial factors are relevant: These are in Kale's estimation,[9]

I. The relative needs and distribution of deprivation amongst the populace, and once again,
2. The healthiness or buoyancy of the society's financial resources or economy.

The relative needs and distribution of deprivation is a function of the relative distribution of incomes and wealth amongst individual members of the society i.e., its dispersion or variability. And since on the basis of this write-up a normal (0, 1) distribution of income and/or wealth for a society implies an optimal or equitable distribution, i.e., a condition tantamount to absence of deprivation, we may say that there is practically no need for government subsidy in a society where income/wealth distribution have attained perfect normalcy because the conditions or the factors that brought such about are deemed fair.

On the other hand, with increasing dispersion in the distribution of incomes and wealth, the government should subsidize to a greater extent in order to offset the corresponding level of suffering of the down-trodden and so hasten the march towards progressive equalitarianism. Hence, we may stipulate that the extent of socialization of any service or an aspect of a service should match the degree

9.   Oladele 0. Kale, 'Prospects of Free Health in Nigeria', *The Guardian*, June 20 & 21, 1984.

or percentage to which the distribution of incomes and/or wealth in the society deviates from the normal (0, 1) distribution, provided the economy is strong enough to sustain same. The society mentioned in the last paragraph may refer to a country, state, local government area or even the whole world. And with respect to free education in Nigeria, therefore, higher education should be subsidized by the Federal Government to reflect the extent or distribution of deprivation for the whole country, while secondary education is likewise subsidized by each state government to reflect the distribution of deprivation within each state. The same applies to local governments and the subsidization of primary education in each respective local
government area.

By the same reasoning, tertiary healthcare should be run and subsidized by the federal government, while the states and local governments take care of secondary and primary healthcare respectively.

It should be left for government and peoples within any given political entity to figure out other areas apart from the health and educational sectors where the above treatment is desirable or applicable.

TERTIARY DISTRIBUTION OF ECONOMIC POWER

In this section, we intend to focus on a system of distribution of wealth or economic power amongst the different nations or countries of the world. This presupposes that there is an existing common pool of funds earmarked for distribution to all nations of the world or at least that such a common pool is bound to be created in the immediate future. Actually, the growing strength of the International Global Security System anticipates an eventual emergence of a comprehensive world revenue system that would bring such a common pool into being. This revenue may come from such sources as contributions, taxes and donations from member nations of the United Nations or as royalties, dividends and interests from companies and national organs operating on international territories and those who may borrow or obtain capital from the anticipated World Bank. See *Chapter 9.* However, since it is not the purpose of this section to go into the production aspect of the envisaged world revenue pool, it will suffice for us to assume for now the possibility of the creation and accumulation of such revenue and then proceed to discourse its use and allocation to nations.

At the tertiary level, as at the secondary level, three factors remain relevant in the distribution of a common resource or fund. These are:

(1) the need to provide fund for the execution of projects of common interest to all mankind. Such projects or problems include:

(a) fighting global pollution, eliminating certain diseases and viruses that afflict mankind generally, and to contain other dangerous natural and man-made disasters, refugee problems, etc.;

(b) providing funds for the maintenance of both the secretariat and other agencies of the central world body. We may refer to this as the Equality of States' principle in that it is aimed at solving problems that are jointly and equally relevant to every nation.

(2) The second factor is to do with the burning need to provide assistance to the poor nations of the world by way of injecting more funds to these countries. This need is borne out of both the inherent danger of the widening gap between the rich and the poor nations of the world, and that humanitarian spirit which enjoins us to be our brothers' keeper. We may refer to this as the Need 'principle.

(3) Finally, we come to the principle of Derivation. Again this arises because common sense dictates that those who provide a nation's or the world's wealth must be given a pride of place in the use and distribution of that common wealth. Under this principle therefore, it is expected that the rich countries of the world or high-tech companies from these countries operating in the said zones would be able to claim a good part of the world revenue allocated to the propensity to produce and therefore to contribute to the world purse.

It may appear rather trivial, irresponsible and downright insensitive to some for one to suggest the allocation of any part, no matter how small, of the world's revenue to the rich countries of the world especially at this time when there is an alarming and unquestionable lop-sidedness in the existing distribution of wealth amongst nations. But we must not allow the present teething problems of the Third World to becloud our judgement. For one thing, those problems are not bound to persist forever. Hence, if the world's revenue is allocated only on the basis of equality and need, it may soon become obsolete in due course as the economic conditions of the poor states change or improve. Secondly, and more importantly, one must not for any reason under-play the inalienable rights of all nations to directly partake of mankind's common heritage and endeavours. Instead, the issue should be how much can the world afford to allocate to that principle at this and subsequent stages in order to meet with the exigencies of the time. Also, for any global revenue formula to be prospective, and to stand the test of time, it must be flexible, taking the facts of the changeability of conditions into account.

On the basis of the above, we propose that the three factors be used in the following ways;

1.   THE EQUALITY FACTOR:

The World Authority, which will be charged with the responsibility for the exploitation of the common territories is to deduct from the annual budget of the organisation all the fund necessary for tackling all problems that come under the equality principle.

2.   NEED AND DERIVATION:

To determine the extent to which each of these two remaining factors is to be applied to the disbursement of the world budget, we evoke once more the abnormality factor in wealth distribution. Thus, a distribution format which reflects the prevailing distribution of wealth amongst nations is imperative. That is, the percentage of the remaining revenue going to the need factor or to be shared according to the degree of deprivation would be represented by the percentage abnormality of the world wealth distribution. This quantity may be distributed to countries by using either the per capita income of each country or the G.N.P., the grand disposable income, capital per capita, etc., or a combination of these values in a way that the poorest countries get the larger shares.

Conversely, the rest of the fund goes to the derivation factor and is to be shared in such a way that the highest producing countries receive the highest amounts, in much the same way as the poorest countries receive the highest shares of the fund shared out on the need principle.

CHAPTER 5

RELATIONS OF PRODUCTION AND POSSIBLE EFFECTS ON COMMON SOCIAL PROBLEMS

The object of this chapter is to show the possible ways the suggested approach to socio-economic organisation is likely to affect some of the common problems that afflict many societies today. We shall take them one after the other.

The first, ownership and control of means of production and exchange has remained a central issue of national policy in all regions of the world. As a source of bitter disagreements and misunderstanding the issue of ownership causes enormous dissipation of energy.

It is evident from the earlier chapters that the economic system envisaged in this thesis is basically a form of mega-co-operation which exhibits a loose association of CAPITAL and LABOUR. Although ownership of the productive property still resides with the owners of the capital used in setting up a company, management and control of the business will not as total as in the capitalist economy. Because Labour income is a function of the total income, one expects that members of the labour force should, at least, be informed about all transactions, expenditure and sales made by the company. And each member should be free to ascertain the accuracy of these periodic reports, for the purpose of preventing fraud. Although this does not amount to direct participation of Labour in the management and control of a business, it does have some limiting effects on the actions of managers. As for such Labour matters as employment of new labourers, fixing of living allowances, etc., the labour association in each company is expected.to have a say.

It will be interesting to watch the evolution of decision making processes in these areas of company management.

The envisaged mode of economic relations is expected to be pre-dominant in the socio-economic system. The system, will accommodate a public sector and a private sector. A private enterprise being defined as a productive or service-providing unit owned and worked by individuals but where the wage-system, in the sense we know it today, will have disappeared or is subsumed by the distribution system herein suggested. It will operate in the non-strategic areas of the economy or in those areas where it serves the best social end. On the other hand, public ownership and control is to be limited to those areas where neither private nor co-operative involvement is desirable or is incapable of providing social harmony and balance. Below are some conditions which may necessitate public involvement or ownership.

CONDITION FOR PUBLIC OWNERSHIP

In a nutshell, public ownership or nationalization of any means of production or exchange should be guided by a proof that such action would do more for the welfare of the nation than private or co-operative ownership. This general principle can be further broken down to the following parts.

1.   EXISTENCE OF NATURAL MONOPOLY

This has to do with such productive or service units derived from natural or communally owned items like river, the sea, vital minerals, etc. Under this may be found water supply and some other utilities. By reaping profits derived from a hydroelectric power plant, for instance, a private or co-operative organisation would be using a communally-owned natural resource to produce electricity only to turn back and charge the same people for the energy. This must be differentiated from, say, an individual drawing a couple of buckets of water from the river or fishing in the river. While the latter case is only transient, harnessing of electric power from the river involves construction of a permanent structure, which could disturb the normal flow of water and also drastically reduce or deplete the quantity with dire consequences to all. In this kind of situation, it would be found that one man or a group of individuals would be taking from the river more than is reasonably due to them and that if other citizens decide to behave in a similar way, there would be chaos – unless, of course, the former is given undue protection by government.

2. TO GUARD AGAINST WASTEFUL COMPETITION

This is in areas where private or co-operative ownership and control would give rise to wasteful competition and may include such public utilities as water supply, gas and light, railways, etc. The case for railways is obvious. This should be compared with road or air transportation where all a private or co-operative organisation has to do is pay the necessary tolls or secure licence to ply publicly built roads and airports.

3. PROTECTION OF WEAK AND DYING INDUSTRIES OR ESTABLISHMENT OF VITAL ONES

The public sector should establish industries or other forms of property and provide service where the non-public sector is afraid to venture (either because of high risk or demand for lots of capital that cannot be mustered by individuals or the private/cooperative sector), as long as such establishment is vital and necessary for the society. The public should also ensure that old productive properties where profit is dwindling do not die away, as long as their continued existence is vital to society.

Examples would differ for different countries. In a developing country like Nigeria, for instance, the iron and steel industry is one such area where for both reasons of huge capital involvement and expected initial losses or little profit, amongst other reasons, make its public ownership necessary, just as development or control of space programmes rest with governments in America, Russia, etc.

Another instance may be that of air transportation. Whereas the capital involved in setting up such an enterprise may be very hard for the private/cooperative sector to come by in a poor Third-World country, the reverse is the case in the rich industrialised countries. Accordingly, ownership of airlines may be the sphere of governments in poor countries while individuals may own them in richer countries.

4. VITAL INDUSTRIES OR PROPERTIES AND SERVICES.

These are productive properties or means of exchange/service that are so vital to the society that their management could not safely be subject to the decisions of private individuals. They may be vital to the society either for monetary reasons, security, international image, etc.

The firearms industry is a case in point. There are also space exploration and other strategic industries.

5. HUMANITARIAN GROUNDS

Public ownership of certain ventures may be advocated on humanitarian grounds. This may entail providing for the less privileged or better balancing of opportunities. It is basically *welfarist*. Major areas include health-care service and education. The extent of public participation here would be a matter of place, people and circumstance, the financial and social costs being important criteria.

The above conditions are by no means final. They are meant to provide a basis for pragmatic evaluation in the process of evolving public participation in production and service delivery. And it is hoped that different peoples and governments would with time formulate and introduce different areas of production, exchange and/ or service where public ownership would be more beneficial for the general good of their societies. But the danger of big-government must be borne in mind at all times. Least possible degree of state interference, fair distribution and balancing of individual self-fulfilment against societal progress and harmony should be the ultimate goal. Nationalization or state ownership or domination of any area of the economy must not be seen as permanent but temporary. When the set of conditions that necessitated state participation disappear, the state should gradually withdraw its control of those areas.

It is hoped that with proper evaluation and formulation of what areas each sector (public or private) is to operate in each country, coupled with the benefits that would accrue from the suggested modes of production and distribution, it will soon dawn on everybody that, as Aristotle observed over 2000 years ago, it is not who owns property that really counts but *how* property is *used.*[1]

UNEMPLOYMENT

The lack of jobs for qualified and willing individuals has become the scourge of modern capitalist and quasi-capitalist societies the world over. It exists in both the rich and poor countries, and has contributed immensely to the

1. a. Bertrand Russel, *History of Western Philosophy*, London, Unwin Paper-back, 1979, Page, 199
b. William Ebenstein and Edwin Fogelman, *Today's –Isms*, Op. Cit., Page, 42

turbulence and despair that mirror social and economic stagnation in most countries today. Yet its magnitude is still on the rise. Recent reports show that unemployment rate has shot up to thirteen (13) or more per cent in some rich developed Western countries.[2] As for the Third World countries, the figures are staggering. Figures are in the region of about 20-30%. That unemployment and its attendant consequences constitute a real threat to both man and society is not in doubt. So also is the payment of "unemployment benefits" as a permanent antidote to unemployment. Experience has shown that no matter the amount of monetary relief or aid given, the unemployed person is still likely to show feelings of inadequacy, rejection, and poor sense of belonging. And in any case, what man can stand idleness – a condition that prevents him from projecting his personality – for a long time. The fact that even the rich industrialised Western societies are unable to accommodate all in the scheme of things by way of full employment of all qualified and willing men is the real pity of the situation.

The root causes of unemployment are: -

1. The wage system – which does not relate the so-called Labour price to income or profit made by the enterprise.
2. Increasing reliance on automation and all forms of artificial contrivance in the production process, and
3. Company tax rebates (reliefs) for depreciating values of fixed-capital assets.

2. Op. Cit.

These factors are easily understandable when viewed against the background of profit maximization. The essence of any business enterprise is to make profit. As such it behoves the entrepreneur to exploit whatever rules that guide the conduct of business activities. With respect to the wage-system, the entrepreneur can exploit its weakness for the purpose of maximising his profit in two ways:

(a) by paying low wages and salaries, and
(b) by employing low number of workers.

At the early stages of the industrial revolution, employers of labour relied more on the first, i.e. (a) above, than the second way. But with the advent of strong labour unions and strong legislations the latter has become more fashionable. Although labour unions do fight against lay-offs or retrenchment of their members, they have little or no powers over increase or decrease of the work force. Employment of new hands into a company is basically the prerogative of the management or owners of the business both at inception and thereafter. As such many enterprises employ the barest minimum (not the optimum number of workers) as a way of reducing the cost of labour. The result is that many enterprises are understaffed with the employers using all forms of "Big-Brother is watching you" tactics to compel the inadequate labour force to provide the extra-labour needed for the proper running of the enterprise. This means that many would-be workers are rendered idle and unemployed.

Another method of achieving higher profit is the use of automation, advanced computers, robots, etc., in place of human labour in the production process. Apart from the higher efficiency and speed which some of these contrivances may have over men or human labour, they are also generally cheaper – at least in the long-run. Hence, there is an increasing tendency towards the use of these artificial contrivances in production while men are employed only where human labour is of absolute necessity. The result: displacement of many men from work.[3]

It is not that one does not realise that some of these machines do relieve men of certain mean and dangerous works or that they could be more efficient and time-saving. But when this "relief" gets to a point where many men are practically thrown off jobs without adequate means of livelihood, while owners of businesses reap millions of extra cash that would have gone to the displaced workers, then one must agree that automation is going beyond healthy bounds. Who really wants to sacrifice the happiness of millions of people for the one-sided "relief", efficiency and quickness of machines. It is nauseating to walk the streets of Lagos and observe these monster-like contrivances digging gutters (just scooping earth with their bucket-like appendages) while unemployed labourers stand idly-by wondering where their next meals would come from, or watch a single computer manned by a few individuals in a multi-million-naira business organisation doing the job that would otherwise be done by many clerks while many qualified men are out of jobs. Surely, there must be a limit (an optimum level) to the degree of automation or the use of any of these advanced contrivances, for any given society. We must first ensure that the available human resources are put to use before employing some of the contraptions.

Of course, the fact that many are out of work today because of increasing reliance on machines, robots, etc., is

3. (a) Peter McGill, 'Japan's employment system plagued by high technology', *New Nigerian*, September 24, 1983

b. *Newsweek magazine*, February 14, 1983, pp. 54-55.

c. Enwere, Dike, 'The dilemma of choice of technology', Lagos, *The Guardian*, August 10, 1987.

no new discovery! Many governments have, in fact, tried to limit the tendency towards automation by introducing controls and guidelines as to what machinery entrepreneurs should go for. But this approach has generally failed either because of the difficulties in policing such measures or because the guidelines can hardly be comprehensive. On the other hand, the entrepreneurs always out-manoeuvre the governments and the inherently defective measures. And why not! The premium is so high: for a relatively low initial and running cost (compared to men) one obtains a device that would save him millions of man-hour (and pay), and Labour problems in a system that emphasises little more than profit maximization.

Our third factor applies to countries that give rebate for the depreciating value of fixed capital assets in taxation. Where the official annual depreciation value or the rebate (relief) due such a depreciation is high, then the tendency would be for investors to rely more on capital intensive (automation implied) mode of production rather than labour-intensive ones. This is because the provision causes a sizeable portion of the costs of purchasing these robots and sophisticated equipment to be passed unto the government in the long-run. Thus, the provision inadvertently ends up promoting unemployment.

It is our stand that the best way to fight unemployment is to strike at these three root causes. Now it has been stipulated in chapter (3) that Labour income should be a fraction of the total company income or value-added. This condition would have a very favourable effect in the fight against unemployment or its three root causes. Let us consider a situation where a certain percentage (x) of the income made by a company goes to Labour. This would mean that no matter whether the company relies more on labour-intensive approach or on high capital outlay (automation, high tech, etc.) in achieving a given income, it still spends the same amount or % of its income on Labour.

Therefore, in order to maximize its own income, it would pay the entrepreneur to increase the contribution made by human labour in the production process rather than over dependence on any manmade contraptions – (Provided also that the tax rebate for fixed capital assets is not too high). Because there is a limit to what degree more work could be exacted from his already overstretched meagre staff, the tendency would be for him to increase staff rather than invest more on machines.

The above situation considered only one company. In a. society with many employers of labour, there would be a mass scramble by different enterprises for more staff. That would mean that there would be so much scramble for more workers by companies that the unemployed would practically disappear from the streets. Thereafter, of course, market forces would come to play, determining who retains what number of staff in his company. But the important aspect of this envisaged scramble is that it will leave no person without some form of employment even if he is "under-employed" at the initial stage. Also production and purchase of certain machines, i.e., those that would have become incompatible with the new situation would fall.

However, it is hoped that with growth in the economy and the attendant increase in volume of necessary work, a more pragmatic approach to development and use of machines will evolve. But this production and purchase will no longer be at the expense of human labour. In other words, the problem of directing entrepreneurs as to what machines should be produced or used in work and industry by external or governmental agencies would have been relegated. The same tendency to profit-maximization would become the prudent policeman nudging investors along the right path – a path that puts the gainful employment of fellow men before those of machines. Only then can unemployment be severely curtailed or totally eliminated.

INFLATION

Inflation – the steady or periodic jumps in the cost of commodities and services is another terrible scourge of modern societies, especially the capitalist-oriented ones. Its rates in different countries vary, with the less stable economies recording the highest figures.

Inflation is a direct result of the free interplay between the consumers, producers and middlemen (distributors). As such it might be regarded as a phenomenon that must remain with us, so long as non-public-owned enterprises exist, and profit-motive remains a central purpose in our economic life. Since this writer is not against the profit motive either in individual or co-operative life, there is no attempt at seeking complete or total elimination of inflation in societal life. Instead, inflation is seen as a phenomenon a society has to live with, provided it is rendered practically toothless and ineffective. In order to achieve this, we need ask ourselves what the main consequence of inflation is.

The main problem with inflation is that it is partial, affecting different categories or groups of people differently. While one group of people are adversely affected; the other group may prosper by it. This may be seen from two angles. The first is sectorial while the other is more related to factors. The partial effect of inflation may be considered sectoral when we consider that the rates at which prices change for different types of products and services are not the same. Hence, if the prices of manufactured goods are rising at a rate higher than that of agricultural produce, then obviously, the real income level in the agricultural sector of the economy will be falling at relatively higher rate than in the manufacturing sector. This means that the agricultural sector is being more adversely affected by the inflationary trend.

The factor-related model refers to the different modes by which different groups or categories earn their income. We may differentiate those who earn their living or income from wages/salary and those whose income are based on profit. The former are usually workers while the latter are the self-employed.

In any free-market society, the self-employed has the freedom to sell his products or service at prices that take the general inflationary trend into account. As the prices of other goods or services rise, he raises his own prices (to the extent that the interplay between demand and supply allows) in order to off-set the adverse effects of inflation on himself. This way, he reduces or nullifies the adverse effect of inflation on himself because there is little or no increase on the real price he pays for goods/services he purchases from others. As a matter of fact, if he has workers (remunerated by wages) under his employment then, we witness a situation where he now produces his goods/services at a lower labour price in real terms (at least for the period before salaries are adjusted). The sum total of this is that the self-employed might and usually does end up getting richer as a result of inflation.

On the other hand, the worker finds that the rising cost of commodities/services now decreases the real value of his pay or its purchasing power. And this would continue until there is a salary adjustment – which in any case, hardly takes care of all the inflationary rates, and usually lags behind the inflationary. This means that inflation redistributes income in such a way that the wage earner is often hurt while the self-employed and employers of labour benefit.[4] It is therefore a vital ingredient to the continued increase in inequality of

4. a. Richard Nixon, *The Real War*, Op. cit. Pg. 237.
b. Richard 0. Lipsey, *An Introduction to Positive Economics*, ELBS & Weinenfeld and Nicolson, G. Britain, 4th Ed. 1970, Pg. 785.

wealth distribution.

Although both the sectoral and factor-related effects of inflation are capable of giving rise to the above conditions, the sectoral factor is often largely neutralised in the existing capitalist system. This is usually by way of movement of many or some members of the adversely affected sector to other sectors of the economy. The process is always referred to as labour mobility by economists.[5] This leaves the factor-based partiality the major problem of inflation. Here then is where the suggested approach to income distribution becomes relevant in the march to rendering inflation practically toothless, ineffectual and therefore containable.

The above statement is better appreciated when we consider the fact that in the proposed new relations of production, labour income is a percentage of total company income. This means that like the self-employed or employers of labour the income of the worker would take the inflationary trend into account since the total company income based on sales of products/services are partly determined by inflationary rates. The end result of this is that inflation can no longer effectively redistribute wealth in such a way that a factor benefits while the other loses. In which case, its effects would become cosmetic – amounting principally to a mere rise in the quantity not quality of cash exchanged for a given commodity over a given time. It may also mean some problems to calculating machines, computers, etc., which could be reduced by periodic redefinition of the unit value of money (not devaluation).

Only then can inflation seize to give us the kind of concern it presently does.

5. Ibid. pp. 359 - 362, 404

Note that the reason adduced here as the major cause of inflation is not necessarily opposed to either the neo-Keynesian or the monetarist models, or their theories about how inflation could generally be reduced. To me, both theories have their strong points. Extremists who tend to disregard the virtues of either fiscal or monetary policy miss the point. The two views (neo-Keynesian and monetarist) are both important and the one that takes the upper hand depends on a particular circumstance. The whole dispute is akin to the controversy (now mellowed) amongst physicists about the supremacy of either the particle or wave theory of matter.

Back to the task at hand, all we want to stress is that even if all other factors or conditions were kept constant, the mere tendency on the part of producers and middlemen to profit-maximization is enough to cause increases in the prices of commodities; which, essentially, is what inflation is all about.

LOW PRODUCTIVITY

The application of the principles expressed in the preceding chapters of this book is expected to boost production or the rate of economic growth in the case of the management of an economy. This statement is based on the fact that, generally speaking, people who seem irretrievably lethargic and unenterprising show amazing bursts of energy when given sufficient self-interest in economic activities. In other words, their seeming laziness is induced by lack of incentives.

In the capitalist economy only the owners of property have sufficient self-interest that induces one to contribute his utmost in economic activities. The worker hardly has enough self-interest to strive towards contributing his optimum in the productive process. His salary (barring periods of depression or recession) is more or less assured and may not necessarily rise above the fixed value just because he shows greater enthusiasm in the work. In contrast, when his total earnings become a direct function of the total income made by the company, the worker (individually and collectively) would be faced with an added incentive to put in more of his energy in the work, since he realises that the higher the company income, the higher his own individual (factor) income. As such, his output would no longer depend solely (or approximately) on the severity of the prevailing 'big brother is watching you" mechanism presently in fashion. The contribution of the worker to the productive process would now depend more on the dictates of his own internal gyroscopes of values and those established by the workers' collective attitudes which are bound to become more positive.

Secondly, the anticipated improvement of the remunerations for the labour force is bound to curtail the prevalent mis-employment of many individuals and the existing improper allocation of our human resources. In Nigeria, poor salaries and wages have continually led to the movement of many workers from the manufacturing, construction, agricultural, mining and services sectors of the economy to retail trading. Even those who have managed to remain at their posts now show marked ambivalence and disloyalty. Thus, many university professors and teachers, for instance, are part-time lecturers and part-time traders and distributors in practical terms. They oscillate between the classroom and their shops to the detriment of research and proper guidance to students.

In short, the thrust of specialization and professionalism is diluted by poor incentives and financial rewards. These go to weaken the productive apparatus of this country. It is conceivable therefore that the adoption of the distributive model enunciated in this book will go a long way to correcting and adjusting the structures of our productive organs and the economy in general. The sum total of the above would surely lead to increases in production even when the quantity, quality or value of fixed capital assets remain constant.

Furthermore, as long as the percentage of company income or profit which goes to labour (labour-income) is reasonable – reflecting the prevailing propensity to invest, interest rates, rate of economic growth etc. – the chances are that we may never experience long-term depression of the economy.

This point is better appreciated if we recall that the big depression of the 1930s is widely attributed to the lack of parity between increases in wages (or labour-price) and the technological increases in productivity during the 1920s in the economies of the advanced Western countries.[6] Technological increases in productivity during this period have been put at about 43% per factory man-hour while factory pay rose by less than 20%.[7] The fact that the former did not match the latter means that the public's capacity to buy finished goods and services fell.[8] According to *Time magazine* of February 1, 1982, 'The collapse of the over-inflated stock market, therefore started a downward spiral in both demand and the ability to pay'. Put in another way, the consumers – made up mainly of the working class, which constituted an important, if not a crucial factor in the productive process – could no longer find the means to procure the very goods they had jointly produced with owners of capital (or the owners of means of production and exchange) but appropriated by the latter. Talk about "surplus value"!

This means that the rich had gotten relatively richer and the poor relatively poorer, even as the G.N.P. was surging upwards, to the extent that it caused the collapse of the entire economic system – a condition long predicted by

6. *Time Magazine*, February 1, 1982. Page 16.
7-8. Ibid

Karl Marx but largely ignored by Western leaders. Needless to say, the 'recovery' that later came about marked essentially a new era (that was a far cry from laissez-faire) due mainly to President Roosevelt' sagacious economic management, the philosophical insight of Dr J. M. Keynes, as revealed in his General Theory of Employment, Interest and Money published in 1936, though largely neglected but for the expediency of executing the Second World War.

One lesson one learns from the above, is that there is a critical need to ensure that the rate at which labour-income rises must not fall below that at which productivity rises. And that this is better assured by governmental interference in income distribution between factors of production rather than the prevailing forces of individual or even collective bargaining in the so-called labour market. When labour income becomes a definite reasonable percentage of total output of an economy, in terms of goods and services produced we will expect that the above anomaly would no longer occur and therefore chances of a depression in economic activities would tend to zero – other factors being constant.

Lastly, application of the ideas expressed in the preceding chapters of this book to national economic management would ensure adequate labour mobility and help provide for a permanent and sustained structural adjustment of the economy consonant with the vagaries of time.

TAX EVASION AND RAPID POPULATION GROWTH

Income tax evasion by companies is fast becoming prevalent in most societies and the techniques employed in achieving this is fast developing into a science of its own. So common-place is the practice in certain countries that many people no longer frown at it. The task of forestalling tax evasion has thus become a tedious and energy sapping venture. And as many governments record increasing failure at extracting adequate tax from increasing number of companies, the tendency to evade tax increases amongst the populace. Also, because company taxation is an important source of revenue for execution of public projects, its evasion by a high percentage of the companies as obtains today means poor infrastructure, social stagnation, etc. Moreover, this practice contributes to inequalities in wealth distribution. Yet, tax evasion can hardly be eradicated by only preaching its adverse effects on society.

The reason why tax evasion has been difficult to check or control by various governments is due to the fact that tax evaluation is at present between company owners (or their representatives) and the tax-officials. This system not only leaves room for collusion between the company owners and the tax-officials, it also allows the company-owners to load the expense column (cost of production, overheads, rents, etc.) in such a way that profits (the basis for taxation) are as small as possible. In Nigeria, the techniques range from inflating the number of employees in the work-force (and therefore the labour-price) to false declarations with respect to fixed capital assets. Although workers in the company may know about these false declarations, they usually feel indifferent, the reason being that their wages/salaries do not depend on the amount of tax paid by their employer.

The suggested approach to the whole economic organisation or distribution of economic wealth contains a very strong deterrence to the existing practice. Because the Labour-income is a percentage of the total company income after taxation, the attitude of the workers is bound to change – individually and collectively. If the income declared by the company is small or less than it would have been so also would the company income after taxation and therefore the Labour Income. As such, the workers would take steps to ensure that the profit declared by the company before taxation and the value of the fixed capital assets submitted to the tax-man are factual – because the size of their income depends on these factors.

Thus, a system would evolve which places tax evaluation on the shoulders of three independent and contending groups: the tax-official, the employer/investor and the labourers/workers. And as long as the percentage of company income due to Labour, taxation rates, etc., are adequately controlled by government the chances of collusion between these three groups will always tend to zero, making for reduction, if not eradication, of tax evasion by companies. This, by implication, also means that evasion on personal income tax would be reduced since in the new system, individual (worker) income tax is agreed to have been deducted alongside the company income tax. This would reduce the size of paper work that is usually done in the process of evaluating and taxing individual incomes, since only those in the informal sector of the economy need be individually assessed by the tax-man.

What is more, since this taxation system does not allow tax-rebates on account of marital status or family size, it is bound to go a long way in discouraging high population growth which is already ranked amongst the world's major problems.

It would be interesting to witness the evolution of the envisaged tripartite relationship i.e., tax evaluation by the tax-man, labour and the investor, referred to above!

CRIME

High crime rate, we have already observed is partly due to unemployment, poverty and inequality – human behaviour being dependent on both innate and environmental characteristics. Since some people take to crime because of poverty or excessive deprivation, it is hoped that with the increasing egalitarianism which the ideas expressed in this book are bound to provide if put into practice, the crime rates we witness in some countries today will surely decline.

That would also entail reduced spending on crime-fighting and the amount of force governments need to employ in the task of maintaining social harmony and survival. This would also give governments the opportunity to turn more attention to those other issues or problems like environmental pollution, security from external aggression, etc., which they owe society.

POOR ACCOUNTABILITY

One of the weaknesses of the capitalist system is that it assigns to corporation managers too much powers in the day to day running of business organisations. Whereas they possess the power to make decisions that affect shareholders, employees and sometimes the society at large, accountability (at least to their employees) is hardly extracted from them. This runs counter to the basic principles of democracy which limits the powers at the disposal of public office holders through the demand of probity and accountability on them. The situation is even worse in the case of small-scale private enterprises that are usually managed by their sole-owners. Lack of accountability encourages those who wield such enormous powers to abuse or use the powers in irresponsible ways. It makes for corruption and other shady deals that are often detrimental to the society.

The situation above is bound to be greatly reduced in the co-operative type of structure advocated in this book. Obviously, the secrecy that surrounds the activities and actions of business owners and managers are bound to decline at least to the extent that they have to be accountable to their employees. It is expected that so long as these decision-makers are conscious of the fact that most of their decisions, transactions, etc., are to be ultimately disclosed to the labour force of the corporation, they would be cautious about what they do. Even those people outside the particular business set-up with whom the managers/owners of a business are dealing with will likely sit up knowing fully well that the wall of secrecy that normally covers shady deals has been cast away. This is inevitable since bribes given out by company executives would become public knowledge as soon as the executives render annual reports, unless of course, they are prepared to use their own private funds for such purpose. In this way societal rules and laws regarding business activities would become more applicable. The sum total of this is that the near-absolute powers business owners and managers wield would be brought to manageable proportions.

THE RISING TREND TOWARDS BIGNESS

From the foregoing, it is obvious that application of the ideas in this book is bound to reduce tremendously the present size of governmental involvement in many areas of societal life. With the expected rise in equitability or fairness which would be buttressed by mass employment, low crime rates, etc., the enormous burden being borne by many governments would decline. Some welfare programmes, law enforcement agencies, etc., of many nations would have to be trimmed down in line with the new order. Those countries that are presently finding it difficult to separate business from politics can now find a way out. In short, the trend towards bigness on the part of governments would certainly decline.

Furthermore, the envisaged reduction in the size of governments and the limitation of their areas of operation and control in the economic or business sector would help sanitise the political processes in many modern nations. It is widely known that in countries with predominant state presence or involvement in economic activities, "politics is the master-key to economic prosperity, social prestige and recognition, personal self-fulfilment, and enhanced group identity."[9]

This is because, "governments and their parastatals possess the biggest contracts of all categories, import and export licences, concessions in land and minerals, etc. To be in government thus means to be in a position to control a lot of these and to be out of government means exclusion from them; elections in this context, then become life and death affairs rather than lose or win competitions which must be seen as that."[10] This is imperative because electoral victory in such setting determines who gets ministerial, board and other political appointments and therefore who controls what government contracts or enjoys other perquisites.

In Nigeria, for instance, governmental involvement in virtually all facets of economic activity, amounting to her participation even in domestic production and distribution has made politics the primary determinant of what individual or group gets what financial reward and social amenity. Consequently, political struggles have become an

9. Michael Olisa, Way out of electoral malpractices. Lagos, *Sunday Times*, March 13, 1983.
10. Ibid

intense cut-throat affair. This has led to the invasion of the political scene by many ill-equipped, vile and self-seeking men and women. This is partly responsible for the nightmares our various attempts at democratic politics have been.

In the light of the above, it stands to reason that the more governmental dominance in business is curtailed, and/or the more governments concentrate on their basic functions – protection of the individual from fraud, violence and external aggression, etc. – the more our political life and processes would be purified and stabilized. Also the baser men will refrain from going into the mainstream of Nigerian politics.

In the business arena, drastic changes would also occur. A combination of the distributive method enunciated in this book and the new approach to income taxation is bound to defuse the tendency toward unlimited profit and acquisitiveness derivable from monopoly, monopsony and other consequences of big business.

What is more, with the enhanced diffusion of capital into the hands of many, which will come about alongside the trend towards normal (0, 1) distribution of incomes and wealth in the society, there would be a corresponding diffusion of the number of owners and therefore number of enterprises or businesses. Such a trend would also go a long way to curbing monopoly, and collusion that presently work against the forces of supply and demand in the market place. This is because, the larger the number of companies producing the same product or service, the more difficult it would be for them to forge alliances or associations, or reach agreements/consensus about prices of their products.

Even when such agreements are reached, application would be difficult as the task of identifying and penalising defaulters would be too high. In sum, this would discourage the on-going trend towards undesirable big business.

WORLD SECURITY

It has been pointed out in Chapter One that one of the major factors responsible for the present global insecurity, local wars and threats of an all-out global War is the virtual division of the world into two ideological camps. The bloody struggles between capitalists and communists cum socialists within different countries today need no elaboration, nor the more portent antagonism between ideologically opposed countries.

The potency of the existing hostility is heightened by the fact that there are only two major ideological blocks: - the Capitalists and the Communists. As such, opposition is easily identified and directed. In contrast, if three or more strong (political) ideologies were in fashion, hostility between the three would be less directed: the chances of open confrontation between any two would be greatly reduced because those two would not like to create a situation which may be exploited by the third ideological camp. If any two engage themselves in a violent conflict, the third might standby only to assume a dominant posture once the warring two have sufficiently weakened themselves. This in essence means that the advent of a third strong socioeconomic/political ideology might forestall or at least greatly reduce the chances of an ideological-based global war by merely re-defining and redirecting the lines of opposition.

And who knows, given the existing state of social and economic stagnation which is afflicting many countries today and the mid-way nature of the suggested third socio-economic mode of societal organisation, the existing ideologies might be ditched by their present adherents thereby making the whole world a mono-ideological, peace-conscious society.

PART III
SOCIO-POLITICAL FORMAT

CHAPTER 6
ELEMENTARY DISTRIBUTION OF POLITICAL POWER

It has already been pointed out that just as the mode of distribution of economic power or wealth may affect the liberty of the individual in a society so also could the mode of distribution of political power. It is a truism that where wealth or power is concentrated in few hands, the stability of the society and the liberties of its individuals could in the final analysis be jeopardised. As a result of the above, this chapter is devoted to the issue of equitable distribution of political power.

Distribution of political power amongst individuals in any given polity herein referred to as elementary or primary distribution of political power is dependent on the form of government in operation. Traditionally, three distinct forms of government have evolved in mankind's long and chequered history of political posturing and inquiry. These are: monarchy, aristocracy and democracy. For purposes of clarity, we need restate the meanings or definitions of these labels, appraise each of them and weigh the relevance or appropriateness of each of them in the light of this thesis.

MONARCHY

Monarchy is probably the earliest form of government known to man. Ancient history is replete with the travails of monarchical rule. Simply put, monarchy is government by one man. Theoretically the monarch is not subject to legal limitations and is therefore free to do things according to his own will. He is the absolute ruler. Thus, monarchical rule involves the concentration of political power in one single individual. However, the extent of power a monarch might possess or wield varies from one to the other depending on whether it is an absolute monarchy, constitutional monarchy, etc. It can also be hereditary with father or mother passing the throne onto one of their offspring.

Although monarchy is often differentiated into two forms: absolute and constitutional, our focus here is on the former as the latter, constitutional monarchy, involves a power-sharing arrangement between the monarch and parliament or the representatives of the people. The constitutional monarch has to seek the consent of the representative bodies, accept advice from ministers, respect the letter of the Constitution, etc. In which case, it may well be argued that constitutional monarchy is no monarchy in the real sense of the word and so belongs to a different form of government altogether.

Proponents of monarchy often argue that a single ruler is a must for the achievement of the unity and oneness of purpose necessary for the attainment and maintenance of a stable polity. According to Bodin (1530 – 1596) monarchy is best adopted to deal with emergencies, as the monarch does not need to engage in time-consuming consultations before taking action.[1] Furthermore, monarchy is deemed to provide the most satisfactory government in a situation where low political consciousness, illiteracy, etc. make orderly government difficult. Lastly, there are those who hold the view put forward by Francis Bacon (1561 – 1626) that monarchy is a natural institution as obedience to a King is as natural as the obedience of a child to its parents. Or as Filmer put it, that the state can be likened to the family with the King and father occupying identical positions.[2]

Looking at the first three of these arguments, one notices that they all assume that the monarch always has

---

1.   A. Appadorai, *The Substance of Politics*, Op. Cit., Page 133.
2.   Ibid.

the interest of the people at heart, that he is always committed or inclined to pursuing policies favourable to all and sundry. However, experience shows that that assumption is not always true; that the monarch may turn out to be self-centred and so unmindful of the yearnings of his people as to become a tyrant. Even when an able, conscientious monarch is found there is no guarantee that those qualities would be inherited by his offspring or successors.

As for the last argument that the state is equivalent to the family, one only has to fall back on records of earlier political philosophies to debunk that claim. In his criticism of Plato, Aristotle pointed out the illogicality of drawing a strict analogy between the family and the State.[3] According to him, the State is made up of adults who should therefore not be likened to children in the family. The child is a minor. Thus while one can justify parental control over children we cannot so justify the King's control of citizens. These arguments therefore go to weaken the case for monarchy as a viable form of government.

Again, looked upon from the standpoint of equitable or fair distribution of power, which is a central concern of this thesis, monarchy can hardly be recommended since it represents the concentration of political power in only one man instead of striving at the attainment of a spread that approaches normal distribution.

ARISTOCRACY

Aristocracy is government by a few individuals that constitute themselves into a ruling class. It is the second form of government evolved by man. The aristocrat is not bound to seek the opinion or support of the ruled for it is presumed that they (the aristocrats) possess superior knowledge and intellect to deal with the affairs of the

3. G. H. Sabine & T. L. Thorson, *A History of Political Theory*, Op. cit., Page, 99.

nation or community without recourse to a people's mandate.

Despite the fact that aristocracy embraces a wider dispersion of power than monarchy, it is still bedevilled by most of the points raised against monarchy. Its chances of success are again dependent on the benevolence of its operators. Where these fellows are not equal to the task, aristocracy becomes (like monarchy) a terrible burden. In this sense, it could degenerate into oligarchy.

Furthermore, aristocracy is weakened by problems arising from succession. Because its members virtually have to occupy their positions for life, an element of rigidity and conservatism always bedevil aristocratic governments thereby making them un-adaptive to changing social and economic conditions. Thus, while it is desirable to have the best men always at the decision-taking levels of government, aristocracy cannot be recommended because of these limitations.

DEMOCRACY

Democracy is a form of government in which the citizens exercise the governing power either directly or through their elected representatives who may be changed or re-elected periodically. Thus, a state is termed democratic if she has institutions for the expression of the people's supremacy and right to self-determination on vital questions of social direction and policy.[4] It is the third and perhaps the most popular of all the forms of government known to man.

Constitutionally, democracy is expressed by the provision of equal rights for all normal adults to vote and stand for elections; periodic elections; freedom of speech

---

4. A. Appadorai, *The Substance of Politics*, Op. Cit. Page 137

and association, etc. In so far as these rules or rights provide opportunities for mass political participation, it can be said that democracy makes for dispersed power. And that all things being equal it approximates the normal distribution of power which by this thesis is a cardinal requirement for lasting social cohesion and political stability. Democracy cannot therefore be criticised on these grounds.

Theoretically, democracy is superior to the other two forms of government. It gives to every person, a sense of responsibility and recognition, while at the same time ensuring that his interests or rights are not whimsically disregarded. Thus, where anyone is genuinely interested in pursuing his legitimate interests and possesses the ability so to do, he cannot be discounted. It gives all men, theoretically speaking, equal access to power and voice in the affairs of the community.

Furthermore, democracy provides possibility for a nonviolent change of government. Where the existing government is found wanting, an election can readily provide an alternative government. Even where a government is not changed, realisation of the ever-present possibility of change, makes those in power to work harder and more conscientiously. This therefore, checks the tendency to corruption and decadence, making the pursuance of common interest and welfare uppermost in the minds of those in power. In this sense, democracy makes authority a trust.

Because democracy allows for the freedom of opinion and association amongst others, it guarantees the safety of the individual from internal enemies. It curtails effectively the possibility of using state power against anyone. Where these safeguards do not exist as in monarchy and aristocracy, any form of dissent may be misconstrued and punished accordingly. In the light of all these, one can say that even if democracy may not be referred to as the ideal government, it must be recognised as the best alternative. While one may not deny that it could possess characteristics that could be negative to proper social and political organisation, it must be pointed out that when appropriately harnessed, it stands to guarantee a most lasting and healthy polity.

Deficiencies of democracy lie mainly on its applicability and workability in societies where there are high rates of illiteracy, low political consciousness, social and economic inequalities, etc. Where these conditions exist, democracy may appear indeed to be government by ignorant fools as some critics often say. Therefore, to make for true democracy, it is necessary to eliminate or push to the barest minimum the existence in society of the above-mentioned maladies.

As for the criticism that the rule of the majority is not necessarily the rule of the best ideas; that the majority is not always right, one can only quip that the rule of the minority as represented by monarchy and aristocracy does not fare any better in this direction. They can be found wanting on that score too since the minority can also be wrong.

Finally, democracy is widely criticised on the grounds that it carries within it a supposedly ill-fated component; the party system. The point put forward against the party system is that it encourages insincerity and intellectual dishonesty because in the bid to abide by party norms and rules, the party-man could become so loyal to the party that the interests of the larger society is compromised or relegated to the background thereby paving the way for undue exploitation of the community by certain individuals within the party.

Although the question of party: to be or not to be, is peripheral to the central issue of what form of government is best suited for a society, it nevertheless cannot be overlooked. However, while one may agree to some extent with the point against the party system, it has to be pointed out that the system has its strong points. In the first place, to the extent that the party is organised principally upon the basic criterion that the interests, aims and opinions of its members are identical and therefore worthy of pursuit in a collective way, the party spirit appears natural to the democratic process. It marks the accentuation of the old adage that birds of the same feather flock together. In other words, a form of ganging up is inevitable in democratic politics if not in all societal processes.

Furthermore, it must be recognised that the party system fulfils certain basic functions that are necessary for the sustenance of democratic politics. This is the vital need for organisation and for the identification and articulation of the muted interests and opinions of the people, as a guide to the formulation and presentation of principles and policies upon which a popular and viable government may be constructed. It also represents a forum for educating the electorate politically in order to reduce the chances of having governments elected and perhaps run by fools. The party also helps to maintain a sense of continuity in public policy. Where the party does not exist, it is conceivable that each successive government being moulded upon an individual would entail widely varying policies. The party system also works against ethnic or tribal politics especially where there are two or more parties and the constitution demands fair national spread from the parties. Also, the two-party or multi-party system helps to keep the government of the day in check, for in the absence of an organised opposition as represented by the other party, it would be very difficult to change or bring pressure upon the incumbent administration in any decisive way. Thus, a dictatorship might result.

Arguably, two brands of Democracy thrive side by side in the now world: the two or multi-party democracy and the one-party democracy, with their respective merits and demerits.

Finally, despite all beneficial aspects of the party system, the issue of party tyranny and its tendency to dictate to elected officials cannot be overlooked, in the drive to establishing and sustaining noble democratic ethos in society. In this regard, we believe that certain constitutional provisions designed to insulate elected government officials (especially those in the executive arm) from possible party blackmail and intimidation are necessary.

Experience shows that party stranglehold on elected officials stems from the officials' fear of party sanctions or from constant and incessant party threats of actually denying "erring" officials of party-nomination for the next election. Thus elected officials often succumb to party whims in order to be assured of being put forward as candidates for the forthcoming elections. Therefore, to insulate the elected officials from undue party influence, this stranglehold must be defused. And the surest way to achieve this is to insert a clause in the constitution which makes it possible for incumbent presidents, governors and council chairmen – that is, those just finishing their first term – to stand the next election as independent candidates where or if, for any reasons, their respective parties chose not to nominate them for the second term.

Will the above provision boomerang, making elected officials to be swollen-headed, opinionated and unresponsive to party wishes? It depends. Every astute politician is aware of the immense benefit derivable from his retaining the support and backing of his party especially for electoral battles. He is aware that there is a slimmer chance of his winning the election for a second term as an independent candidate as compared to when he is contesting on the ticket of his party. Therefore, it is conceivable that the prudent incumbent chief executive would never want to antagonise and lose his party's backing unless the issue between him and his party is one of extreme and crucial nature; one that is a matter of boom or doom for the larger society. And the shrewd and astute chief executive would be sure that his case is self-evident, obvious and acceptable to the electorate before he can take any gamble that would pitch him against the party or that will cause him to ditch his fellow party-men.

MOBOCRACY

Just as monarchy may degenerate into tyranny and aristocracy into oligarchy, so could democracy degenerate into "Mobocracy" to borrow El Chinoy's terminology. *Mobocracy* then represents a decadent, polluted and abused form of democracy in which one group or the mob takes the law into their hands, intimidating the other group(s) or the opposition and employing coercive tactics to beat them into line. The democratic form of government thrives most in an atmosphere of tolerance and mutual respect. People must accept the principles of live and let live, for there to exist freedom of speech, association and the other cardinal attributes of democracy. As such, intolerance and/or lack of respect for the feelings of the other man, becomes the chief source of friction and of pollution of democracy. When people or groups, because they have the upper hand, decide that they cannot co-exist with those they perceive to hold different and opposing views, the ultimate result is mob action and persecution. It is therefore crucial that individuals within a democratic set-up must eschew intolerance if democracy is to produce the desired results.

Intolerance and mob action within a polity could result from two sources: instigation from political parties or politicians, and indirectly from the populace or a section thereof. Where the former is the case, its elimination could be effectively carried out by using the state machinery and by carefully making adequate constitutional provisions. Generally, where there are adequate provisions relative to people and place, for separation of powers in addition to other rules concerning party organisational procedures, this malady could be checked or curtailed. With adequate separation of powers, the chances, for instance, of the ruling party using state power against the opposition is contained.

In Britain, separation is supplied by the Westminster Parliamentary system, while in the U.S.A., they have the

Presidential system. A study of these two systems, readily reveals their adaptation and suitability to the two different cultures and/ or peoples and their peculiar circumstances. However, while they may each work very well for these two peoples, it cannot be guaranteed, as experience has shown, that they would work out the same way if transposed or if either of them is exported wholesale to other lands. Thus, it behoves other nations and peoples who have been brought up under different regimes to evolve their own systems or adopt variants of the above models which meet the realities of their own peculiarities. This decision indeed, is what different nations and peoples are beginning to brace-up to. (For a discussion of a suitable model for Nigeria, see the Part Five of this work).

Where intolerance in democratic politics is widely spread or resides with the people, solutions do not come so readily. Experience shows that in the many regions of the world where intolerance based on differing political beliefs thrive amongst the people; governments tend to resort to brute force or some form of police action to combat the problem. While one may not entirely discount the possible effectiveness of this method, we cannot but think that there could be other more positive means of achieving the same end. To put this solution into the right perspective, one needs to contrast the modern democracies with the earlier ones or rather the different conditions under which they operated.

CHAPTER 7

**SECONDARY DISTRIBUTION OF POLITICAL
POWER**

Just as a fair distribution of political power among individuals in a polity may favourably affect the degree of freedom the citizens enjoy and the likely degree of cohesion, understanding, solidarity and oneness of a people, so could the perceived fairness in the distribution of power amongst the sub-national or ethnic groups that make up that polity do the same. Where political power is perceived to rest mainly with one section of the populace, the other section or sections are likely to show resentment about the status quo. In extreme cases, this could lead to agitations, separatist movements and even civil wars.

As a result of this, the mode of power distribution among ethnic or sub-national groups in a country has always been of central concern and importance to nation-builders. It is widely recognised that a good or fair power-sharing arrangement is crucial in the process of organising and building a nation. Hence, over the years, there have emerged different power sharing models in the governance of countries or nations. Before we can make any meaningful statement as to the appropriateness of this or that system or mode of power distribution among sub-national or ethnic groups in national politics, we need first to examine the existing models, their evolution, acceptability and relevance to prevailing realities.

MODES OF POWER DISTRIBUTION AMONGST (ETHNIC) GROUPS IN NATIONAL POLITICS

Ever since the dawn of democratic government in the Greek City-States and its subsequent adaptation by emergent country-states, there has been steady development in the

171

modes of power-sharing and distribution arrangements between communal or territorial groups that have come to make up modem nation-states. In the Greek city-states, the problems of ethnicity – its demand for power-sharing and communal political participation – were largely absent because the polis, as the Greeks called their states were comparatively small, both in land area and population. And because the inhabitants of each state were practically of the same stock, each city-state boiled down to what we may today refer to as a single constituency.

On the other hand, the largeness of the modern country-state with its often heterogeneous groups, differentiated from one another in intricate and diverse ways, coupled with the attendant divergence in interests, opinions, goals, etc. makes political organisation and the process of mustering consensus and solidarity, a complex and sometimes wary business. As such, nation-builders have come to realise that these smaller geographic territories, ethnic or communal groups and the political power elites who govern them cannot be ignored if a truly strong and virile nation-state is to emerge or is to be sustained from the aggregation of communities or ethnic groups who usually make up the modern country-state.

In turn, this has led to the obvious conclusion, that some sort of acceptable power-sharing and distribution scheme is necessary in the large country-states not only for the sake of preserving and accommodating certain differences in the cultures of the different units but also to ensure reasonable and commensurate communal political participation at the centre. This is viewed now as the only lasting and peaceful method to achieving and maintaining a true nation-state where a high degree of passionate identification and allegiance to the centre is necessary to overcome the numerous internal differences of the units that often jeopardise national stability and survival. Needless to say, it is a truism that without creating the proper national political climate upon which the appropriate national sentiment can be built, the equation of a country-state to a nation-state would forever remain suspect, as the former is more of a geographical expression while the latter is basically a political concept.

In keeping with the above, two basic patterns of organising and institutionalising national power have thus far emerged. The first is the establishment of tiers of government and the second is the concept of assuring, even if to different degrees, that adequate political participation at the centre is not denied any community. The creation of tiers of government is borne out of the tendency or desire to preserve and accommodate regional cultural differences. It is therefore designed to deal with what areas of policy-making or governance the different tiers of government or groups are to preside. The direct result of this concern is the emergence and survival of the Unitary and Federal systems of government.

Generally, it must be observed, where the units are powerful and the people tend to cling to their different communal traditions, the federal system is more favourable, while the unitary system is usually adopted in places where the units are either weak or possess relatively homogeneous cultural traditions. The United States, India and Nigeria are typical examples of countries organised on the principles of the federal system from inception, while Guyana, Haiti, Panama, etc., represent typical unitary states. *It is little wonder that the current notorious inclination, indeed attempt at running Nigeria as a unitary state instead of a federation, which augurs well with its large size and diversity, is causing a lot of hiccups in that country. It is easy to see that unless Nigeria is returned to federalism, the present political turbulence in the country will persist, in fact deepen.*

The concept of assuring political participation of the different communities at the centre, designed to placate every territorial or ethnic group's sense of responsibility and acceptance, and therefore elicit their commitment to the nation is a more tenuous and intricate business. Because it is designed to deal with the composition of the central government, the policies it must pursue, whose views must dominate, etc., this aspect of power-sharing remains a more potent source of friction since different territorial groups often advocate different policies at different times in the course of a nation's life. As such, it has from time immemorial demanded a thorough and continuing examination of the factors – their number and relevance – upon which a true and equitable power-sharing scheme acceptable to all or at least the majority of the groups, must be based. The fact that up to now the matter has not been settled in comparison to the relatively entrenched tier system in the political cultures of perhaps all modern nations underlines the fact that it is relatively more complex in nature.

Traditionally and historically, power-sharing process has been based upon the perceived strength or power of the different territorial or communal groups that make up a nation. However, the complexity of this process in the modern country-states has been accentuated in recent times by the advancement of scientific and technological know-how which has led to revolutions in the fields of transport, communication and warfare. This last development has especially confused the axiom upon which a group's possible strength or power is traditionally measured or estimated.

In the olden days, the probability that a particular group would come out victorious in an inter-group warfare depended largely, if not solely, on the relative numerical strength of the combatants. Hence, the most populated group was always expected, and indeed usually came out the winners in such struggles. Consequently, at the dawn or emergence of the country-state, this morbid right to dominate or dictate to the less populated was transformed into a civic or political right to have more say at the centre for the most populated. Hence, the numerical strength or population of each constituent territorial group within the larger society was viewed; or indeed enthroned, as the sole determinant of the magnitude of political clout or influence each group or unit must exercise over the affairs of the union. This would appear to be in keeping with the partly valid principle that voting or national democratic politics is a civilized way of fighting the erstwhile inter-ethnic or inter-communal battles that determined which group dominated the other in the past.

In practical terms, the above mode of power-sharing was expressed in the one man, one vote precept. This therefore, assured the most populated ethnic or territorial group a larger vote or control over national affairs. In the legislature, this was to give rise to the Unicameral system.

Faced with the ever-present threat of reversion to physical confrontation and possible defeat at the hands of the most populated group(s), the less populated communities or territorial groups simply had to succumb to this pattern of power-sharing arrangement. Hence, the population of each ethnic or territorial group became acceptable as the chief index of power-distribution among the constituent units of a country-state in the early times.

However, contemporary history reveals that a second factor, namely; the equality of states principle has since been introduced to complement the earlier population principle in many emergent nations of the world. In 1970, for instance, of the 108 countries with national legislatures, fifty-six of these were unicameral (single chambered) bodies, with group votes weighted solely along the lines of numerical strength while the remaining fifty-two were bi-cameral, with group votes weighted both along the lines of numerical strength and 'equality of each group' to one another regardless of size of inhabitants in each unit.[1]

As one might expect, federal systems fall overwhelmingly into the latter category. That is, they produce more bicameral legislature than the unitary system. The second or upper chamber of federal countries generally reflect a kind of formal recognition of sub-national territories or communal groups, thereby giving them equal representation or vote regardless of size or population. As such, we can say that the Upper Chamber symbolises power concessions made to groups, especially the less populated ones, in order to elicit their passionate allegiance and therefore improve the viability of the nation-state.

Certain factors favour or discourage the introduction of either unicameralism or bicameralism. The reasons can be drawn from both theoretical and practical standpoints. We may summarise these as below:[2]

1. **SIZE:** In general, nations that are territorially small tend to prefer unicameralism. Where small states are bi-cameral, it usually signals the existence of some very special pattern of guaranteed representation. For example, there is the need, as some have argued, to ensure that the activities of the popular representatives, which is regarded often as rash and inexperienced or ill-advised, is curbed by the deliberations of a more conservative second chamber. This type of second chamber is therefore clearly different from that based on the equality of each unit in the union.

1.Roland Young, *Approaches to the Study of Politics*, Evanston ILL., North-western University Press, 1962.

2.Ibid.

Equally relevant is the fact that size affects structure in other directions, With the glaring exception of China, which is a very old nation, the largest countries seem to detest unicameralism or require bicameralism or even something more than that, in order to achieve or to attain nationhood. This is not only because of territorial expanse or spread but also because ethnic, regional, religious, linguistic and developmental factors as well as racial divergence often accompany large size.

2   .**DIVERSITY:** This is a vital factor influencing the basic structure of national legislatures and vote-weighting for elections to national executive offices. Where potentially conflicting interests are not easily reconciled or over-ridden by brute force, where sub-national centres of power must be recognised, the bicameral mode of power-sharing naturally suggests itself. This is true for states or countries which were created out of a number of sovereign and independent nations as exemplified by most African countries. In Nigeria, for instance, British colonialism led to the amalgamation of many erstwhile unconnected and independent ethnic groups, with their linguistic, religious cultural and developmental diversities, into a modern country-state.

However, it must be pointed out that although the underlying motivation for bicameralism is most evident in federal states, it can also be detected elsewhere. Thus, in unitary Great Britain, we notice that bicameralism resulted from historical evolution based on the fact that the nobility and the higher clergy were represented in the House of Lords, while the general public were represented in the House of

Commons. It must be noted that because the nobility only represents themselves, the House of Lords is of little consequence vis-a-vis power-sharing between primary groups within that society!

3. **IDEOLOGY**: Ideological commitment is another factor that often influences the type of legislature a country adopts. This stems from the very peculiarities of each ideology. Thus, it is conceivable that a collective society with her 'single people', ruled by a single party and dedicated to a single collective purpose should not under normal conditions require a second chamber. Strictly speaking, second chambers naturally belong to those ideologies which recognise and accommodate individualistic and sectional pursuits, while the centralised planning and control noticeable in socialistic states make unicameralism a natural choice for left-leaning states, other factors being constant. Notice that most communist states were unicameral. The remarkable exception of USSR, Yugoslavia, and Czechoslovakia was probably due to the overwhelming influence of size and diversity. Indeed, the large size and divert of these countries were so acute and demanding that with the collapse of communism these countries became so insupportable that even bicameralism could not keep them together, and they had to dissolve irretrievably.

Finally, we would like to point out that the introduction of the principle of equality of states as a factor in power-sharing schemes is partly due, in concrete terms, to the probable realisation that numerical strength or population does not always determine the direction of victory in inter-ethnic or inter-group squabbles. Such other intangible assets or characteristics as courage, skill, tactics, even luck, which one group may possess over and above the other, has historically often swung victory to the side of relatively less populated groups, especially in the modern world where technology alone could make all the difference. These therefore make 'jungle elections' as these inter-group contentions may be called rather unpredictable.

Furthermore, the fact that the aggregate magnitude of contributions made towards national survival by different units within a union is not always dependent on the numerical size or population of each unit must have made policy-makers or nation builders to reassess the traditional or predominant basis for power-sharing. Needless to say, the contribution referred to above may either be in the area of bolstering national defence capabilities or in the calmer waters of international competitions in trade, industry, sports, etc.

Therefore, to accommodate the simple but important fact that the very quality of being a group could be as important as the size of a group, nation-builders introduced the concept of 'equality of each unit' as a thriving factor in the formulation of power-sharing schemes. Therein lies the 'crude' motivations behind the introduction of bicameralism or the symbolic concession made to minority groups in power-sharing schemes noticeable in some countries, especially the federal states.

Bicameralism is perhaps most exemplified in the American federalism. As such, we need to take a look at the American bi-cameral system as an illustration of the mode of power-sharing arrangement.

POWER-SHARING AMONG AMERICAN STATES

The United States of America is a federation of about fifty states. Power-sharing amongst these states is noticeable from the number of representatives each state has in Congress, the U.S. Legislature. That legislature consists of two chambers; the Senate and the House of Representatives.

Within the Senate, the States are each represented by two Senators.[3] This means that the States have equal voting power in that chamber, since all senators are basically of the same status. On the other hand, the House of Representatives is composed of some 436 members apportioned among the states according to their populations.[4] Thus, the larger the population of a state, the more the number of her members in the House of Representatives. Since each member of the house has one vote, this arrangement amounts practically to a distribution of power in direct proportion to the numerical strength or population of the constituent states. And in view of the fact that the Senate has equal powers with the House of Representatives (in ordinary legislation), we may conclude that power-sharing among American States is roughly two-dimensional, resting on:

(1) the numerical size of each state; and,

(2) the equality of states principle.

The two-dimensional distribution of power is no doubt a more recent development in the tangled business of power-sharing among ethnic or territorial units in national politics. This mode is adopted in many countries where the luxury of unicameralism is considered incapable of satisfying all the units or eliciting their commitment to the larger society.

In comparison, unicameral states like Costa Rica, Guatemala, El Salvador, Guyana, Haiti, Panama, etc., are relatively small in size, exhibit little diversity and are sometimes also buttressed or strengthened by a relatively collective ideological atmosphere. Bicameral USA, though with large territorial and numerical size, individualistic ideology, exhibit little diversity in culture, language and religion for the constituent states.

1.   A. Appadorai, Op. Cit., p. 333   4. Ibid.

PART IV
THE INTERNATIONAL ARENA

CHAPTER 8

THE INTERNATIONAL ARENA AND THE FREEDOM OF THE INDIVIDUAL

It is a common knowledge that the freedom of the individual is dependent not only on the forms of government or the types of state but also on the relations of the individual's own state or country with other states. As such, these interstate or international relations are of great importance to political theory. In the preceding parts of this discourse, we considered at length the first factor, i.e. the reconciliation of the individual and the subnational entities with the state. In this the fourth part of the book, however, we are going to focus largely on the latter, that is, inter-state relations vis-à-vis individual freedom or safety.

THE PLACE OF NATIONALISM IN WORLD AFFAIRS

Modern states are sovereign states. They are supposed to owe allegiance to no other and are deemed to be independent from interference by other states. Each modern state is a unified political entity, organised on a national basis and strengthened by national sentiments. These sentiments are usually made up of three traits:

> one of these lies in the past and centres upon the possession of a common heritage of memories or cultural past.[1]

Because the individual is to a large extent a product of his social environment and experience those who have been brought up in the same fashion and territory tend,

1.   A. Appadorai, *The Substance of Politics*, Op. cit., page 145.

183

generally speaking, to be more like one another, and to differ from those born and reared under another regimen. Hence, we find that the psychological traits common to those who have been socialized in the same fashion or brought up under the same regimen constitute a social character. This is potentially related in diverse ways to values and beliefs as well as the prevailing systems of social relationships upon which a people's social inertia is tied.[2]

The second trait lies in the present:

> It centres on the emotional needs, drives and feelings of the people which act together in defence of cherished characteristics.

Finally, there is the future. The import of this is contained in the nature of goals or ideals each people set for themselves or strive to attain or bequeath to their offspring. Needless to say, these goals may be absurd or downright unrealisable – like the aim by some societies at utopian equality or classlessness. Nevertheless, where there is a general or collective will to pursue that or any particular ideal or course of action, that consensus is transformed into a binding force, a sentiment that becomes part of the essential conditions of a people's being.

Nationalism is a powerful sentiment and could be beneficial or destructive depending on what is at stake, how it is organised or exploited and to what purpose. That it has considerable value is generally recognised. For one thing, nationalism saves the world from the monotony of a global empire which could hamper the continued evolution or, at least, the rate of evolution of political advancement and

2.   El chinoy, *Society*, Op. cit. page 84.

sophistication on the planet.[3] This is because political as well as individual advancement are inextricably linked to contacts, cross-cultural influences and competition. The existence of nation-states affords the world a diversity of cultural patterns which represent distinct experiments in social, economic and political management from which one another could benefit, since every nation has the freedom to copy from the other or others those progressive traits or ways of doing things that they cherish or that are superior to their own local ways. Such inter-cultural dependence is noticeable in all components or aspects of cultural heritage – ideas, institutions and material culture.

Furthermore, the existence of many nation-states goes a long way to satisfying diverse shades and colours of local expectations, desires, needs and tendencies. It helps to preserve those special group characteristics of different peoples which, for the sake of all mankind, are good to preserve. For just as collectivism could adversely reduce individuality or inhibit genius so could an attempt to forge a common global custom, creed or empire for all men destroy some special beneficial character or modus operandi which a nation may develop by virtue of her own unique experience geographical/ecological peculiarities or some innate characteristics that are native only to her citizens. It is in this sense therefore, that nationalism may be regarded as beneficial.

Thus, prudent support for nationalism amounts to a recognition that people should differ in their methods of law and governance in keeping with the inherent and contrasting varieties of human groups – their experiences, needs and goals – and that civilization progresses by differentiation, selective acculturation and sometimes by assimilation.

3. Burges, John W., *Political Science and Constitutional Law*, Boston, Gina, 1890-91, Vol.1, pages 38, 39.

What is more, the existing diversity in cultural traits, especially differences in modes of socioeconomic and political ideologies amongst the different peoples and nations of the world makes the establishment or survival of a world government, structured along the lines of existing national governments, an illusion. And that the very attempt at imposing such a government could usher in unprecedented despotism and social malaise.

Yet, these should not make us lose sight of the negative aspects of nationalism. The bad and dangerous aspects of nationalism lie in the fact that it possesses within itself a possible source of its own destruction and that unless carefully curbed of excesses could of itself shake or off-set the very equilibrium upon which our earthly existence and civilization hinge.[4]

Excessive nationalisms, if we may so denote the negative aspects of nationalism, is given vent when nationalistic feelings are tinged with ethnocentrism, greed and covetousness. Sociologists have long identified the tendency by some individuals or groups to regard as natural, what is widespread or conventional in one's own society. This view, christened ethnocentrism, that one's own group or the way they do things, is the measure of man everywhere, constitutes a major obstacle to good neighbourliness, goodwill and peaceful co-existence between nations and peoples. Thus, it has often led to the annihilation of peoples, and the destruction of nations and civilizations.

Same goes for the other factors of greed and covetousness. In pursuance of their mad, inordinate desires for egoistic and material gains, nations have made repeated wars against one another since ancient times. Peoples have been consequently enslaved, pillaged and humiliated just because some more powerful groups think that a marginal improvement of their lot is worth more than the very

4, A. Appadorai, *The Substance of politics*, Op. Cit. Pg. 146.

existence of some other neighbouring groups. Such thinking and actions have not only dealt crippling blows on man's material as well as non-material achievements over the ages but also create fear and mutual suspicion between nations and peoples thereby inhibiting goodwill and good neighbourliness among nations.

Fear, though corrupted or made commonplace by casual and frequent usage over time is really a very potent force. It is a very painful and negative emotion which by itself alone lowers or causes to be lowered, the quality of life a person or persons end up living in this world. It could paralyse a person's imagination, the activity of certain vital organs in his body or the effectiveness/efficiency of some normal bio-chemical processes, thereby off-setting his psychological balance. Generally, it brings up such processes or conditions which could lead to psychological disorder and personality disintegration.

On the group level, fear can retard the social-momentum of a people and transform those psychological effects it induces on individuals into the corresponding sociological phenomena. It therefore brings with it not only social movements, disintegrations or changes but also the more potent international conflicts and tensions. Fear must be seen as a vital force that ushers in a craving for unlimited build-up of military and defence machinery by nations at the end of every round of violent war or conflict. That this was the motivating force behind the cold-war between the Western and Eastern bloc countries, which threatened to blow into the open at every opportunity is not in doubt.

Whereas the maxim 'offence is better than defence' gives credence to the first assertion that individual differences, greed, covetousness, et cetera, cause nations to fire the first shots that start wars, military build-ups result largely from the inherent unpredictability of the intentions of one's or a group's enemies or even seemingly friendly neighbours. And this is reinforced by the historical fact that individuals or groups can hardly preserve their freedom by merely exuding goodwill – say by unilaterally withdrawing from the arms race or a wilful and deliberate suppression of one's own defensive instincts or mechanisms. For it is a historical fact that such an attitude would sooner attract aggression than anything else. Which is perhaps why many a world leader is quick to point out that "there is no immutable law of nature that says only the unjust will be afflicted, or that the just will always prevail. While might certainly does not make right, neither does right by itself make might".[5] This might explain every nation's present preoccupation of producing more and more destructive weapons as well as maintaining large armies.

It is this negative aspect that gives nationalism or more exactly excessive nationalism – like tribalism and individualism – its pungent air, which is usually expressed in national arrogance, attempts to obliterate the fact that civilization is a collective achievement of all mankind, etc. This makes excessive nationalism one of the deadliest problems confronting mankind today. In view of this, there is no gain-saying the fact that the future of all mankind is now partly dependent on how we handle nationalism or nationalistic pursuits in the immediate future.

When viewed from the standpoint of economics, nationalism makes the optimal and positive utilization of

---

5. Richard Nixon, *The Real war*. Op. Cit., page 6.

national economic resources and in a sense that of the whole wide world impossible. Since one function of the state is defence against external aggression, maintenance of national military organisations remains a sine qua non to the continued existence of nation-states everywhere on the globe. This implies the expenditure of large chunks of national economic and human resources towards defence needs to the detriment of optimum or higher rate of economic growth. Statistics show that most nations spend upwards of five percent of their G.N.P. on defence and defence-related matters.[6] There are even countries which spend up to thirteen percent and above of their Gross National Products in this direction.[7]

That there is a strong and direct relationship between the size of national budget, spent on defence and the actual performance of a national economy is no revelation. The fact is, the more the percentage of national budget devoted to defence, the more adversely is the total economy affected. This point may be further appreciated if we cite the performance of the Japanese economy since the end of the Second World War.

Japan is said to allocate less than one per cent of its G.N.P. to defence as compared to about five to thirteen for the United States of America and Russia.[8] This is perhaps the lowest percentage compared with every other major nation with the possible exception of Mexico.[9] According to experts, this relatively low expenditure on defence is partly responsible for Japan's meteoric economic rise. They estimate that if Japan had been spending up to six per cent of its G.N.P. on defence over the past couple of decades, its G.N.P would have been about thirty per cent lower than its current (1980) value of about one trillion (U.S.) dollars, which made it the second highest in the world after the United States.[10]

6-7. Ibid, Page 206.
8 -10. Ibid

Yet, that is only talking about the opportunity cost of military build-ups alone. We can well imagine what happens when nations go to war – ostensibly in defence of national interests, prestige or survival. Maybe, someday, some economic analyst would compute the actual material cost of the two global wars fought in the last century and paint a picture of what the world's economic state would have become today if those wars were somehow averted! That would certainly give us an insight into what malady excessive nationalism portends for us all economic-wise.

Economic burden or toll resulting from nationalism may also be perceived from the standpoint of trade restrictions, tariffs, prohibitions, quotas and customs duties which states set up as a means of protecting their various economies and individual producers from external competition and 'exploitation'. Erecting excessive trade barriers to keep lower-priced foreign goods out of a nation's market may provide short-term relief for the country's economy or producers, but probably causes disaster for that same country's economy and consumers in the long-term.[11]

Protectionist trade barriers are generally beneficial to a country with a heated economy if such measures were from the on-set conceived and publicised as temporary and short-term measures that would be lifted within a given period during which government expects investors and leaders of industry to have taken appropriate steps to restore the competitiveness of their products on both the domestic and international markets. Failure to notify industrialists and producers at large that a protectionist policy or governmental regulation – including "wage" and price-control on the domestic front – is meant to be transient or to give the impression that it is introduced as a lasting policy leads to inaction on the part of producers. It

11. Ibid, Page 237

stifles incentive for the nation's manufacturers or producers to modernise, replace obsolete equipment, techniques and managerial styles. In the long-run that nation would find herself many years behind the others not only in the easily perceptible area of material culture but also in those other important components of culture as Institution and Ideas, which confer wellbeing and respectability on great nations.

On the global scale, nationalist protectionist barriers inhibit trade which is the life-blood of the international economic system. Over-regulations and high tariffs prevent the free flow of trade resulting in an imperfect or non-optimal utilization of the world's economic resources, thereby restraining the natural tendency towards specialization and resource transfer or re-allocation based on comparative advantage.

Economists often remind us that the very advantages derivable from free trade between individuals are also applicable to trade between nations especially when those trades are as unrestricted as possible. It is easy to perceive that if there were to be no trade or some sort of exchange between individuals or families the world would become a very difficult place to live in. Each individual or family would have to make himself/herself self-sufficient in production: each individual or family would have to provide itself all her material needs – food, clothing, shelter, transport, Medicare, entertainment etc.

Although this would be a very extreme or unreal situation which may never occur in practice, it serves as a vivid illustration of what is involved or is at stake – and makes us realise how adversely living standards or quality of life, leisure time, etc., would be affected by extreme curtailment of inter-family contact, trade or exchanges. Trade between individuals allows each person to concentrate and specialise in things he can do well, while purchasing from the others those other items or services he cannot easily produce or provide for himself.[12] As such, trade and specialization are closely connected. Without trade every person has to be self-sufficient; with trade every person can specialise and enjoy better quality of life and leisure.[13]

This same principle is applicable to nations. The more trade-barriers are erected by different nations, the more a nation has to be self-sufficient. The less the barriers, the more nations can specialise, producing different range of goods with minimal difficulty, while at the same time obtaining from other countries those other sets of goods that would have given her much trouble to produce and at equally reasonable cost – the existing stifling polarization in productivity notwithstanding. Thus, the quality of life or living standards of inhabitants of each nation can be raised – i.e., provided specialization and resource reallocation do not boil down to giving a few nations monopoly in the production of particular goods and services.

Finally, there is the question of national currencies and their inhibiting effects on international trade. Because nations possess different and distinct currencies from one another necessitating the introduction of such institutions as International Exchange Rates and Reserves, international trade remains a highly speculative and wary affair. There is no gain-saying the fact that the present dollar standard tied as it were to American production of goods and services (about 70% of world trade is in dollars)[14] instead of a more collective global standard, leaves much to be desired and works against a possibly heightened activity of the international market.

12. Richard C. Lipsey, *An Introduction to Positive Economics*, Op. Cit. Page, 636 - 637.
13. Ibid.
14. Richard Nixon, *The Real War*, Op cit., page 239

In conclusion, we might say that with the increasing smallness of the world brought about by modern civilization and the ever-increasing inter-dependence of nations in respect of capital, skilled labour, raw materials, markets, etc., nationalism has come to cross-roads. The facts are bare. On the one side stands the forces of economics, material culture or technology, the revolutions in living standards resulting from inter-dependence of nations and the steady shrinking of the 'distance' separating states on the globe. These represent a manifest drive or propensity to unity. On the other side are the forces of politics, reaction, pugnacity and ethnocentrism, etc., which fuel or tend to perpetuate the obsolete and rigid division of mankind into sometimes antagonistic nation-states.[15] Whereas it is an undisputable fact that when it comes to business and trade, international borders are as real as the equator, politics and socio-political differences necessitate the erection of "Berlin walls" between nations.

All these bring to the fore a burning need for a redefinition of national sovereignty or the scope of sovereignty vis-á-vis international relations and security of people everywhere on the globe. Unless this is done now or in the immediate future, the steady shrinking of distance between nations that result from modern science and technology could squeeze the nations so closely together that they will ultimately grind one another to pieces.[16] And it must be added that this menace has assumed alarming proportions in recent times with the ever-increasing destructiveness of modern warfare and weaponry.

15-16.
   A. Appadorai, *The Substance of Politics*, Op. Cit., Page 147.

ATTEMPTS AT COLLECTIVE SECURITY

Though warfare in the early or ancient times was not as awesome and destructive as the modern version, it was not by any means less unnerving and nihilistic. The most frustrating aspect of those inter-tribal or inter-state conflicts was probably the length of time each and every particular battle or war lasted. As ancient history reveals, most of those wars were fought for upwards of twenty years: some children were conceived, born and raised while a single war was going on and eventually fought and laid down their lives fighting the same war. The worst thing is that the long periods spent fighting those battles ensured long periods of famine during and immediately after each round of fighting as agriculture was largely neglected or overshadowed by the exigencies of protracting that warfare. The result; recurring periods of hunger, desolation and poor living standards.

The resultant human and material costs of these upheavals have since early times led mankind to devising diverse ways of forestalling wars and ensuring better relationships between peoples or nations. Prominent among the early methods were non-aggression and friendship pacts or treaties. These have been followed in the contemporary world by arms reduction and limitation talks and treaties.

But the beneficial effects of these measures or approach to the issue have always been incomprehensive and short-lived. This was because mutual distrust, fear and ultimately counter-productive exploits of some upstart that thirsts for 'action' or that feels cheated by the prevailing protocols would ultimately shatter whatever treaty or agreement that existed or was forged by their predecessors. Even as I write this today, August 2, 2019, the Donald Trump administration in the United States of America withdrew his country from a 1987 Cold War Arms Limitation Pact between USA and USSR, now Russia, claiming that Russia has not kept her own side of the bargain. The pact was aimed at limiting the production of Intermediate Range Nuclear Arms.

Another major way used as a means of safe-guarding the security of nations and the maintenance of a semblance of peace has been the formation of alliances between friendly nations so as to keep their mutual enemies at bay. Again, the inherent limitation of this approach was to undermine its efficacy and lead men once more to ponder the problem and come up with new solutions. It was this state of affairs that led to suggestions or demands for some kind of collective or joint action by all (major) nations.

The first known idea of establishing some kind of international organisation aimed at the prevention of wars between nations is traceable to the fourteenth century and possibly beyond. Suggestions have been as varied as different backgrounds and circumstances dictated. Notable amongst these is the call for the establishment of international arbitration and judiciary by Pierre Dubois in his work *The Recovery of the Holy Land* (Circa 1305).

Erasmus (1466-1536) in his letters put forward some scheme for the establishment of a league of peace. In the seventeenth century, Grotius and his school put forward some principles, *The Law of War and Peace* (1625) which should govern the relations between states without, however, mentioning the formation of any organisation that should enforce such rules. This gaping omission was to wait until the eighteenth century when the German philosopher, Kant, suggested that something in the form of a federation involving all nations should be formed as the only effective method reconcilable with individual freedom as exists within states.

A tendency towards the implementation of these theoretical schemes is noticeable in the Holy alliance (1815) and the League Conferences (1899, 1907). These were the forerunners of the true international organisations.

The Holy Alliance was a declaration of goodwill, mutual promise to remain friendly and to lend each other aid and assistance as befits 'peoples bound or united by a true and indissolvable fraternity', and was formed between Prussia, Russia and Austria. Later, many other rulers in Europe signed the treaty and were duly admitted into the Holy Alliance. However, the alliance did not last long, nor did member-states take it as seriously as was hoped. Its ultimate collapse therefore did not surprise anybody and may have been due primarily to the vagueness of its terms plus the non-membership of some major powers.

Following the collapse of the Holy Alliance two conferences now referred to as The Hague Conferences (1899, 1907) were summoned on the initiative of the Tsar of Russia as a means to seeking international peace and disarmament. Although mutual suspicion and jealousy bedevilled these conferences, they nevertheless led to the establishment of an international tribunal at The Hague which brought about the settlement of many international disputes by arbitration and in a sense accelerated moves towards the creation of a larger international peace organisation which culminated in the formation of the League of Nations.

THE LEAGUE OF NATIONS

From the preceding paragraphs, it can be seen that earlier attempts to collectively tackle the problems of international nature were partly enfeebled by the absence of a permanent centralised body charged with the important duty of continually surveying the international scene, reminding nations of their obligations towards one another and providing a forum for members to discuss issues as they arise and acquaint themselves with the knowledge of one another's viewpoint. The League of Nations established in 1919 for the promotion of international co-operation, peace and security was devoid of these defects. From the on-set the permanent institutions that would carry out the objectives of the League were made an important part of the body. There was provision for the creation of an assembly, a council, a secretariat and a court of international justice. What is more, the issue of funds for the maintenance of these institutions were attended to. Members of the league were to make contributions for maintaining and running these institutions.

The adverse experiences of the First World War no doubt helped to make the realisation of these goals possible by eliminating or at least, reducing the half-heartedness with which many nations had hitherto approached efforts aimed at the establishment of such a body in the past.

The Assembly was to be made up of not more than three representatives or delegates from each member-nation and each nation was to have one vote. In other words, there was complete equality of strength for all member-states of the League in the Assembly. The Assembly was empowered to deal with all issues within the League's sphere of action, or that were likely to affect international peace and security.

The council, originally envisaged to consist of nine members: five great powers as permanent members and four non-permanent members drawn from the not-so-great powers to be elected periodically by the Assembly, was increased to thirteen, made up of four permanent and nine non-permanent members. This composition was said to be in recognition of the worldwide interests and the overwhelming responsibilities and roles the great powers were expected to play in the success of the League.

The council in practice was to carry out the duties of the League – create and direct the various committees, prepare the agenda for the Assembly and appoint the Secretary-General with due regards to the wishes of the Assembly. As such, it was to meet more frequently than the General Assembly.

The Secretariat which was to be the permanent feature of the League was headed by the Secretary-General, and acted much like government ministries: doing the field work and carrying out the various decisions or instructions of the League.

The Court of International Justice had judges elected by the Assembly and the Council for a nine-year term. Set up between 1920 – 1922, it sat at The Hague and was charged with the onerous task of settling inter-state disputes brought to it and to give opinions on matters referred to it by the Council or the Assembly.

A subsidiary body, the International Labour Office, was also set up to see to the interests of workers as the plight of the working class was also perceived as a major source of international tension.

Pursuant to the principal interest or duty of the League, i.e. collective security and peaceful co-existence between states, the League drew up articles which were to form the essential ingredients of that covenant. Without going into the rather lengthy details of these articles, one can say that it set out to achieve the following:

1. A reduction of arms build-up by member-countries, as unrestrained build-up contributes to out-breaks of armed aggression;
2. To ensure that members respect the political independence and territorial integrity of other states;
3. To ensure that treaties or pacts between states were reported or registered with the League's secretariat because it was deemed that secret treaties had a way of encouraging wars;
4. To promote international co-operation in such areas as communication, transport, trade and;
5. To look into the plight of Colonies or dependent territories lost by the major powers in the First World War.

Members agreed that any issue likely to provoke war must be regarded as the concern of all and should therefore be submitted to the League for arbitration, judicial settlement or inquiry by the Council. And that the nations involved must await the results of the council's probe or the decision of the courts or arbitrators before embarking on any actions of their own. In fact, they pledged to give three months' grace to the League's decision before embarking on any unilateral action.

Where one of the disputing nations accepts and abides by the decisions of the League, the League was to throw her weight behind this obliging state in the event of an armed conflict between her and the defaulting state. The League's line of action in such circumstance ranged from ostracism of the covenant-breaking nation to armed intervention on the side of the favoured nation.

PERFORMANCE AND DISSOLUTION OF THE LEAGUE

Although the formal dissolution of the League did not come until the year 1947, the outbreak of the Second World War in 1939 can be regarded as the effective collapse of the League. The break-up of the League resulted from her inability to settle major disputes that were addressed to her. Hence, as these disputes escalated, the very foundation of the League which was the willingness or agreement of the big powers to act together was eroded to a point where the League became only a paper-tiger.

This deteriorating trend that culminated in the Second World War and the subsequent cessation of the League's existence started with the Sino-Japanese dispute. After the Japanese invasion of Manchuria in 1931, the League made frantic efforts to stop the war. She set up a Commission of Inquiry which came up with recommendations for normalization of relations between the two powers. Unfortunately, as history books tell us, the Japanese Government turned down the proposal and withdrew from the League.[17] The war raged on with the world watching helplessly.

Soon after, the Italians invaded Abyssinia in total defiance of the League's pleas, recommendations and injunctions.[18] Even the application of the League's laid down sanction of ostracism against such erring states, and to which about fifty states joined, failed to deter Italy's aggression against Abyssinia. Eventually, Italy over-ran Abyssinia and like the Japanese, withdrew her membership of the League. The final blow that was to signal the total collapse of the League did not take long in coming. When it did come, the Second World War not only marked the demise of the League but also exposed the inherent structural weakness of the organisation.

It must be pointed out that although the League failed to achieve its primary goal of maintaining international peace and security, it did succeed in settling a number of inter-state disputes. A case in point is the settlement of border disputes between Turkey and Iraq between 1924 and 1926. Another was the normalization of relations between Colombia and Peru (1931 –35) following the crisis over the Leticia Trapezium. Also the International Court of Justice settled several inter-state disputes. On the social, economic and medical fronts the organisation also made remarkable contributions.

17—18. Ibid, Page 154

The collapse of the League of Nations and the devastations of the Second World War opened up yet another round of out-cry for collective security and co-operation by the nations of the world. Statesmen started another round of frantic efforts at forging another international body while philosophers and thinkers combed their heads in search of better ideas that would lead to lasting peace and co-existence. Many formulae were floated, scrutinised and dropped. Amongst those that made the headlines were the suggestion by Oscar Newfang in 1939, that the League of Nations be converted into a World Federation of States with its own Legislature, Executive and Judiciary.[19]

The basis for this opinion is not far-fetched. The evolution of the state has been due in part to man's thirst for security. In the early times, the individual (or family) relied solely on his own strength and means for the protection and security of both his life and property. Then he sought the help and co-operation of his immediate neighbours, towns-folks... . etc., until the nation-state evolved, with an attendant progressive reduction in the self-governance of the smaller units as they abdicate part of their sovereignty to the growing centre.

Subsequently, it came to the turn of the nation-states to go through similar processes. Initially, each nation relied on her own strength for security. Then they began to work out alliances only to provoke stronger or equal counter-alliances. Hence the need, Newfang must have reasoned, for us to go the whole hog and create a World Federation of States in much the same way as different peoples and groups had come together to form nation-states.

19. Ibid. Page 156.

Whatever the merits and demerits of Newfang's proposition, it is now history that the United Nations Organisation which was subsequently worked out by the statesmen of the World largely neglected these suggestions. Perhaps, it was felt that the climate for the emergence of a super-state did not exist and that the nations of the world were unprepared to sacrifice their sovereignty!

THE UNITED NATIONS ORGANISATION

The United Nations Organisation was born on the 24th October, 1945 with an initial membership of twenty-nine nations, but soon expanded to include almost all independent nations of the world.

Essentially, the organisation is similar to the League of Nations: a confederation of world states, although it has a larger platform, drawing memberships from all parts of the world and with all the big powers represented. The United Nations was at the onset made up of six main organs, the General Assembly, the Security Council, the International Court of Justice, an Economic Council, a Secretariat and a Trusteeship Council.

1. The General Assembly

The General Assembly draws representation from all the member-countries with each country represented by not more than five persons. All states enjoy equal status in the Assembly; i.e. each nation has one vote. The Assembly concerns itself primarily with problems of international nature, be they in social, economic, cultural, educational and medical fields. It also looks into labour problems within different nations of the world.

The Assembly is entrusted with the power to elect the ten non-permanent members of the Security Council, members of the Economic Council, and the Secretary-General of the

U.N. though the Security Council has to first of all make recommendations on the matter. Also, the Assembly is vested with the power to admit, suspend or dismiss nations from the Organisation upon the Security Council's recommendation.

2.   The Security Council

This is made up of fifteen states but with two classes of membership: five permanents and ten non-permanent members. The militarily strong nations of U.S.A., Russia, China, France and Britain make up the permanent members while the ten non-permanent members are elected by the Assembly for a two-year term. A retiring member is not qualified for immediate re-election.

The permanent members of the Council are each conferred with a veto-power by which any one of the five can block any decision on non-procedural matters even if supported by a majority of the council. Hence, although the support of only seven members are required for the passage of any bill, the five permanent members must be amongst this number to make the decision binding.

In the area of maintaining international peace and security, the Security Council is imbued with the effective power to make decisions and take actions on behalf of the Organisation. All other members are obliged to toe the council's line of action and to support its moves in whatever way possible. The council investigates a dispute or any potential source of dispute that might jeopardise international security and takes necessary peaceful steps to bring about normalcy. She is also empowered to use coercion to restore order where peaceful methods prove abortive. Technical or logistic arrangements necessary in prosecuting a military strike is to be negotiated between the Security Council and other members of the U.N. Organisation, with the added injunction that the military staff committee, which would assist the Security Council in prosecuting an armed campaign should be made up of the Chiefs of Staff from the five permanent members.

3.   The Economic and Social Council

This is made up of twenty-seven members elected by the General Assembly for a nine-year term with one-third retiring every three years. Its duty is to gather reports and data on international economic, social, cultural, educational, health and related problems, analyse the data and suggest solutions to problems that might emanate from these areas. It also promotes international interaction for exchange of ideas on relevant areas of economic and social affairs.

4.   The Trusteeship Council

This is to look into the affairs of territories or former colonies placed under the international trusteeship system made up of:
    a) states administering trust territories;
    b) all the veto-wielding nations; and,
    c) member-nations elected for a three-year term into the council.

5.   The International Court of Justice

This is established to settle international disputes on the principles of Justice and International Law. Fifteen judges are elected by the General Assembly and the Security Council in separate meetings to decide cases for the court. And a candidate is declared elected on securing a majority vote from both the Assembly and the Security Council. Each Judge enjoys a nine-year term and may be re-elected at the expiration of his term.

In cases where disputes are referred to the court by the Assembly or where the decision of the court is accepted by the Assembly, that verdict is binding on the disputing parties for all stated categories of cases. Where a party to any dispute decided by the court refuses to accept the verdict, the Security Council may be called in to take appropriate measure against the defaulting state, because it is a fundamental provision in the Organisation's covenant that all member-states must comply with the court's verdict.

6.   The Secretariat

The Secretariat is headed by a Secretary-General elected by the Assembly upon the Security Council's recommendation.

The Secretariat sees to the day to day running of the Organisation.

APPRAISAL OF THE ORGANISATION

In many ways, the United Nations Organisation is similar to the defunct League of Nations, though strengthened by the fact that it is made up of virtually all the nations of the world. From the foregoing, it can be seen that their charters are more or less the same – at least in principle. Like the League of Nations, the United Nations is basically a confederation of states, lacking, as it were, all sovereign powers.

Also, any state is free to withdraw from the Organisation when it meets with her exigencies and so conduct her international relations according to her wont. There is absence of a permanently organised force that can be used at any point in time to compel the organisation's will. And, of course, it has no power to tax individual states. Presently, member-nations only make contributions in the form of dues for the maintenance of the Organisation's secretariat and routine operations.

In the light of the above, it can be seen that the Organisation, like the League of Nations, is inherently very unstable being only a loose association of nations which can scatter at the least provocation in the same way the League of nations crumbled. An example is the crisis that hit UNESCO where certain members threatened to pull out from the Organisation. In fact, the United States of America which contributes as much as twenty-five percent of the UNESCO fund has already withdrawn, while Japan with about ten percent contribution is on the verge of following suit.

Coming to the operations of the United Nations since its formation in 1945, it is evident that the organisation has not yet elicited confidence as to its ability to provide the much needed collective security or prevent a possible outbreak of another major global war. It has also not been able to forestall the outbreak of the so many local wars that have been fought all over the world since 1945. Nations are still spending very high proportions of their resources on armament and large sophisticated armies, even when millions of their citizenry are suffering from want and starvation.

The arms race is daily increasing in momentum just as the potency of the new weapons is galloping. Despite the fact that each super-power now possesses enough weapons to single-handedly destroy the world, they are still researching and experimenting with new weapon systems whose deadliness are better imagined than described, as well as mass-producing perfected ones.[20] Presently, we have entered the era of star-war scenario as the super-powers engage in the production of weapons that could be used in space and on satellites.

20. The concept of Mutually Assured Destruction (MAD) is now common knowledge. For summary of available weapons, see next section.

Now, if these nations have any shred of faith or confidence that the United Nations could provide them any meaningful cover from attack by other nations they would not have any business monkeying with these deadly weapons or maintaining large armies for that matter. Mutual fear and suspicion which have always led to the ruin of nations from time immemorial is still very much here with us and there is no gainsaying the fact that the United Nations as presently constituted has not been able, nor can it be able, to defuse this fear and tension.

Notwithstanding the collapse of communism in Russia and the liquidation of the WARSAW PACT, the old tensions in the world have not entirely disappeared. As such every crucial issue are still viewed from the old suspicions. The adverse consequence of such a climate to the efficacy of the U.N. is obvious. Each occurring problem now has the tendency of further driving nations more apart than keeping them together and united.

Moreover, the provision of the Veto for the five militarily strong nations has continued to render the Organisation, and more especially the Security Council, ineffective when it comes to taking crucial decisions on vital issues. Because the five Veto-wielding nations of the Security Council are scattered into three or so different power blocks and therefore different interest groups, the Security Council can hardly be expected to arrive at any meaningful decision on vital issues. The result: a crippled United Nations which roars like a lion but bites like a rat.

However, in fairness to the Organisation, it must be pointed out that it has made many vital contributions to the welfare of mankind on this planet since its formation, especially in the vital areas of providing educational, scientific, cultural and medical assistance to member-nations. And, in the sense that most of these aids are directed more to the poorer countries of the world, the Organisation has done much in correcting the structural imbalance in the distribution of economic power in the world. Even in the limited areas of preventing the outbreak of interstate conflicts or the settlement of same, the U.N. is not entirely lacking of success.

Above all, the Organisation's most valuable contribution is in her continued provision of a common platform for different peoples and nations of the world to meet from time to time, to parley or discuss with one another and therefore either learn or know more about one another's fears, expectations, inclinations, and goals. For without the existence of such a forum, it is doubtful whether there would be any semblance of peace on this planet. What is more, the very existence of that platform provides mankind with a unique forum for initiating new and better ideas or the adaptation of new ways and methods that might lead to the achievement of the true system of collective security which has eluded mankind for so long.

THE RISING NEED FOR EFFECTIVE COLLECTIVE SECURITY TODAY

It is pretty obvious from the foregoing that the U.N. as presently constituted, structured and operated does not have the wherewithal to stem the present tide of frequently recurring out-breaks of local wars, not to talk of forestalling the outbreaks of a global fratricidal war. That the nations of the world do not yet have faith in the prospects of a peaceful future, as already pointed out, is underscored by their various sceptical attitude to the U.N. The mere fact that the big-powers have not gone to war against each other does not imply that they have at any time discarded the chilling notion that war could become the eventual determinant of who reigns supreme in the world someday. With this kind of thinking lurking in the hearts of most of the world leaders, they have set about building monstrous military machines.

As the U.N. itself acknowledges, the military industrial complex has become one of the most dominant in the world, with more than fifty (50) million people engaged directly or indirectly in military activities.[21] It is reported that as much as half a million scientists and engineers are presently engaged in research and development for military purposes.[22]

In 1980, military expenditure world-wide was as high as 500 billion (US) dollars or 1.4 billion dollars daily.[23] Presently, it is estimated that the world has more than 100,000 nuclear warheads, with a combined explosive power two million times the atomic bomb dropped in Hiroshima some seventy-four years ago.[24]

Surely, the continued development and deployment of these weapons 74 years after the birth of the United Nations is, to say the least, instructive. But the most terrifying is the fact that these negative and aggressive postures exist at a time when several other international problems that might ignite the long smouldering embers of jealousy and hatred, are rearing their ugly heads. The danger here is that as the world gets 'smaller' and areas of disagreement increase, there would be a corresponding rise in the chances for inter-state conflicts and subsequent escalation. This is a dangerous trend. Ideally, one would have expected that the ability of the world community to resolve problems should at least keep pace with the rate at which they occur. Instead, every day we are confronted with these mounting problems, only to file them away as if some extra-terrestrial beings would have to come down here and solve them for us.

21-22. Eluem Emeka Izeze, 'The Tottering World of the U.N.', Lagos, *The Guardian*, December 7 & 10, 1984.
23-24. Ibid

The problems which face mankind at present and which in their separate ways underline a burning and ever-increasing need for the development of an effective collective security system are as varied as the various ways in which the nations of the world are getting 'closer' to one another. These range from the aesthetic to the structural, and from the physical to the cosmic. While on the subject, we might as well cite a few of the major ones in order to keep them fresh in our minds.

INEQUALITY AND POPULATION GROWTH

For all the many years of man's existence on this planet, it is only in the past ten thousand years, i.e., since the agricultural revolution, that man has turned himself from a mere gatherer of food to the more settled and paying life of farming and animal husbandry. It is also only in the past two hundred years that we went through the great transition called the industrial revolution, which has further improved our living standards many fold, providing us with longer hours of leisure per day for an increasing number of people and cutting short the effective periods during which man is engaged in virtually unremitting labour. Hence, even as the world population gallops to nearly eight billion people (over the last two centuries) the average per capita income of the world has risen only tenfold: from 200 dollars at the start of the Industrial Revolution to about 2,000 dollars today (in 1979 U.S. dollars).

However, this average per capita income of the world does not in any way mirror the true distribution of wealth or incomes in the world. A world bank source[25] shows that

25. World Bank: Atlas (published by BRD, 1973).

in 1973 the richest ten countries of the world with a combined population of about 10% of world total population had a combined GNP equivalent of about 70% of the world total and a per capita GNP of about 4,440 (U.S.) dollars. This may be compared with those of the poorest twenty countries representing also about 10% of the world population, which had a combined GNP of 0.78% of the world total and a per capita GNP of only 78 (US) dollars. This indicates that the first group is richer than the latter about ninety times over and that the average man from the first group enjoys a monetary income some fifty-six times that of the average man from the poorer group.

Meanwhile, in 2006, the richest 10% of adults in the world own 85% of global household wealth, the bottom half collectively owns barely 1%. Even more strikingly, the average person in the top 10% owns nearly 3,000 times the wealth of the average person in the bottom 10%. These are some of the results that emerge from a study of the distribution of household wealth undertaken for the UNUWIDER project on Personal Assets from a Global Perspective.

Today, adults with less than $10,000 in wealth make up 64 percent of the world's population but hold less than 2 percent of global wealth. The world's wealthiest individuals, those owning over $100,000 in assets, total less than 10 percent of the global population but own 84 percent of global wealth.

While a small proportion of the world is basking in immense affluence, the other portion is wallowing in abject poverty. Indeed, so many live so close to the poverty line that slight negative variations in weather conditions, like those that bring drought, soil or marine erosion and therefore poor crop yields, in the developed countries have been known to bring about immediate deaths by starvation
to many in poor and developing countries.[26] Reports have it that as much as 600 million people, mainly from poor

countries live day to day on starvation diets, while 500 million cannot get adequate medical services. An estimated 800 million people (mainly from Third World countries) cannot read and write, while some 250 million children roam the streets out of want and neglect.[27] And the situation continues to grow from bad to worse with the passage of each day!

A glance at Africa's economic barometer more than substantiates this statement. According to *Newsweek* magazine, [28] in the early independence years of the fifties and sixties when Europe and Japan were rebuilding their war-ravaged economies and the U.S. enjoying rapid growth, newly independent African States enjoyed a surge in commodity prices. Their export commodities — cocoa, rubber, copper, coffee, groundnut, palm produce, etc. — were just the raw materials the industrial nations needed to rebuild their economies and industrial machinery. As such, the continent's rate of economic growth jumped well ahead of the records mentioned earlier. However, this was short-lived. In the '70s' with less demand for her products, oil price hikes, political instability and astronomical increases in the prices of finished goods, the trend simply reversed. Many were turned to beggar-nations. The nightmare in Ethiopia and some other countries in Africa's Sahel hardly needs any introduction.

Commenting on the situation a voice for UNIDO, the United Nations' office for Industrial Development said that "African countries would have to import more than eight out of every ten items of agricultural equipment they need by the end of the last century unless they could develop

26.   Richard, G. Lipsey, *An Introduction to Positive Economics*. Op. Cit. Pg. 734.
27.   Eluem Emeka Izeze, Op. Cit.
28.   *Newsweek magazine*, July 19, 1982, Pg. 20—25.

their local industry".[29] In the meantime, Africa's (minus South Africa) GDP (1979) was only about 3.5% of the World total.[30] Lack of capital remains a major barrier to any appreciable increase of this figure. Available channels for capital transfer remain inadequate.

Plagued by excessive borrowing, the majority of Third World debtor-countries are finding it extremely difficult to honour their agreements or service their debts. Some are even beginning to think that strict adherence to the terms of these loans might end up making them net exporters of capital, a situation that is directly opposed to the very reasons for which these loans were sought for in the first place.

The above situation is worsened by the adverse effects of the Malthusian problem that now plagues the poor nations. Their high rates of population growth discourage national capital accumulation. Energies directed towards raising the living standards of the peoples by increasing productivity are dissipated by corresponding increases in national population figures.

The Malthusian problem is today a central concern for Third World countries because their low economic growth rates are combined with higher population growth rates. This contrasts with the economies of the developed countries, where low population growth is combined with higher economic growth. A United Nations survey[31] indicates that the Third World has the highest population growth rate while Western countries record the least population growth. Africa has the highest population growth rate while Western countries record the least population growth. Africa has the highest rate of 2.9% annual rate of population growth as compared to only 0.1%

29. *Daily Times*, August 6,1984.
30. Computed from a UN source
31. United Nations, 1984

in Western Europe. A further breakdown shows that many Third World countries like Kenya, Botswana, Algeria, Rwanda, Uganda and Brazil have growth rates of about 4% each, while many Western countries are now recording zero or negative population growth. Germany had maintained a constant population for some years before it turned negative; ditto United Kingdom.

The high population growth of the Third World, particularly Africa, presents a study in what sociologists refer to as 'cultural lag'. According to this theory, first advanced by W. F. Ogburn[32] in the 1920s, there is always a different growth rate or rate of change for the various sectors of culture and society. He argues that the non-material culture, which is made up of beliefs, customs, norms, laws, etc., change less rapidly than material culture, consisting of technology and other artefacts erected by society. Hence, the non-material culture 'lags' behind the material culture.

In Africa as well as most other Third World countries, we have continued to witness an influx of the fruits of modern technology — improved Medicare, better transportation facilities, foods, etc. — ever since the continent came into contact with the rest of the world. These have resulted in better quality of life, higher life expectancy (from 47 years in the '50s' to about 60 presently)[33] as well as low infant mortality. Whereas these factors naturally encourage higher population, those modern psychological and sociological attitudes that discourage high birth rates in industrial or associational societies have hardly penetrated African societies. Those traditional norms and belief systems which discourage birth control and promote family planning are still very

32. Ogburn, William F, *Social Change*, New York: Huebusch, 1923
33. Nnamdi Obasi, 'Issues before the Mexico Population Conference'. Lagos, *National Concord*, August 8, 1984

much with us. They have refused to keep pace with our technological development or those other material benefits we derive from our association with the more technologically advanced countries.

Governments in countries like China and India have for a long time been taking drastic steps to control the rate at which their countries' populations are growing as a means of improving their living standards. Ironically, in Africa the official position is that of naive complacency, while many citizens are bent on exploiting modern medical science and techniques for increased births. Polygamy is still rife, with women reducing the traditional three-year birth-spacing period to only one year. The result: high population growth and a corresponding negative economic conditions.

The matter is not helped by the facts of cumulative nature of growth.[34] Pragmatic economists never fail to reckon with the immense contributions or difference a fractional change in the net rate of economic growth could make in the level of living standard of a people even over a short period of time. Hence, if two countries have different rates (however marginal) of net economic growth, it would be possible for their living standards to widen so progressively that the country with the lower net rate of economic growth could easily become like a primitive society relative to the other within a short space of time, even if they were equally developed at the initial stage. Therefore, given the trend of events in different areas of the world, we may well imagine what the situation would be in the next few decades. Surely, the extreme skewness in the distribution of wealth that is bound to occur would certainly give rise to new fears and new crises.

Third World's plight could have direct and painful effect on the economies of the technologically advanced countries. This may be so since these nations depend on the

34. Richard C. Lipsey, *An Introduction of Positive Economics*, Op. Cit. pp. 736 — 739

Third World for most of their industrial raw materials. Furthermore, the Third World still represents valuable markets for finished products from the industrialised nations. Hence, a subsequent inability to buy from the developed nations, which the economic collapse of some of these third world countries may bring about, could stifle international trade and perhaps lead to a depression of the magnitude the world has never experienced. What is more, the adverse economic weather that might afflict the developing countries could lead to the collapse of many governments – with the citizens doing everything to migrate to the developed countries as indeed is already happening. The wave of African migrants trying to get into Europe by crossing the Mediterranean is a case in point.

It can also be argued that the collapse of governments and established political norms could pave the way for a risky scramble by the big powers to control or even re-colonise Africa – a situation that would bring the super-powers face to face and ultimately into a mad war. Already, the weakness, that is, military as well as economic, of most third world countries have resulted in countless armed intervention by the big powers in either the civil affairs of the weak nations or their disputes with neighbouring states. Africa's vulnerability to foreign intervention is an established fact.

The contemporary history of Angola, Ethiopia, Zaire, Chad, etc. are cases in point. Also, a good percentage of African and Third World countries now play host to foreign troops, military bases and advisers. Certainly, one of the gravest threats to international peace today is, in the words of Kenya's former President Arap Moi, "the impulses that spring from hopeless poverty"[35] and lopsided distribution of wealth and incomes on the globe.

35. *Newsweek magazine*, July 19, 1982, Page 20

COMMON PROPERTIES

Not too long ago, different groups and communes on the face of the earth were so far flung apart that national borders were only hazy conceptions and loose expressions used to denote the relative limitedness of a group's territorial assets. Those were the days when the population of man on the planet was scant, resources abundant, begging for exploitation. Man's interests as far as exploiting nature was concerned ended with food gathering and later farming. No one thought of the treasures that might lie beneath the land surface, the sea waves or above. Contact between groups was hardly frequent, thereby making each man or group of men self-sufficient with regard to the area or extent of the earth surface they were entitled to roam and to exploit.

However, with galloping population, jet-age technology and aggressive inquisitiveness and curiosity, the situation has reversed. Contact between peoples is now very common, distant journeys that used to take a long time to accomplish are now covered in minutes or hours. Also man's ability to exploit the planet has been pushed to the subtle reaches of the globe and beyond. Indeed, the globe has 'shrunk' in size.

As nations get nearer and nearer to one another, the issue of national borders and demarcation lines between them have made a sharp transition from hazy, semi-formed or crude concepts to rigid and scientific propositions. National boundaries have so narrowed down that they have strictly become linear concepts. Along national borders one false step can put one on another nation's territory with possible apprehension, interrogation and sanctions for trespassing. This goes to say that the issue of national territorial boundaries in all its ramifications, has become crucial and could make or break good relations between nations. The problem could be examined from the different physical dimensions of contact between peoples or nations.

LAND

The first and oldest territorial problem that man came to grapple with was that of Land. Many inter-personal quarrels, inter-family, inter-clan, or inter-tribal strife and the now prevalent international disputes are traceable to disputes over land. As it is, it is probably more difficult to point out or enumerate instances where border or land disputes have led nations to war in mankind's contemporary history, than where it has not. From the nations of Africa and Asia to those of Europe, America and Australia, the story is the same. Even the immediate causes of the first and second world wars are linked with territorial claims and counterclaims by different nations.

Old as territorial disputes are and despite all the efforts made by mankind to resolve and put an end to the matter, it is still very much with us, threatening daily to shatter the fragile peace this planet has known since World War II. Again this phenomenon is world-wide. In Africa, international border disputes are common. Despite the fact that the Organisation of African Unity's founding Conference in 1963 declared that respect for post-colonial national boundaries is a cardinal principle of the OAU, the continent still has many records of claims and counter-claims of chunks of territories across national borders.[36]

This is mainly due to the divide and rule tactics adopted by European Colonialists during their partition of Africa, whereby African territories were divided up amongst the imperialists without regard to traditional lines of cleavage, language and cultural affinity, etc., or those vital factors that the evolution of nation-states and harmonious co- existence of groups are traditionally based on. Flourishing

36. *Newsweek magazine*, July 19, 1982, Page 21

tribal nations were haphazardly divided and thrown into the webs of different European powers, traditional social and trade links were disrupted to the bewilderment of the African people while European imperialists tried to create new patterns of trade relations, solidarity and political consensus. But traditions die hard! After several decades of these experimentations and subsequent withdrawal of the colonial masters, different groups of African peoples still yearn for contacts with their kith and kin across the so-called national borders. They exhibit doubtful attachment to their countries' governments or political processes and in some cases campaign for the redefinition or re-drawing
of national boundaries. The result is that inter-state border disputes are rampant with occasional skirmishes or strife.

Nigeria, for instance, has in recent times found herself at the brink of war with virtually all her neighbours — Cameroun, Chad, Niger and Benin Republic — due to conflicting border claims. Somali's invasion of Ethiopia which led to the continent's most serious inter-state conflict, with the attendant super-power backings was due to territorial claims. All these and more seem to signal that the taboo on violation of colonial frontiers as enshrined in the O.A.U. charter is rapidly eroding.

In Asia, the major and most dangerous border dispute is that between the USSR or Russia and China. The conflict has its deep roots in the past, dating back to the mid 1600's when the two ancient empires first encountered each other on the mouth of the Ussuri River.

According to historical accounts,[37] intermittent warfare raged along this border until the mid-nineteenth century when the Russians over-ran the area seizing two huge chunks of land estimated at about 650,000 square miles from the Chinese. Subsequently, the treaty of Peking (1860) gave the Russians title to a Seaport within this territory and was named Vladivostok — Russian for rule of

37. See also Richard Nixon, *The Real War*, Op. cit., pp. 62—64.

the East. This was followed by a long period of uneasy peace and suspicion between the two giants until the Communist victory when the new Russian rulers issued what is now known as the Karakhan Declaration of 1919. This declaration renounced the "conquests made by the Tsarist Governments". They promised to annul the treaties the Tsars made with China and return to the Chinese everything that was taken from them by the Tsars.

This led to a relaxation of tension, even of friendliness between the two powers. But it was short-lived. The promise was never fulfilled. In 1929, the Chinese fought an undeclared war with the Soviet Union following the entry of the Red Army into Mongolia. The battle was followed by another period of cold relationship punctuated only for a brief period in the fifties due to the inevitable rapport the Chinese revolution brought to the two countries. But once again, this new friendship did not last. Many reasons have been adduced for this split which followed within one decade of co-operation between the two communist giants. But it is not our intention to go into that here.

However, the parcel of land 'seized' some 150 years ago by the Russians may have been a contributing factor. What we do know is that in 1960 the Soviets withdrew their technicians who had been working on many development projects in China. We also know that the Chinese are still demanding that the U.S.S.R. relinquish control of the captured territory to her. Between 1960 and now, that territorial dispute has brought about several armed clashes between the two countries. Even now, many army divisions from both sides are still permanently stationed along the entire 4,000-mile border. To these two snarling armies, the United Nations or its resolutions have little or nothing to contribute to the fragile restraint existing between them now. Only harsh logistic calculations and "balance of terror" is presently keeping the guns cold. The interpretation of the military balance by either country in its favour might spark off an armed confrontation which could easily escalate.

There are similar and equally dangerous border disputes in other parts of the globe. In the Middle-East, the Arab-Israeli war which started with an outright Arab refusal to accommodate the Israelis in the region, has mellowed, we hope, to a disagreement as to which areas should be occupied by whom. In other words, the situation is fast becoming another border dispute — a knotty one for that matter.

In the face of all these, we can only recommend that better measures, based on collective efforts, be taken to forestall the eruptions that stem from land or border disputes.

THE WATERS

It might sound absurd or even irrelevant to those not familiar with the vagaries of Maritime or International Laws of the Sea to discuss territorial boundaries under this subheading. But on the contrary the waters – oceans, seas, even rivers have always constituted major areas of international friction. This controversy centred on the territorial claims of coastal nations on the extent of their sovereignty over waters immediately adjoining their shores. For some time now, there have been series of claims and counter claims over portions of the seas or oceans. These have made it difficult to reach agreement and draw codes of common international law that would be binding on all nations.

These problems have a long history. Yet the law of the sea remained in a state of upheaval until about the mid-eighties. Among the reasons for this complication is the ever improving technological know-how of man which brings about new ways of using the seas or waters and also increases the levels of activities in many well established uses of the waters. The result: a continual and rapid rate at which acceptable proposals on the law of the sea become obsolete.

Claims to ownership of wide areas of the sea is traceable

to the middle ages. In the 15th century, Spain and Portugal claimed control over the western part of the Atlantic Ocean.[38]Since then, there has been a running spate of claims and counter-claims. Also, various concepts have been adopted to guide the formulation of law of the sea. Under these, the seas are sub-divided into two areas with separate regulations proposed for each. All the proposed guidelines deal with:

    (a) Guarantee of free navigation for ocean going vessels;

    (b) Security considerations and,

    (c) Fishery interests and conservation.

TERRITORIAL SEA

Historically, a three-mile territorial sea influenced international sea laws. Although there may not be any theoretical grounds for choosing this distance, there is however a normative one; the major maritime nations had, for a long time adhered to this limit. However, this is not conclusive. The Scandinavian countries had for centuries advocated a four-mile limit. And the decision of the International Court of Justice on the Anglo-Norwegian fisheries dispute of 1951 has at once debunked adherence to the 3-mile limit as well as strengthened dissension on the somewhat traditional three-mile limit.[39]

The U.S.S.R. inherited a 12-mile zone or limit from imperial Russia.[40] In 1927, the twelve-mile claim was

38. Rene-Jean Dupuy, *The Law of the Sea*, Oceania Publications, Inc., N.Y. p. 50
39. Ibid, p. 54.
40. Amado, F., *The Exploitation and Conservation of the Resources of the Sea*. Leyden, Sijthoff, 1963. Pg. 31 —42.

embodied into the first comprehensive statute on territorial jurisdiction by the Soviets. Since then and despite countless efforts to establish a uniform law many other states have unilaterally or under limited multilateral proclamations setup their own separate limits – with widening disparity on distances, terminology and purpose. Chile, Ecuador, and Peru unilaterally legislated 200-mile maritime zone and later, in 1952, joined in the Santiago Declaration which proclaimed the sovereignty and jurisdiction of each of these nations over the sea adjacent to their respective shores up to a distance of 200-miles into the sea, though with the important concession that "innocent" passage would not be restricted.[41] In 1955, Costa Rica joined the group.

This state of affairs has invigorated an increased quest for development and codification of International Law of the Sea. But the conferences have continually run into one blank wall or another, notably the continued insistence by the big maritime nations for a 3-mile limit and 12 miles by nearly all the rest of the world, including U.S.S.R., Asian, African and Latin American countries. It must be mentioned though that a 1960 U.N. sponsored conference voted 54 in favour, 28 against with 5 abstentions for a proposal which sought to grant coastal states a six-mile territorial sea, plus a further six-mile fishery zone with a further provision that foreign fishery rights would be phased out within a certain limited period and that preferential fishing rights even beyond the 12-mile belt would be granted to coastal states.[42]

That proposal supposedly needed only the abstention of only one of the opposing states to make it law, but it never came. As it were, the world had to wait another 14 years before an agreement could be reached on a common draft law of the sea. In December 1984, an overwhelming

41. Rene-Dupuy. *The Law of the Sea,* Op. Cit. Pages 4-8
42. Oda Shigeru, *International Law of the Resources of the Sea*, Lieden, Sijthoff

majority of member-nations of the UN endorsed a new proposal at Law of the Sea Convention held in New York.[43]

This is a very welcome development. Prior to this time, the world had been bedevilled by mounting dramatic, even violent, disputes because of the non-existence of any universally acceptable laws regarding the use and exploitation of the seas. A case in point is the 1981 shoot-out over the Mediterranean between planes of the U.S. Navy and the Libyan Air Force, in which the Libyans lost two Soviet built SU-22 air-crafts.[44] The scene was over the Gulf of Sidra, claimed by the Libyans as their own 'internal sea'. When therefore, two American destroyers slipped into the northern reaches of the Gulf, the Libyans sought to demonstrate their annoyance at this "deliberate intrusion into their territorial waters"[45] by sending in the two SU-22 sortie, which subsequently met their waterloo.

Luckily, that quarrel did not escalate! But the development is instructive. True, the new Law of the Sea covenant is bound to drastically reduce the chances for such misunderstanding as public opinion is bound to deter noncompliance. But that does not mean that there will not be some form of deviance every now and then. The ongoing faceoff between Iran and the British, on the one hand and the US, on the other, in the Strait of Hormuz is a case in point! How shall we handle a defaulting nation or a crisis similar to the above, especially if a big-power is involved? Can we afford to let some super-power play the policeman or shall the whole world be able to, as things are, embark on any worthwhile coercive, or even democratically inspired countervailing, action? These are the questions that must be answered if the new laws are to really become something to fall back on when the need arises.

43. *National Vanguard*, Lagos, December 13, 1984
44-45. *Time magazine*, August 1981

AIR SPACE AND OUTER SPACE

Starting with the Paris Conference on Air Navigation of 1919 to present day, international activities have resulted in studies and agreements on not only the rights to 'peaceful' use of another country's airspace, but also marked statements on sovereignty in the air. For instance, Article I of the International Convention for Aerial Navigation of 1919 – an off-shoot of the Paris Conference – states that all parties (or states) must recognise that every power or state has complete and exclusive sovereignty over the air space above its territory. This implies that flights over foreign air space is a privilege and not a right. Consequently, this has paved the way to confusion and misunderstanding over other related matters thereby giving rise to international concern and efforts to resolve the issues involved. This has given rise to such conventions as law conferences on aerial discovery and rights, aerial rights over international waterways, contiguous and air defence identification zones, unauthorized flights and flights at high altitude as well as flights over prohibited zones.

Although these conventions and other subsequent ones have made remarkable progress in terms of setting out rules and regulations governing the use of the air-space, the concept of air sovereignty is still very much a loose term and therefore continues to generate wary arguments and frictions between states. Many ugly incidents have occurred as a result of these loop-holes. The Soviet destruction of a South Korean liner in 1983 with its more than 200 passengers is a case in point.[46]

After more than two decades of debate, the U.N. is yet to establish where the air space ends and outer-space begins. Many theories have been advanced and many solutions offered. While some have suggested that specific

46. *Time magazine*, 1983

distances ranging from 25 miles to 600 miles be regarded as air space, others have suggested that the limit of a state's effective control over the area above its territory be taken as the area of her sovereignty. There are also those who hold the view that the limit of the earth's gravitational effect or pull be used as the dividing line between air space and outer space. Yet, others want it equated to the aerial belt. There are many more! The suggestions are as diverse in origin and as conflicting in detail as there are different and opposing interests.

At a U.N. conference on space held in Vienna, tagged UNISPACE '82, two particular technological break-through caused some political concern.[47] Firstly, Third World countries were worried that the space powers would grab off all choice locations on the geostationary orbit. Currently, communication satellites are parked along the equator producing a ring that, at the time, was made up of about 95 to 100 satellites. But on the basis of existing technology, these satellites cannot be conveniently stationed less than 2 degrees apart, making the available satellites slots on the equator to be only 180. This left only about 80-85 satellite slots vacant along the equator. This was a source of concern to Third World countries, especially those situated along the equator, who at the UNISPACE '82 claimed "air-right" to everything above them, in the hope of securing sovereignty over satellite slots directly above them.

The question of distribution or ownership of satellite slots is a vital one given the intrinsic benefits derivable from modern communication satellites. Therefore, barring the development of more powerful geostationary "Super-satellites" with such immense capacities as to alleviate the

47. *Time magazine*, November 22, 1982. Pages 48-51

subsequent overcrowding of satellites (above the equator), the question of rights to satellite slots would become vital. Although scientists and engineers are optimistic that three 'super-satellites' spaced at equal distances along the equator could handle all the world's telecommunications and therefore diffuse the issue of slot-rights, its realisation is still distant because it is still a little more than a dream. Again it may not be able to take care of the wide range of national communication policies that are bound to come up in the near future.

The second technological break-through in space is NASA's 'remote-sensing' satellite called Landsat. First launched in 1973, this observatory can literally see, in a variety of colours (some of them beyond human vision) what is happening on different spots on earth and relay the information and photographs back to manned earth stations. Because they are designed to travel via the polar regions, the Landsat passes a different patch of the world as the planet rotates underneath. As such, the Landsat collects all types of information – ranging from the natural to the cosmic – about everything below it and in every country of the world. Because the Landsat can give information about mineral deposits deep below the earth's surface, know about a nation's natural resources, plus other uncanny abilities, they have come to be regarded by many countries especially in the Third World, as economic spies. Hence, the protest that the Landsat systems should not take any further photographs of their countries except with express permission from the country in question. Funny, as this may sound, many Third World countries re-echoed their distaste for the Landsat at UNISPACE '82.

Scientific and technological developments have intensified the wrangling over air-rights which hitherto seemed vain and unimportant. The place of this, the third dimension of sovereignty, with regard to international security is no longer in doubt, nor the need to bring the rule of law to that region of man's activities. Although an Outer Space Treaty was signed in 1967, this dealt only with demilitarization of outer space. Even then, since the crash in 1978 of Soviet Cosmos 954 spreading about 45Kg of nuclear (radioactive) debris from enriched uranium over an area in Canada and era of interceptor-destructor satellites or hunter-killer system,[48] the safe use of outer space (including the use of nuclear powered space vehicles) has again become one of the most dominant topics in world security circles.

EXPLOITATION AND USE OF MANKIND'S COMMON PROPERTIES

It is noticeable that presently while some parts of the planet are partitioned and owned (or at least claimed) by different people or nations, certain other areas of planet earth remain principally uninhabited and unclaimed by any nation. These areas, which we will henceforth refer to as mankind's common properties include the high seas, the deep ocean floors, the moon, and the Antarctic. Because of their status as common properties, there is a consensus derived from the basic prerequisites of commonality surrounding these properties that the exploitation of the resources (supposed as well as proven) within these areas be undertaken in the interest of all nations.

Ironically, the concept of sharing the resources from these territories could not have bothered the average man or occupied the statesman and the intellectual in the not-so-distant past. It was a merely harmless notion which some philosophers may retreat into by way of relaxation after doing the day's job or discuss with some patronising colleagues only as small talk or academic exercise. Today,

48. Ibid.

however, it is no longer so: thanks to the giant strides man has made in the field of science and technology.

Speculations that there may exist vast resources in these territories have become real, with categorical assertions on the ways to tap these resources. Some nations or individuals can actually put some of these ideas into practice and flood the world with 'goods' from these territories. Yet, they are held back by one major obstacle: the absence of consent from other nations of the world and therefore absence of guarantee that their lives and tools would be secure once they venture into tapping resources in these territories. This lack of authority, it must be pointed out, stems from an absence of consensus as to how the ensuing benefits from these territories would be shared.

This state of affairs came about after Ambassador Pardo, permanent representative of Malta to the United Nations first, (in 1967), drew the attention of the UN General Assembly to the many proposals and schemes by some governmental bodies and private individuals aimed at exploiting or using these vast untapped areas, and the problem that could result from the implementation of any such schemes.[49] Consequently, the United Nations General Assembly in Resolution 2340 (XXII) on the "Examination of the question of the reservation exclusively for peaceful purposes of the sea beds, the ocean floor and the sub-soil thereof, underlying the high seas beyond the limits of present national jurisdictions and the use of their resources for the interest of mankind", appointed an Ad-hoc Committee to study and provide practical guidelines for international co-operation in the exploration, use and conservation of the resources of the deep ocean floor.

The committee sat and later (in 1968) issued a report but never agreed on any set of legal principle or norms that

---

49. Rene-Jean Dupuy, *The Law of the Sea*, Op. Cit. Page 4.

would govern these activities. This was due to different interests of the diverse groups that were represented at the negotiating table: the interests of the capitalist countries ran counter to those of the socialists, while the developing countries differed from the developed countries, etc. However, there is overwhelming support for exploitation under International Control as opposed to exploitation under the jurisdiction of flag states. This is based on the argument that the former proposition assures security of those who would eventually carry out exploratory and exploitative activities in the territories. Secondly, the interests of the developing and geographically handicapped countries would be taken care of under an International Regulatory Agency.

The continuing inability of the UN to work out guidelines and agreements as to how nations should behave themselves in these areas is causing a lot of frustration on countries where huge capital has already been spent on research for the exploitation of the territories under consideration. This in turn brings about a lot of tension and anarchic tendencies as many nations are practically adopting unilateral actions to protect their interests or imagined interests. Even now, no acceptable definition on the extent of the deep ocean floors, and the continental shelf has been agreed upon. The trend towards anarchy is noticeable from the goings-on in the Antarctica.

THE ANTARCTIC

Antarctic, the cold frozen continent in the south-pole has for centuries been regarded as a doomed unattractive territory. The explorer, James Cook who navigated the Antarctic continent in the eighteenth century opined that the world would never derive any benefit from the Antarctic. However, with the wealth of scientific and technological know-how at man's disposal today, coupled with the changing weather conditions and the increasing prospects of mineral resources, "Cook's words no longer ring true".[50] Or does it? Perhaps, it is only when we consider the fact that a scramble for the so-called immense wealth of the Antarctic could, like the historical scramble for Africa, alienate and plunge nations into another mad war that one might want to take another glance at Cook's words.

William F. Ogburn has told us that the non-material culture always lags behind the material culture. And that since the various elements and components of culture are closely related to one another, this lag inevitably produces a mal-adjustment. Ogburn's theory is as true today as it was in the twenties when it was propounded, and very much applicable to the Antarctic debacle. But what is not so certain or clear is whether the non-material problems or mal-adjustments that result from the material progress made by man in the Antarctic would be eventually eliminated by re-arrangements in laws, customs and norms, if any, guiding man's activities in the region. And, come to that, whether any such re-arrangements would be effected violently or peacefully.

According to Roger Wilson,[51] at the time some seventeen countries were exploring the Antarctic without any meaningful guideline concerning their relationships especially in the important area of exploitation and ownership of patches of the territory. Although there is an Antarctic treaty comprising 14 strong nations operating in the area, the treaty side-stepped two contentious issues. Firstly, it did not take cognisance of the fact that many of the signatories already have territorial claims to parts of the continent. Secondly, the possibility of exploiting the

50. Roger Wilson, 'Antarctic Minerals and the Third World', Lagos, *Daily Times*, April 6, 1983.

51. Ibid.

continent for mineral and marine resources, or how these should be carried out and by whom was not mentioned.

Furthermore, not all the countries then operating in the region were signatories to the so-called Antarctic treaty. These were India and China while Brazil was not a full member. There is thus, a raging disagreement, which if allowed to get out of hand or to escalate, could cause a lot of bad blood and perhaps in the end give credence to James Cook's opinion that "the world would never be benefited by a country doomed by nature never once to feel the warmth of the sun's rays, but to be forever buried under everlasting snow of ice".[52]

ENVIRONMENTAL PROTECTION AND NATURAL DISASTERS

On several instances, we have had cause to draw attention to the rapid and immense scientific and technological progress man has made in the course of the last two thousand years. These strides have contributed to the existence of very high standards of living in many parts of the world. Growth rates in industrial production and economic activities have similarly increased. All these are healthy developments and it is expected that in the future the level of industrial production and therefore living standards will increase considerably.

However, growth is never unidirectional. The principle or doctrine of dualism always play a part. Thus, industrial growth and technological progress or more generally, all man's positive activities on this planet are not without their partners or equally powerful side-effects. Technological progress, scientific advancements, etc., must by the very nature of things, elicit equally powerful negative movements. As Isaac Newton rightly observed many

52. Ibid.

centuries ago, "action and reaction are always equal and opposite".

One of the many negative effects of our rising material progress is pollution and destruction of our natural environment. In the course of producing and using those choice commodities and artefacts that man savours, a mountain of items that he does not need or want is created. And because of the rapidity with which consumer items are produced to meet the demand of the ever-increasing number of consumers, man finds himself surrounded by an equally large number or volume of disposables. A problem therefore arises; how to free our surroundings of these unwanted items or pollutants. And because this problem has international dimensions, there is a question as to whose responsibility it is to clear the said pollutants.

Pollutants come in different shapes, sizes and states. There are pollutants in the form of solid wastes, as well as liquid and gaseous ones. They are also found on different mediums – land, water and air, and even beyond. These range from traditional excrements discharged on the surface of the earth or its aerial space, through the ordinary residues from industrial processes to the sophisticated radioactive wastes from nuclear power plants and fuels.

Mundane and local as any of these may sound, they all have possible international dimensions. The methods (or lack of methods) devised by nations for dealing with their respective waste problems and the effects or possible effects of these on the global ecosystem and international relations may be discussed under three broad headings:

(1) activities physically affecting other states through the medium of shared resources;
(2) activities affecting shared resources, and
(3) national environmental regulatory activities affecting the entire globe.

1.   That certain human activities pose as threats to the lives of others in distant places or nations is not often self-evident. But in reality, the stability of the global ecosystem is partly dependent on what goes on in each and every spot of the planet as the 'vibrations' from these sources are often transmitted through the medium of shared resources to all parts of the globe. The most important resource use problems stem from urbanization, and technological developments. The cumulative impact of urbanization and deforestation which convert spongy, low-heat conductivity surfaces into high-heat absorbents, for instance, cannot be overlooked. Along with other activities which generate enormous heat and/or increase the percentage of carbon-dioxide in the atmosphere, urbanization, deforestation, etc., cause drastic changes in regional and global climates or temperature leading to changes in everything from agricultural production to the physical state of many areas of the world. Drought and desertification are partly due to this phenomenon. Also the green-house effect which is partly responsible for the rising levels of the oceans plus the attendant marine erosion, the vanishing of beaches and choice relaxation spots in many coastal states is also traceable to this phenomenon. Since the 1930s, it has been observed that oceans have been rising at a rate of one and a half-foot (45cm) per century because trapped heat in the atmosphere melts parts of the Antarctic icecap.[53]

53. *Time magazine*, 1983.

Also large scale modifications of the earth's landscape such as is noticeable in the construction of dams, canals, etc., affect distant countries who may have been benefiting from the natural or normal state of things or of a common resource. This may therefore lead to friction between the states involved. Think what would happen to Egypt's Aswan dam if Tanzania or some other country along the Nile, decides to erect a super-dam across the Nile within their own territory. What happens to Nigeria's major Kainji dam if Niger or any other country up the River Niger decides to do anything that would effectively reduce the volume of the Niger? Certainly, such actions which may incapacitate the huge investments of these countries on these 'shared resources' – the Nile and Niger – could lead to very unpleasant and dangerous developments. Pollution of a common resource is also known to be rampant and to constitute a thriving source of friction among nations. When nations pump fumes and gases from industrial plants into the air, they may be laying the ground work for the incidence of acid rains that destroy forests and other property across their own borders. Water pollution on the other hand is known to affect every other country especially coastal states or those who share a given lake or river with the offending country. There is also the issue of offending nuclear radiation which may originate from the activities of other countries either within or outside their own territories.

2   The Aswan dam provides yet a typical example of how one nation's activity may affect a shared resource. According to reports,[54] the annual sardine catch in the eastern Mediterranean has declined by up to seventy per cent (from 18,500 to 5,000 tons since

the erection of the Aswan dam because the supply of flood-born nutrients for marine life from the river Nile is now being trapped in the silt behind the dam. This means that Egypt enjoys the fruits of her Aswan dam partly at the expense of some other coastal states in the Mediterranean whose fishermen could have been enjoying higher fish yields than they presently do.

Water pollution from the numerous oil rigs that dot the surfaces of the world or from oil tankers is yet another example.

There are also discharges that penetrate the earth's crust and finally pollute ground waters deep below the ground.

In the upper reaches of the sky, the exhausts from chemically fired rockets continues to damage the protective ozone layer thereby exposing everything beneath to harmful radiations from the sun.[55]

In the outer-space, abandoned or lost objects whirling around the earth pose serious danger to space-crafts and satellites: According to reports,[56] of the 2891 or so manmade objects in space in 1982 only 1277 of these were operational, while the rest

54. *International Law of the Resources of the Sea*, Op. Cit.

55. James Mpinga, 'Stripping of Earth's Ozone Layers', Lagos, *Daily Times*, December 21, 1984

56. *Time magazine*, November 22, 1982, pp. 48-51.

are either lost satellites, empty fuel tanks, the remnant of boosters and test debris. Any of these high speed (17,000 mph) objects could hit useful space crafts or satellites of any nation any day. And in these days of hunter-killer systems, wrong interpretations and conclusions may be given to such accidents. In any case, the continued existence of the space-garbage is not in the best interest of mankind.

3   The question of the national environmental regulatory activities affecting the entire globe is self-explanatory.

In conclusion, it must be observed that although modern man may have had the unique experience in history of witnessing great triumphs of human genius, great achievements and conquest hitherto unobtainable, all these do not guarantee that man's future is secure.

It is not the existence or validity of international law that gives cause for doubt. In its long history, International Law has so improved in scope and substance that reference is often made to provisions contained therein today. But has it been effective? Have its provisions been adhered to by nations of the world? Well, to a large extent! What then are we talking about? While one may not contest the need for our law makers to put in more efforts in order to create a stronger framework upon which the behaviour of nations may be guided, one must not be tempted to blame existing laws or the law making processes for the plight of the world at present. It is a fact of social kinetics that laws always lag behind. They always come after the forces they are erected to check have been operating for some time. Therefore, the fact that

International Law lags behind the immense material and ideological forces they are meant to combat or check, should not be misconstrued. The real problem is that our laws are not backed with sufficient force to make them beneficial to mankind.

It is a truism that in every society laws have always existed side by side with effective organs for the physical enforcement of the ensuing laws. In this regard, the police force has become a permanent feature of every human society. No society can expect to survive today without the police force. Unfortunately, it does not seem that it has dawned on us that the world has now become one single society or one global village, as it is said. And that without an effective means of enforcing the existing or would-be international laws, the appalling state of international affairs is bound to continue. And that the survival of the global society would continue to be uncertain and unpredictable.

CHAPTER 9

THE ORGANISATION FOR EFFECTIVE GLOBAL COLLECTIVE SECURITY

The spate of antagonism and rivalry among nations that has become a feature of the global system constitutes a major source of worry. From the impoverished countries of the Third World to the affluent nations of Western Europe, America, Asia and Australia the story is more or less the same. In every part of the world, strife or impending strife appears imminent. Vast human and material resources are daily being channelled to armament and war preparations even as millions of people die of poverty, hunger and disease. The situation has become so grave that even at the grassroots, many movements and demands for more positive action to check the increasing insecurity of life and property are now springing up in virtually all parts of the globe. Many ideas have equally been put forward in recent times on ways and means of securing global peace and security. Prominent among these is the proposal by Grenville Clark and Louis B. Sohn (*World Peace through World Law*, 1962)[1] asking for the creation of a supra-national body in place of the U.N. to handle and settle all disputes or problems that are capable of jeopardising world peace and security.

The proposed body is to have carefully defined powers under limited law, designed to operate only in the area of maintaining peaceful and harmonious relationship between nations. All other powers pertaining to national sovereignty would be reserved and enjoyed by the nations.

---

1.   G. Clark and L. B. Sohn, *World Peace Through World Law*, Harvard University Press, 1962. See also, A. Appadorai, Op. Cit. Page 1 68.

The essential points advanced in this proposal are as follows:

1. A general and total disarmament by all nations of the world. This presupposes that as long as nations continue to build or make weapons and maintain armies, the tendency for frequent unilateral military actions on the part of nations would remain.

   What the authors appear to be saying here is that power held in reserve has always played important and often dangerous roles in group affairs. And that partial disarmament will never work as mutual suspicion and mistrust would always put the discussions and agreements at a disadvantage.

2. The formulation of an enforceable universal law (to which all nations must subscribe) against the use or threat to the use of force by nations in international relations. This is to go with the establishment of a World Police Force that would have monopoly of major weapons of violence and that would carry out the decisions of the proposed World Peace Authority.

3. Establishment of a World Legislature with limited but adequate power to approve the annual budgets of the Authority, enact appropriate sanctions or penalties and other necessary regulatory rules against the violation of World Laws, and to monitor the activities of other organs and agencies of the Authority.

4. Appointment of a World Executive to control and direct the various organs and agencies of the Authority as well as exercise other necessary

executive functions.

5. The establishment of a World Equity Tribunal to
    deal with cases that cannot be satisfactorily settled
    or decided by the application of legal principles.
    This is to complement the efforts of the
    International Court of Justice.

6. The creation of an adequate world revenue system to
    support the supra-national body and her agencies, as
    well as for the development of poor countries of the
    world since poverty and under-development
    constitute a vital source of revolutions and
    international tension.

The proposed Authority is to be devoid, according to the authors, of the 'VETO' which has hitherto crippled the United Nations.

REVIEWING THE PROPOSAL

The validity of the core proposal above, i.e. "the idea of creating a supra-national body in place of the U.N. to handle and settle all disputes or problems that are capable of jeopardising world peace and security" or its relevance to diffusing international tension and creating lasting peace on the globe is not in doubt.

AMENDMENTS TO THE PROPOSAL

Of course, the proposals of G. Clark and L.B. Sohn could be amended in certain areas, or built upon to produce a more acceptable proposal or idea upon which the international community could act upon.

Our take on this is partly as follows: We do not agree with the authors' suggestion for "a general and total disarmament by all nations of the world", as contained in the first item above. We do not think that that is the way to begin. The evolution of states has been due in part to man's thirst for security. But nobody set a pre-condition of the general disarmament of the eventual subnational groups for the creation or sustenance of the nation-state.

What generally took place was that as the state stabilised and began to assure constituent communities or peoples of its ability to protect everybody then the constituent parts began to gradually surrender some of their weapon systems as well as the propensity to create new ones to the state.

Indeed, the emergence of the nation-state has not translated into the denial of the individual or family the right to bear arms or the possession of guns and other means of self-defence, nor has it given the state a monopoly of the means of coercion. Sub-national groups, towns and villages still maintain a modicum of arms bearing institutions. The creation of the World Peace Authority should not therefore amount to a wholesale denial of the possession of arms or some level of the means of self-defence on nations.

We should not set a pre-condition that nations must disarm in order to foster or encourage the creation of the advocated new Authority or supra-national body "to handle and settle all disputes or problems that are capable of jeopardising world peace and security". It is only after the body is created and is seen to be succeeding in the requisite task that nations will hopefully have the confidence to gradually give up the arms race and even begin to dismantle some of their deadly stockpile of weapon systems, by their own volition.

Conversely, considering what has taken shape within the nation-states, the proposed World Peace Authority would not need to have monopoly of all means of coercion. Nations must reserve the right to have armies or to voluntarily relinquish them.

Finally, on the issue of the veto, we would suggest that as a precaution the use of the veto by members of the big five should be allowed for the first four years or the first term of the World Assembly. An extension of the right to use the veto beyond this point would then depend on the mood of the Assembly.

REALISATION OF THE PROPOSAL

It is one thing to evolve a sound theoretical framework upon which an effective collective global security system should be built and quite another to work out an equally practical or tactical method that would see the actualization or realisation of this noble proposal through. Although the proposed World Peace Authority, including our original input into the matter have been around for quite some time despite the fact that they have received the support of many – at least in principle – the idea has not as yet been seriously considered at the United Nations. As things are, it is on the verge of being consigned to the scrap-heap history as other proposals before it. This is why we make this re-visitation.

So we ask again: What are the major obstacles militating against the adoption of the core proposal?

From the foregoing, we can see that the proposal has practically suggested the abrogation of the Security Council, assigning all legislative powers to a possibly unicameral legislative assembly of all the nations of the world and at the same time suggesting the abrogation or removal of the veto- power that is traditionally reserved for the big-five militarily strong nations of USA, Russia, China, Britain and France. In other words, all nations regardless of size or power are to have the same status or voting power within the proposed new Authority. This provision may therefore be the Achilles heel of the proposal. For one thing, it runs counter to all known organisational framework or power-sharing arrangements that mankind has evolved over the ages and to which all nations, democratic or totalitarian, subscribe. And for another, it does not tally with the normal tendency or propensity to gradation or differentiation that has almost become natural in human affairs or group life. As such, it may never elicit the support of the big nations as that would amount to their surrendering or giving up a universally accepted 'right' to lead or dominate. Therefore, it seems to us that before the proposal can attract a listening ear from the comity of nations, this later matter must be somehow resolved.

The provision of the veto in the UN charter, it is argued is in recognition of the valid principle that power must be linked to responsibility, and that the unanimity of purpose of the big- five is fundamental to the continued existence of the organisation. If the big-five split on any major non-procedural matter, a decision to enforce any view as a means of resolving the matter or problem would not work. In fact, attempts to enforce such a view could easily lead to a global conflagration since each of the world powers is generally recognised as capable of more or less taking on the rest of the world. Therefore, unless the big-five agrees, we may as well say good-bye to any form of enforcement in any dispute, at least as things are.

While one may not dispute the wisdom behind the concept of 'linking responsibility to power' or assigning greater influence to powerful nations, one cannot help but question the criteria upon which the power of a nation is measured in the present scheme of things. One wonders whether the existing model is in the best interest of mankind and whether there are no other methods which if adopted would in the long-run serve a more useful purpose than what we have now while at the same time taking the might of the big nations into account.

Presently, veto-power or veto-status, is assigned solely on the basis of a country's military strength or might. The first two countries that enjoy veto status, USA and Russia are military super-powers, while each of the other three, China, Britain and France are each regarded as a 'world power'. We do not contest the probable military strength or prowess of any of these five. But the question is: what are the immediate and long-term effects of using this militaristic criterion in distributing the veto-status?

The veto-status is a very respectable title. It confers a lot of influence and prestige on any country that possesses it. The veto also draws a mixture of admiration and envy from the rest of the member-nations of the UN. Because of the far- reaching benefits derivable from possessing the veto-power, nations aspire to attain that status or to become members of that exclusive club. And since military strength is the sole yardstick for determining what country qualifies to wear the veto-medal, each aspirant must strive to develop and improve her military capabilities in order to become a member of that influential class of nations that wield veto-powers in the comity of nations. She has to maintain big armies, develop new strategic weapon systems and at any opportunity demonstrate to the world the effectiveness of her military power.

Even the big-five powers are not excluded from behaving in this same way as they have to at least keep one step ahead of the hordes of medium powers that are daily gravitating towards the top reaches of the military stratum or to overtake any of the present big-five nations and therefore lay claims to membership of the exclusive veto-club. Little wonder therefore that some nations look for avenues to reveal to the world that they have developed this or that new deadly weapon, sponsor local wars where some of these could be tested, and generally throw their weights around. In the end, the world finds herself with more destructive weapons, more wars and increased international tension. In other words, a clause in the charter the United Nations, which is meant to safeguard the security of all, ends up promoting the arms races in some sense.

We do not say that purely defensive or even offensive needs borne out of mutual fear and mistrust are not partly responsible for the on-going arms-race. What we are saying is that these are not by any means the only factors at work.

Status consciousness, stronger (political) influence even at the UN, and the prestige that goes with being recognised as a big-power must be seen also as very vital factors. Or how else can we explain most of the face-saving military actions often undertaken by nations over what could after all have passed as trivial issues!

The use of military might as the basic criterion for assigning the veto-status or expressing the valid principle that power must be linked to responsibility runs counter to the aims and goals of the UN – not only because it creates structural rigidity or cripples the Security Council, but also because it is downright negative and unfair. What

'responsibility' are we talking about or linking to the power or influence a nation wields in the world community? Is this responsibility viewed from the standpoint of positive contributions that nations make to the advancement or improvement of civilization on this planet or merely from the standpoint of just the perceived destructiveness a nation is capable of wreaking on the globe? Which of these two should we consider as reasonable?

The answer to these questions must take cognisance of the fact that nations like human beings try to conform to societal expectations and sanctions as a means of attracting favourable rewards. And that if the world society makes the acquisition of destructive power the hallmark of responsibility, then she should not have any business discussing disarmament and/or peaceful coexistence of nations on the planet for that matter.

Finally, we think that issues of insecurity and peaceful coexistence on the globe; problems of environmental pollution and other problems of common nature to mankind ought to be openly and democratically discussed, debated, rationalised and packaged with a view to securing the allegiance and support of all concerned. The present system of leaving such matters to a few selected countries in the Security Council leaves much to be desired, more so since the composition of that council and the frequent use of the veto to block decisions in the Security Council constitutes a stumbling block to progress of any sort.

In view of the above, the following questions may be asked: what yardsticks should we use for assessing national strength and therefore for expressing this vexed but valid principle that responsibility must be linked to power in international affairs? In other words, how do we propose to distribute or assign statuses to different nations in the proposed World Legislature or World Peace Authority? Would this formula be able to direct men's energies away from the armed race? And finally, would the formula elicit the support of the big-five and so become admissible in the comity of nations?

To answer the first question, we need to delve a little into what we may refer to as the true axiology of national power. Basically, national power or strength is a three-dimensional concept, resting upon:

(I) Economic Power;
(2) Numerical Strength or Population; and
(3) National Will (Capacity for Innovation/Tenacity of purpose)

At the national level, power-sharing between subnational groups – states, regions, etc. – is based roughly on the application of two factors, namely:

(1) the numerical size of each state; and,
(2) the equality of states principle.

But at the international level, we have to add Economic Power to the above two to make up a three-dimensional power-sharing model that should befit the international arena, hence:

(I)   Economic Power;

(2)   Numerical Strength or Population; and
(3)   Equality of States

The relevance of population and economic power needs no elaboration. Willpower, however, refers to that intrinsic quality of being, luck or resilience which could give a group some advantages over the other especially when other factors are held constant. In fact, it corresponds to that same factor upon which the 'equality of states' principle got introduced into power-sharing schemes in national politics. That is, it is same as that factor responsible for the second (upper) chamber or Senate in the national legislature.

Each of these factors contributes to national power and is very vital to national survival at any point in time. When a country possesses a healthy dose of all these three attributes, she becomes really great or dominant and may then channel the enormous powers that derive from these sources into either peaceful or aggressive purposes. If the nation chooses the first option, that is, channelling her immense resources to peaceful pursuits, she would, as things are, turn out to be a benign, affable giant often contributing positively to the welfare of lesser powers and to the progress of mankind, in general. If on the other hand a nation chooses the second option, it could develop an immense and fearsome military machine, intimidating the lesser powers and possibly winning herself a veto-status by the existing scheme of things.

By way of definition, a nation's economic power relative to another may be estimated from the size of their respective G.N.P or G.D.P. The economic power of a nation affects the ultimate strength of that country in diverse ways. For one thing, it partly determines the value, quality or quantity of goods (military or non-military) and services a country can produce or acquire, the degree to which that society can sustain the welfare or material needs of her populace and to some extent the state of evolution of her material culture.

The numerical strength or population of a country on the other hand, reflects the number of individuals in that country and the probable 'manpower' she can deploy in the pursuit of any task or goal, be it peaceful or aggressive. Hence, in a war as well as in peace time, the available number of men needed to operate the nation's available weapons or machines of industry, and to take any actions, tangible or intangible, necessary for the pursuit of the nation's goals, depends on that country's population. It is therefore no surprise that where all other factors are constant, population becomes the crucial determinant of which nation is mightier.

Finally, national will, which informs the concept of equality of states, deals with a people's resolve and determination to pursue any chosen line of action and make the best of it. It roughly equates to entrepreneurship. National-will may be embedded in belief systems, moral, philosophical and theological inclinations of a people. It may also be anchored on a feeling of self-righteousness or upon the experiences of a people. Whatever the foundations upon which a people's will may hinge, Will-power or tenacity of purpose, unlike the other two factors is basically a subjective concept which is not amenable to empirical measurement. Any attempt to give national Will-power an objective analysis is illusory and may land us onto the threshold of ethnocentrism. However, that does not obviate the fact that different peoples at different times possess different degrees of Will-power which energises and galvanises their beings into great actions and achievements.

The intrinsic relationship and inter-dependence of these three factors is not debatable. That they feed into one another in diverse and intricate ways is sure. While each is extremely significant, taken together they prove irresistibly presage. They form the tripod upon which a nation's true power rests. And it is from this power that military might could flow. Where any of the three factors is weak we find that the potency of the country's power, military and otherwise, is suspect.

Military might apart, the USA and Russia can lay claim to super-power status because they each have a strong economic base buttressed by advanced technological know-how, and at least the optimal population to back up such development. China, with its present number two status as an economic power and an overwhelming population figure cannot be ignored in this regard.

On the other hand, and despite their respective strong economic and technological base, Britain and France suffer from relative low population count, though they are influential enough to mobilise manpower support and assistance from around the world. Saudi Arabia with all her petro-dollars lacks the right size of population that is a sine qua non to global greatness. Despite its ranking fourth position on the world population index, Indonesia's greatness and global reach is fractured by her relatively weak economic and technological base.

On the basis of the above, we feel strongly that national economic power, population and will-power represent the real factors upon which national power rests. To deviate from these axioms and equate national power or responsibility to national military capability is in our considered opinion fraudulent, short-sighted and dangerous. It is fraudulent because industrial and economic giants like Japan and Germany which could literally build themselves monstrous military machines overnight are denied their rightful place in the scheme of things and the comity of nations.

It is short-sighted because the probable consequences of that mode of assigning 'responsibility' are not taken into consideration. And finally, it is dangerous because it taunts such truly great nations like Japan, Germany, India, Brazil, etc., and could subsequently draw them into the arms race, big time. What is more, if a country is capable of contributing to a relatively large portion of the world's economic well-being and material progress, then it stands to reason that she should be given some prominence in the world community.

Surely, we should not wait until countries like Japan build themselves monstrous military capability before we assign them positions commensurate with their true powers in the comity of nations.

POWER SHARING WITHIN A PROPOSED WORLD ASSEMBLY OR THE NEW UN

We have established that the voting power of each nation should be based on the nation's economic power, population and will-power. These form the true determinants of a nation's real strength – and ultimately underlines the degree to which her military strength can be raised. Pursuant to this therefore, we suggest that in the proposed world legislature, these three factors should be used to weight each country's vote.

The way we apply these factors will depend on what type of Legislature we opt for: whether it would be take the three factors as equal in every material particular or whether we make some distinctions amongst them. If we look at these factors as equal and allot equal powers to each, we can easily and conveniently arrive at a Unicameral Legislature. On the other hand, if we make any distinctions between them, then a Tri-cameral Legislature would suggest itself.

GRADATION OF THE THREE FACTORS/INDICES OF LEGISLATIVE REPRESENTATION & TRI-CAMERAL LEGISLATURE

But let us face it, in the bicameral legislature of National Assemblies, the House which draws its membership on the basis of the Population factor or index is regarded as the Lower House (and suffers all the implications of that categorisation) while the Upper House, the Senate, is that that draws its membership on the basis of the Equality of States principle. If we have a tri-cameral legislature at the world level, which draws its membership on the basis of the three factors of

Population, Equality of States principle and Economic Power (read hi-tech and ability to produce the food, medicines and the other material innovations that sustain life) which of the three Houses should be the Uppermost House? Of course, to my mind, there is no doubt that the House founded on the Economic Power index should take it.

So, how do we reflect the above sentiment in a proposed World Legislature or the United Nations? Perhaps we should have a tri-cameral Legislature at the world level after all, with the House founded on the basis of Economic Power playing the role of the Uppermost House in much the same way the Senate play the role of Upper House in National Legislatures, and with this Uppermost House enjoying even more than all the rights, privileges, perquisite and leadership role that is reserved for the Senate in National Legislatures. Of course, the elected head of the Uppermost House is to become the leader of the entire World Legislature!

VOTING POWER/SEATS FOR COUNTRIES IN EACH OF THE THREE HOUSES OF THE PROPOSED WORLD ASSEMBLY OR THE UNITED NATIONS

We now publish hereunder the projected voting powers/ Seats for all the countries of the world in each of the three Houses in a proposed Tri-cameral World Legislature beginning with the Uppermost House, with each House projected to have about 1,000 seats. Of course the Upper House (that based on Equality of States principle) will have equal number of seats for each of the 233 countries of the world. If we chose to make it 4 seats per country, then the House will be a (233 x 4) or 932-member legislative House.

THE UPPERMOST LEGISLATIVE HOUSE

Distribution of Seats for Countries in the Uppermost House of the Proposed World Assembly

Using the GDP of nations, it can be shown that a total of 91 countries qualify to have seats in the Uppermost House of a future Tri-cameral World Legislature or Parliament with their respective number of seats as follows:

TABLE 9.1

Rank	Country	GDP (US$million)	% world GDP	No of Seats
	World [2019]	87,265,226		
1	United States	21,439,453	24.57	246
2	China	14,140,163	16.20	162
3	Japan	5,154,475	5.91	59
4	Germany	3,863,344	4.43	44
5	India	2,935,570	3.36	34
6	United Kingdom	2,743,586	3.14	31
7	France	2,707,074	3.10	31
8	Italy	1,988,636	2.28	23
9	Brazil	1,847,020	2.12	21
10	Canada	1,730,914	1.98	20
11	Russia	1,637,892	1.88	19
12	Korea, South	1,629,532	1.87	19
13	Spain	1,397,870	1.60	16
14	Australia	1,376,255	1.58	16
15	Mexico	1,274,175	1.46	15
16	Indonesia	1,111,713	1.27	13
17	Netherlands	902,355	1.03	10
18	Saudi Arabia	779,289	0.89	9
19	Turkey	743,708	0.85	9
20	Switzerland	715,360	0.82	8
—	Taiwan	586,104	0.67	7

21	Poland	565,854	0.65	7
22	Thailand	529,177	0.61	6
23	Sweden	528,929	0.61	6
24	Belgium	517,609	0.59	6
25	Iran	458,500	0.53	5
26	Austria	447,718	0.51	5
27	Nigeria	446,543	0.51	5
28	Argentina	445,469	0.51	5
29	U Arab E	405,771	0.47	5
30	Norway	417,627	0.48	5
31	Israel	387,717	0.44	4
—	Hong Kong	372,989	0.43	4
32	Ireland	384,940	0.44	4
33	Malaysia	365,303	0.42	4
34	Singapore	362,818	0.42	4
35	South Africa	358,839	0.41	4
36	Philippines	356,814	0.41	4
37	Denmark	347,176	0.40	4
38	Colombia	327,895	0.38	4
39	Bangladesh	317,465	0.36	4
40	Egypt	302,256	0.35	4
41	Chile	294,237	0.34	3
42	Pakistan	284,214	0.33	3
43	Finland	269,654	0.31	3
44	Vietnam	261,637	0.30	3
45	Czech Rep	246,953	0.28	3
46	Romania	243,698	0.28	3
47	Portugal	236,408	0.27	3
48	Peru	228,989	0.26	3
49	Iraq	224,462	0.26	3
50	Greece	214,012	0.25	3
51	New Zealand	204,671	0.24	2
52	Qatar	191,849	0.22	2
53	Algeria	172,781	0.20	2

54	Hungary	170,407	0.20	2
55	Kazakhstan	170,326	0.20	2
56	Ukraine	150,401	0.17	2
57	Kuwait	137,591	0.16	2
58	Morocco	119,040	0.14	1
59	Ecuador	107,914	0.12	1
60	Slovakia	106,552	0.12	1
—	Puerto Rico	99,913	0.12	1
61	Kenya	98,607	0.11	1
62	Angola	91,527	0.11	1
63	Ethiopia	91,166	0.10	1
64	Dominican Rep	89,475	0.10	1
65	Sri Lanka	86,566	0.10	1
66	Guatemala	81,318	0.09	1
67	Oman	76,609	0.09	1
68	Venezuela	70,140	0.08	1
69	Luxembourg	69,453	0.08	1
70	Panama	68,536	0.08	1
71	Ghana	67,077	0.08	1
72	Bulgaria	66,250	0.08	1
73	Myanmar	65,994	0.08	1
74	Tanzania	62,224	0.07	1
75	Belarus	62,572	0.07	1
76	Costa Rica	61,021	0.07	1
77	Croatia	60,702	0.07	1
78	Uzbekistan	60,490	0.07	1
79	Syria[n 4]	60,043/Na	0.07	1
80	Uruguay	59,918	0.07	1
81	Lebanon	58,565	0.07	1
—	Macau	55,136	0.06	1
82	Slovenia	54,154	0.06	1
83	Lithuania	53,641	0.06	1
84	Serbia	51,523	0.06	1
85	Congo, D Rep	48,994	0.06	1

86	Azerbaijan	47,171	0.05	1
87	Turkmenistan	46,674	0.05	1
88	Côte d'Ivoire	44,439	0.05	1
89	Jordan	44,172	0.05	1
90	Bolivia	42,401	0.05	1
91	Paraguay	40,714	0.05	1

				971

NB: Calculated by the author with Data from the IMF

THE LOWER LEGISLATIVE HOUSE

Distribution of Seats for Countries in the Lower House of the Proposed World Assembly

Using the population of nations, it can be shown that a total of 133 countries qualify to have seats in the Lower House of a future Tri-cameral World Legislature or Parliament with their respective number of seats as follows:

TABLE 9.2

# Country	Pop (2019)	% World Pop	No. of Seats
World (2019)	7,713,468,100		
1 China	1,433,783,686	18.59 %	189
2 India	1,366,417,754	17.71 %	177
3 United States	329,064,917	4.27 %	43
4 Indonesia	270,625,568	3.51 %	35
5 Pakistan	216,565,318	2.81 %	28
6 Brazil	211,049,527	2.74 %	27
7 Nigeria	200,963,599	2.61 %	26
8 Bangladesh	163,046,161	2.11 %	21
9 Russia	145,872,256	1.89 %	20
10 Mexico	127,575,529	1.65 %	17
11 Japan	126,860,301	1.64 %	16

12 Ethiopia	112,078,730	1.45 %	15
13 Philippines	108,116,615	1.40 %	14
14 Egypt	100,388,073	1.30 %	13
15 Vietnam	96,462,106	1.25 %	13
16 DR Congo	86,790,567	1.13 %	11
17 Germany	83,517,045	1.08 %	11
18 Turkey	83,429,615	1.08 %	11
19 Iran	82,913,906	1.07 %	11
20 Thailand	69,625,582	0.90 %	9
21 U K	67,530,172	0.88 %	9
22 France	65,129,728	0.84 %	8
23 Italy	60,550,075	0.78 %	8
24 South Africa	58,558,270	0.76 %	8
25 Tanzania	58,005,463	0.75 %	8
26 Myanmar	54,045,420	0.70 %	7
27 Kenya	52,573,973	0.68 %	7
28 South Korea	51,225,308	0.66 %	7
29 Colombia	50,339,443	0.65 %	7
30 Spain	46,736,776	0.61 %	6
31 Argentina	44,780,677	0.58 %	6
32 Uganda	44,269,594	0.57 %	6
33 Ukraine	43,993,638	0.57 %	6
34 Algeria	43,053,054	0.56 %	6
35 Sudan	42,813,238	0.56 %	6
36 Iraq	39,309,783	0.51 %	5
37 Afghanistan	38,041,754	0.49 %	5
38 Poland	37,887,768	0.49 %	5
39 Canada	37,411,047	0.49 %	5
40 Morocco	36,471,769	0.47 %	5
41 Saudi Arabia	34,268,528	0.44 %	4
42 Uzbekistan	32,981,716	0.43 %	4
43 Peru	32,510,453	0.42 %	4
44 Malaysia	31,949,777	0.41 %	4
45 Angola	31,825,295	0.41 %	4

46 Ghana	30,417,856	0.39 %	4
47 Mozambique	30,366,036	0.39 %	4
48 Yemen	29,161,922	0.38 %	4
49 Nepal	28,608,710	0.37 %	4
50 Venezuela	28,515,829	0.37 %	4
51 Madagascar	26,969,307	0.35 %	4
52 Cameroon	25,876,380	0.34 %	3
53 Côte d'Ivoire	25,716,544	0.33 %	3
54 North Korea	25,666,161	0.33 %	3
55 Australia	25,203,198	0.33 %	3
56 Taiwan	23,773,876	0.31 %	3
57 Niger	23,310,715	0.30 %	3
58 Sri Lanka	21,323,733	0.28 %	3
59 Burkina Faso	20,321,378	0.26 %	3
60 Mali	19,658,031	0.25 %	3
61 Romania	19,364,557	0.25 %	3
62 Chile	18,952,038	0.25 %	3
63 Malawi	18,628,747	0.24 %	2
64 Kazakhstan	18,551,427	0.24 %	2
65 Zambia	17,861,030	0.23 %	2
66 Guatemala	17,581,472	0.23 %	2
67 Ecuador	17,373,662	0.23 %	2
68 Netherlands	17,097,130	0.22 %	2
69 Syria	17,070,135	0.22 %	2
70 Cambodia	16,486,542	0.21 %	2
71 Senegal	16,296,364	0.21 %	2
72 Chad	15,946,876	0.21 %	2
73 Somalia	15,442,905	0.20 %	2
74 Zimbabwe	14,645,468	0.19 %	2
75 Guinea	12,771,246	0.17 %	2
76 Rwanda	12,626,950	0.16 %	2
77 Benin	11,801,151	0.15 %	2
78 Tunisia	11,694,719	0.15 %	2
79 Belgium	11,539,328	0.15 %	2

80 Burundi	11,530,580	0.15 %	2
81 Bolivia	11,513,100	0.15 %	2
82 Cuba	11,333,483	0.15 %	2
83 Haiti	11,263,077	0.15 %	2
84 South Sudan	11,062,113	0.14 %	1
85 Dominican Rep	10,738,958	0.14 %	1
86 Czech Republic	10,689,209	0.14 %	1
87 Greece	10,473,455	0.14 %	1
88 Portugal	10,226,187	0.13 %	1
89 Jordan	10,101,694	0.13 %	1
90 Azerbaijan	10,047,718	0.13 %	1
91 Sweden	10,036,379	0.13 %	1
92 U A E	9,770,529	0.13 %	1
93 Honduras	9,746,117	0.13 %	1
94 Hungary	9,684,679	0.13 %	1
95 Belarus	9,452,411	0.12 %	1
96 Tajikistan	9,321,018	0.12 %	1
97 Austria	8,955,102	0.12 %	1
98 Papua New Guinea	8,776,109	0.11 %	1
99 Serbia	8,772,235	0.11 %	1
100 Switzerland	8,591,365	0.11 %	1
101 Israel	8,519,377	0.11 %	1
102 Togo	8,082,366	0.10 %	1
103 Sierra Leone	7,813,215	0.10 %	1
104 Hong Kong	7,436,154	0.10 %	1
105 Laos	7,169,455	0.09 %	1
106 Paraguay	7,044,636	0.09 %	1
107 Bulgaria	7,000,119	0.09 %	1
108 Lebanon	6,855,713	0.09 %	1
109 Libya	6,777,452	0.09 %	1
110 Nicaragua	6,545,502	0.08 %	1
111 El Salvador	6,453,553	0.08 %	1
112 Kyrgyzstan	6,415,850	0.08 %	1
113 Turkmenistan	5,942,089	0.08 %	1

114 Singapore	5,804,337	0.08 %	1
115 Denmark	5,771,876	0.07 %	1
116 Finland	5,532,156	0.07 %	1
117 Slovakia	5,457,013	0.07 %	1
118 Congo	5,380,508	0.07 %	1
119 Norway	5,378,857	0.07 %	1
120 Costa Rica	5,047,561	0.07 %	1
121 Palestine	4,981,420	0.06 %	1
122 Oman	4,974,986	0.06 %	1
123 Liberia	4,937,374	0.06 %	1
124 Ireland	4,882,495	0.06 %	1
125 New Zealand	4,783,063	0.06 %	1
126 C. African Rep	4,745,185	0.06 %	1
127 Mauritania	4,525,696	0.06 %	1
128 Panama	4,246,439	0.06 %	1
129 Kuwait	4,207,083	0.05 %	1
130 Croatia	4,130,304	0.05 %	1
131 Moldova	4,043,263	0.05 %	1
132 Georgia	3,996,765	0.05 %	1
133 Eritrea	3,497,117	0.05 %	1

1006

Calculated by the author using Population data from Worldometers (www.Worldometers.info) 2019. Elaboration of data by United Nations, Department of Economic and Social Affairs, Population Division.

WHAT THE PROPOSED WORLD ASSEMBLY IS NOT!

The proposed World Assembly is not by any stretch of the imagination to be likened to a world government. We make the distinction that just as it is wrong and futile to run a large heterogeneous country-state like Nigeria as a unitary state, instead of a federation that it should be, so will any attempt to run the world as a federation of states end up in chaos, ruins and regrets. The proposed World Assembly is therefore conceived to be a confederal organisation like the League of Nations and the United Nations before it that can only act on specific mandates given to it by nations of the world.

Like the United Nations, it is meant to take charge over a few matters of common concern to member countries – matters like world security, curtailment of environmental pollution, global warming, etc. But unlike the UN, distinction has to be made that the new organisation we propose must be inclusive. All the nations or countries of the world are to be part of the decision-making process of the organisation in line with democratic traditions.

In the UN, it is only the few nations that are in the Security Council that are imbued with the power to take charge over the all-important security matters of the world while the vast majority of nations are side-lined and consigned to languish in the talk shop called the United Nations General Assembly, UNGA. The Security Council is not only there to make the rules but is also empowered to take direct action without reference or recourse to the UNGA.

Furthermore, the five permanent veto wielding members of the council are each empowered and entitled to veto any decision the council might make without minding where the rest of the members (permanent and non-permanent) stand. As a consequence of this provision, the Council is perpetually mired in grandstanding and stalemates thereby giving room for unhealthy and dangerous competition between especially the United States and Russia over which of them that becomes the world's policeman, with the EU, China, etc. waiting on the wings or playing a waiting game. This is akin to returning the world to primitive politics!

While this unhealthy competition is going on at all fronts, the international civil servants that man the executive arm of the UN dither not wanting to be consumed by the rivalries among the big powers. The result is a mammoth weakening impact of the UN in its allotted area of responsibility and action. The situation is indeed most destabilising to the goals of the UNGA and the United Nations itself.

It is for the above reasons that we propose the tri-cameral Assembly that should remove a major problem that has for too long dogged and enfeebled the United Nations and in fact kept it from performing efficiently or excellently. It is our viewpoint that the veto is to be abrogated. In its place each of the three Houses of the World Assembly is to establish its own house committee on security. And whatever decisions these committees reach in their respective domains are to be tabled for the ratification of each House, and these are to be harmonised in a joint seating of the three houses in the usual legislative manner. The Assembly can then decide on sanctions or ostracism for erring member nations, and where necessary, practicable and plausible apply force by rallying member nations. It is expected that the kind of support issues receive in the Assembly would go a long way in stimulating compliance by all and sundry.

Finally, we intimate that we are not particular about what name the Assembly should bear. If there is the will to restructure the UN to meet this proposal, then the name United Nations could be retained to carry on with the new mandate!

PART V

ATTAINING NATIONAL STABILITY & PROGRESS
– A CASE STUDY
ON THE SOCIO-POLITICAL DIMENSION

CHAPTER 10

THE UNDERLYING CONSTITUTIONAL CRISIS IN NIGERIA

It is not only in Nigeria that politics has remained a battle between different ethnic groups each of which aspires to seize the instrument of state power and exclude every other group from influence, patronage and status. Throughout the African continent, it is precisely this problem that has made the state so fragile and unstable. In Nigeria, Somalia, Sudan, Niger, Mauritania, Guinea, Sierra Leone, Liberia, the Central African Republic, Congo, Rwanda, Burundi, Uganda, Mozambique, Angola, and South Africa, the ethnic struggle for supremacy has ended in civil wars with the attendant massacres and refugee problem, and the disruption of developmental initiatives and projects.

To put it succinctly, ethnic pluralism is the ogre standing between Africa and development. Until this problem is solved through dialogue, openness, commensurate power sharing and equity, no other problem can be usefully addressed. Peace is a pre-condition for prosperity, and it is only in freedom that people fully mobilize their creative powers. In Nigeria, as in the other African countries, programmes of economic re-construction will continue to fail until we get the politics of national reconstruction right. In other words, the most important reform Nigeria needs is political. We first need to effect a thorough restructuring of the captive Nigerian state that will in turn reconcile the different Nigerian peoples and hence liberate the suppressed genius and complementary energies of the people for social and economic advancement.

265

Since the end of the Nigeria-Biafra war, many of us have been canvassing that the country be returned to true federalism which practice has been disrupted by military rule and which constituted a vital part of Nigeria's covenant of union at independence. For the avoidance of doubt, the federal system is a constitutional arrangement in which there are two or more levels of government that are equal and coordinate in their respective spheres of influence.

Some Needed Key Constitutional Changes

The ebullitions of the Nigerian military via its advent into the governance of the country following the series of military coups that have shaken the federal foundations of the Nigerian state, culminating in the replacement of the 1963 Republican Constitution with the 1999 Constitution is at the centre of Nigeria's present travails and political turmoil. The 1999 Constitution was not decided by the peoples of Nigeria. Rather, it was crafted by a tiny minority that is determined to impose itself upon other Nigerians, and was foisted by military fiat on Nigerians, and has been sustained by brute force.

The direct and inevitable consequence of the above is widespread dissatisfaction that has today produced all manner of agitation against the status quo, including armed insurrections that could reproduce the typical unfortunate African scenario recounted above. Indirectly, the imposition of the 1999 Constitution and the attendant alienation, marginalization and weakening allegiance to the Nigerian state by many subnational groups that have simmered in its wake have turned the country into a Babel, an anarchic state, in which individuals and groups scramble to corner national assets and social goods by fair or foul means.

Therein lies the root of the major evils plaguing the country today, including ethnicism, corruption, electoral fraud, political instability, decayed infrastructure, etc. The grim reality is that for as long as the present Constitution remains in force, Nigeria will remain in technical dissolution until it is reconstituted into a federation.

When the social and political upheavals plaguing the country are put side by side with the enormous economic stress on ground, it becomes quite evident that Nigeria is at crossroads. It is obvious that the country is being run aground. Indeed, there are grave fears that the country is heading for an implosion.

When matters are put forth in this manner, one might get the impression that the collapse, if it does come, would take the shape and form of the disintegration of the Soviet Union, in which all the groups and nationalities mutually consented to go their separate ways without let or hindrance. But given the simmering discontent and rising belligerence and chaos in the nation, we very much doubt that Nigeria's demise, if at all this would come about, will take such a non-violent route.

In fact, from the way things are going, there is every cause for worry, for one to believe that the darkling clouds hovering over the country will, if unchecked, precipitate unimaginable cataclysm and bloody upheavals that will make what is happening in the Congo look like a child's play. To redress the political and institutional decay and the silent war of attrition plaguing the country, many have proposed that a duly elected Constituent Assembly, made up of true representatives of the peoples of Nigeria, in which the six geo-political zones of the country will have equal representation, be constituted immediately to give the country a new constitution.

Of course there are those who think that what is required is for the present National Assembly to effect needed amendments to the present constitution (perhaps by drawing from the outcome of the 2014 National Conference) and elevate it to a level that will gain acceptability from all and sundry.

To the extent that the real contention in Nigeria today is whether the country should be run as a unitary or federal state, we table below the general principle that guides the choice between those two systems for a country:

MODES OF POWER DISTRIBUTION AMONGST (ETHNIC) GROUPS IN NATIONAL POLITICS

Ever since the dawn of democratic government in the Greek City-States and its subsequent adaptation by emergent country-states, there has been steady development in the modes of power-sharing and distribution arrangements between communal or territorial groups that have come to make up modem nation-states. In the Greek city-states, the problems of ethnicity – its demand for power-sharing and communal political participation – were largely absent because the polis, as the Greeks called their states were comparatively small, both in land area and population. And because the inhabitants of each state were practically of the same stock, each city-state boiled down to what we may today refer to as a single constituency.

On the other hand, the largeness of the modern country-state with its often heterogeneous groups, differentiated from one another in intricate and diverse ways, coupled with the attendant divergence in interests, opinions, goals, etc. makes political organisation and the process of mustering consensus and solidarity, a complex and sometimes wary business. As such, nation-builders have come to realise that these smaller geographic territories, ethnic or communal groups and the political power elites who govern them cannot be ignored if a truly strong and virile nation-state is to emerge or is to be sustained from the aggregation of communities or ethnic groups who usually make up the modern country-state.

In turn, this has led to the obvious conclusion, that some sort of acceptable power-sharing and distribution scheme is necessary in the large country-states not only for the sake of preserving and accommodating certain differences in the cultures of the different units but also to ensure reasonable or commensurate communal political participation at the centre. This is viewed now as the only lasting and peaceful method to achieving and maintaining a true nation-state where a high degree of passionate identification and allegiance to the centre is necessary to overcome the numerous internal differences of the units that often jeopardise national stability and survival. Needless to say, it is a truism that without creating the proper national political climate upon which the appropriate national sentiment can be built, the equation of a country-state to a nation-state would forever remain suspect, as the former is more of a geographical expression while the latter is basically a political concept.

In keeping with the above, two basic patterns of organising and institutionalising national power have thus far emerged. The first is the establishment of tiers of government and the second is the concept of assuring, even if to different degrees, that adequate political participation at the centre is not denied any community. The creation of tiers of government is borne out of the tendency or desire to preserve and accommodate regional cultural differences. It is therefore designed to deal with what areas of policy-making or governance the different tiers of government or groups are to preside. The direct result of this concern is the emergence and survival of the Unitary and Federal systems of government.

Generally, it must be observed, where the units are powerful and the people tend to cling to their different communal traditions, the federal system is more favourable, while the unitary system is usually adopted in places where the units are either weak or possess relatively homogeneous cultural traditions. The United States, India and Nigeria are typical examples of countries organised on the principles of the federal system, while Guyana, Haiti, Panama, etc., represent typical unitary states. It is little wonder that the current notorious inclination, indeed attempt at running Nigeria as a unitary state instead of a federation, which augurs well with its large size and diversity, is causing a lot of hiccups in that country. It is easy to see that unless Nigeria is returned to federalism, the present political turbulence in the country will persist.

All in all, it is our considered opinion that the new constitution envisaged for Nigeria must satisfy or reflect certain other sentiments in order to meet the yearnings of majority of Nigerians and hence douse the tension in the land. Given the centrality of some of these matters to Nigeria's progress and survival, we shall endeavour to highlight some of these key requirements and their relevance hereunder:

1) Merit/Federal Character Principle

The fundamental concern here is to return Merit to its traditional pride of place in national affairs, especially in such non-political matters as the admission of students into educational institutions. The relegation, as it were, of merit in favour of mediocrity in this regard has produced more problems than solutions. It has bred acute cynicism and ill-will that cast serious aspersion on Nigeria's nationhood and oneness of its people. All this have led to indiscipline and endemic corruption, and have compromised ethical standards and national wellbeing.

The Federal Character Principle, Nigeria's equivalent of "Affirmative Action" in the USA has not been as successful or even as acceptable as the latter is in the United States. This is largely because affirmative action in the USA is meant to favour a very small group that constitutes perhaps only about 10% of the entire population. Consequently, its impact is not very visible or disruptive of the fundamental principle and use of Merit in that country's national affairs. In Nigeria on the other hand, the targeted beneficiaries of the Federal Character principle constitute of groups that represent as much as perhaps half the population of the country. Consequently, its impact becomes very visible and disruptive of the concept of merit and its application in the ordering of national affairs and priorities. In this regard, the application of Federal Character becomes disruptive of national cohesion and unsustainable for national integration and must therefore be fine-tuned and made subject to meritocracy.

To this end, it should be stipulated that in applying the Federal Character principle – in employment in Federal establishments – the actual physical demand of each state or region for placement, defined by the actual size or number of applicants from respective states/regions who possess the stipulated minimum qualification for employment, shall be put in perspective. Indeed, appointments, intake or enlistment should be based on the following factors (with each carrying equal weight): (a) Individual qualification or Merit; (b) Equality of states/region; and (c) the actual physical demand of each state/region for enlistment or intake. Minimum qualification standards or levels are to be stipulated and shall apply across board. And beyond the point of entry, promotions shall be strictly on merit.

2). Federating Units of the Federation

The present partially adopted six-zonal structure appears more attractive and logical to adopt as the federating units of the Federation. This is in view of their large size and actual potential for forging economies of scale as well as whittling the huge disproportionate recurrent expenditures that are annually deployed in servicing the wasteful mushrooming state bureaucracies across the country. The issue of creating administrative divisions within each zone or region (States or Local Government Areas, LGAs) shall be the exclusive prerogative of respective zones or regions. Statutory revenue allocation from the centre or the federal level shall go to the zones or regions each of which shall share whatever it gets with its component states or local councils on the basis of an agreed ratio. Direct statutory revenue allocation from the centre to the so- called third tier, the local government councils, is to be abolished.

3). Return to Parliamentary System of Government

A return to the Parliamentary system of government in which a Prime Minister shares power with a President (or Presidential Council) is here advocated. As usual the President shall take charge of the regulatory functions of state. The President (or the Presidential Council) shall have executive power over the National Electoral Commission. He shall appoint the chairman and commissioners of an independent electoral commission, thereby relieving the Prime Minister of the burden of performing such role; of acting as both a player and referee in the electoral process.

The President or Council shall also have the power to call on a candidate duly elected Prime Minister to form a government. Similarly, the President or Council shall also, with advice of the National Judicial Service Commission, appoint judges to the Supreme Court and the Court of Appeal. He shall also appoint and supervise the chairman and commissioners of the National Population Commission; the Code of Conduct Bureau; the Revenue Mobilization, Allocation and Fiscal Commission; the Federal Character Commission, etc., as well as have control over Federal Audit.

There shall be established a National Presidential Council comprising of six eminent Nigerians drawn from each of the six geo-political zones/regions in the country. The said eminent citizens shall be raised through the respective traditional/cultural processes in each zone. It shall be the duty of the Council to elect from among its members a chairman, who shall be designated President of the Federation. A similar arrangement should equally be worked out in the zones or regions, with zonal Governors (and zonal governorship councils) that will share power with Premiers or Heads of Zonal/ Regional Governments.

The idea is to reduce the powers of the Head of the Federal and Regional Governments, to make the system less dictatorial and more amenable to a multi- ethnic polity as we have. We view the presidential system as currently being operated in the country as a kind of democratized monarchy that can easily degenerate into autocracy and dictatorship. Allowing the President so much power as he presently has smacks of giving one individual excessive powers over the affairs of the nation. As the saying goes, such excessive or absolute power corrupts absolutely.

When the President is constitutionally authorized to appoint auditors of his government's finances, the chairman and commissioners of the Independent National Electoral Commission, etc., it is obvious that the society is deliberately courting disaster. We should not predicate the political health of the nation on an individual's goodwill or high-mindedness; in the vain hope that a

President will always do the right thing and that he would never want to abuse his power or use it capriciously. It is better to erect institutions to check possible abuse or misuse of power at all time.

4). Representation (Legislative)

In view of the fact that census figures in Nigeria have remained contentious, unreliable and divisive, the use of population as a factor in revenue allocation and political representation are to be suspended until such a time that Nigeria is able to produce a reliable census data. Conversely, we recommend equality of zonal representation in the central legislature in both the senate and house of rep. Specifically, we recommend 15 senatorial seats per zone or region and one senate seat for the Federal Capital Territory (FCT), Abuja, to bring the total number of senators to 91. For the House of Representatives, we propose 60 members from each zone or region and another 4 members from the FCT, making for a total of 364 representatives.

5). Onshore/Offshore Mineral Rights

It might be too much to consign the ownership of Nigeria's territorial waters or exclusive economic zone in the Atlantic Ocean, stretching some 200 nautical miles into the open sea, to the littoral zones/regions of the Federation. But it makes good sense to regard a portion of this huge territorial space as part and parcel of the territory of Nigeria's littoral zones/regions, for purposes of derivative revenue sharing. By this token, we shall only be emulating the international community which in its wisdom allowed coastal nations to have the said 200 nautical miles of the ocean as their exclusive economic zones at its 1982 Law of Seas Convention. Borrowing from that gesture, we should regard not more than 20 nautical miles of Nigeria's 'territorial waters', starting from the shoreline and moving outwards into the continental shelf and the open sea, as the 'economic zone' of the littoral zones/regions of the Federation.

6). Fiscal Federalism & Derivative Revenue Formula

At independence in 1960, Nigeria had a revenue sharing formula of 50 per cent in favour of Derivation. That was an important article in the covenant of union at the emergence of Independent Nigeria which deserves to be respected; something that should never be thrown overboard without consultation and agreement by all involved. We must therefore explore the possibility of returning Nigeria to that maxim as part of an overall plank in addressing the resentment of the Niger Delta over the subsisting poor 13% Derivation fund for mineral revenue from the area and in fact every other sub-national territory. Indeed, we recommend that the zones/regions shall have the power to exploit, under federal supervision, the mineral resources within their respective land area and 'economic zones' in the Atlantic Ocean as well as gather value-added tax (VAT) in their respective regions, and pay 50 per cent of these revenues into the Consolidated Federal Revenue Fund.

Similarly, the Federal Government of Nigeria (FGN) shall have the power to exploit the mineral resources in the Nigerian 'territorial waters' in the Atlantic Ocean (minus the part of it ceded to the littoral zones/regions as their own 'economic zone') and distribute 50 per cent of the revenue to the zones/regions, on equality basis, as derivation fund accruing to the zones or regions. Furthermore, the FGN is also to collect excise duties throughout the federation and pay each zone/region 50 per cent of the fund generated from its territory as derivation fund.

7). Decentralisation of Power from the Centre

We recognize the crying need to decentralize and de-concentrate power from the centre and devolve authority to the zones or regions. As a result, we recommend that as part of that overall concern, the list of items in the Exclusive Legislative List of the Federal Republic of Nigeria is to be drastically reduced from the present 68 and transferred to the Concurrent List. Zones or regions shall thereby be empowered to establish Regional Police services; electricity boards or commissions for the generation and supply of electric power, railways, the exploitation of available mineral resources in the region, etc. The duties or functions of the federal government should principally be limited to Defence, Foreign Affairs, Currency and Exchange and such other items that affect more than one region.

8). Electoral Reforms

Until our democracy matures and becomes internalized, the Open-Secret-Ballot system shall be used in all elections, and results of elections are to be announced at each polling station before being forwarded to the central collation stations.

9). Political Party System

The multi-party system remains attractive. However, in view of the undue proliferation of political parties in Nigeria today, we recommend that we jettison the present practice of giving annual federal subventions to political parties, which we think is the catalyst behind the said proliferation. This move should help prune down the number of parties to a manageable level. We might add that there should be provision for independent candidacy in elections.

10). Land Policy

The 1978 Land Use Decree should be abrogated and its vague occupancy rights replaced with a true and registrable property rights. Indeed, we should curb the excessive power of the state over land matters and assure speedy access to the land for all those who within the confines of economic possibility, practicality and tradition wish to acquire land.

BIBLIOGRAPHY

Achebe, Chinua, *Morning Yet on Creation Day*, London, Ibadan, etc. Heinemann, 1977.

Ajayi, J. F. Ade, *History of West Africa*, London, Longmans, 1971.

Amado, F. V. Garcia, *The Exploitation and Conservation of the Resources of the Sea.* (A Study of Contemporary International Law), Leyden, Sijthoff, 1963.

Appadorai, A., *The Substance of Politics.* New Delhi, Oxford University Press, 11th Edition, 1975.

Aristotle, *Politics.* Translated by William Ellis. London, J. M. Dent (Everyman edition). 1912.

Billyou, De Forest, *Air Law.* New York, Ad Press, 1964. Birch, Anthony Harold, *Representation.* New York, Praeger, 1971.

Boguslavsky, B. M., et al, *ABC of Dialectical and Historical Materialism.* Moscow, Progress Publishers (English translation) 1978.

Brezhnev, Leonid I., *Reminiscences.* Translated from the Russian by Robert Daglish, Moscow: Progress Press, 1981.

-       *Socialism, Democracy and Human Rights*, Oxford, Pergamon Press, 1980.

Broom, L. and Selznick, P., *Sociology.* New York, Harper & Row, 1963.

Brown, Norman 0., *Life against Death*. New York, Random House, Modern Library Paperback, 1960.

Burgess, John W., *Political Science & Constitutional Law*, Boston, Gina, 1890 —91

Center for International Studies Princeton University (ed. Sponsors). *World Politics* (a quarterly journal of International Relations) Volume XVI, October 1963 — July 1964.

Chase, James Hadley, *The Whiff of Money*. London, etc. Panther Book Ltd., 1970.

-        *Tiger by the Tail*. London, etc. Panther Book Ltd., 1966.

Chinoy, El, *Society; An Introduction to Sociology*. New York, Random House, 2nd Ed, 1967

Christenson, Reo M. (et al), *Ideologies and Modern Politics*. New York, Dodd, Mead, 2nd Edition, 1975

Cloward, Richard A. & Lloyd E. Ohlin, *Delinquency and Opportunity*. New York, Free Press, 1960

Cohen, Albert K., *Delinquent Boys*. New York, Free Press, 1955.

Cohen Maxwell (editor), *Law and Politics in Space*. Leicester University Press, 1964.

Dahrendorf, Ralf, *Class and Class Conflict in Industrial Society*. Stanford, Calif., Stanford University Press, 1959.

Dalen, Hendrik Van & Zeigler, L. Harman, *Introduction to Political Science*, Prentice-Hall, Inc. Englewood New Jersey 07632

Daniel, Wayne W. & James C. Terrell, *Business Statistics*, Boston, Houghton Mifflin Co. 2nd edition, 1979

Davidson, Basil & Buah, F.K, *The Growth of African Civilisation*. (A history of West Africa 1000 — 1800) London, Longman, 1965.

Demaris Ovid, *The Last Mafioso*. New York, Bantam Books, 1981

Dupuy, Rene-Jean, *The Law of the Sea* (Current Problems) Oceania Publications Inc. Dobbs Ferry N.Y., A. W. Sijthoff-Leiden, 1974.

Durbin, E. F. M., *Problems of Economic Planning*. London, Routledge and Kegan Paul, 1949.

Durkheim, Emile, *The Rules of Sociological Method*, Translated by Sarah A. Solovay & John H. Muller, Chicago, University of Chicago Press, 1938.

Eagleton, Clyde, *Responsibility of States in International Law*, New York, Kraus Reprint Co. 1928, Reprint 1970.

Ebenstein, W. & Edwin Fogelman, *Today's –Isms*, Prentice-Hall. Inc. Englewood Cliffs, New Jersey, 8th Edition, 1980.

English, M C., *An outline of Nigerian History*. London, Longmans, 3rd Impression, 1961.

Fage, J. D., *Introduction to History of West Africa*, London, Cambridge University Press, 3rd Edition, 1966.

Fawcett, James E. S., *International Law and the uses of Outer Space*, Manchester University Press, 1968.

Femi, Laura, *Mussolini* The University of Chicago Press, 1961

Freud, Sigmund, *Civilization and its Discontents*, New York, Doubleday Anchor Books, 1958.

Goodrich, Leland M., *The United Nations in a Changing World*, Columbia University Press, New York & London, 1974

Gosch, Martin & Richard Hammer, *The Luciano Testament*, London, Pan Books/MacMillan, 1976.

Gotlieb, Allan, *Disarmament and International Law*, The Canadian Institute of International Affairs 1965.

Hitler, Adolf, *Mein Kampf*, with introduction by D. C. Watt, translated by Ralph Manheim, London, Hutchinson & Co.

La Palombara, Joseph G., *Politics within Nations*, Englewood translated by Ralph Manheim London, Hutchinson & Co., Cliffe, N.J. Prentice-Hall, 1974.

Hook, Sidney, *The Hero in History*, London, Seeker & Warburg, 1945.

Hopkins, A. G., *An Economic History of West Africa*, London, Longman Group, 1973.

Isichei, Elizabeth, *A History of Nigeria,* New York, Longman, 1983.

Jarman, Thomas L., *The Rise and Fall of Nazi* Germany London, The Cresset Press, 1955.

Jennings, Sir Ivor, *Party Politics II. (The Growth of Parties)*, Cambridge, at the University Press, 1961.

- *Party Politics III. (The Stuff of Politics)* Cambridge, At the University Press, 1962.

Jhingan, M.L., *Micro-economic Theory*, New Delhi, Vikas Publishing House PVT Ltd. 1977.

Johnson, Harry H., Sociology, *A Systematic Introduction,* New York, Harcourt Brace & Co., 1960.

Johnston, Norman. et al (editors), *The Sociology of Punishment and Correction*, John Wiley and Sons, Inc. New York, 2nd Edition, 1970.

Kardiner, Abram, *The Individual and His Society*, New York, Columbia University Press, 1939.

Katz, Leonard, *Uncle Frank – The Biography of Frank Costello*, New York, Pocket Book ed., April 1975.

Kecskemeti, Paul, *Meaning, Communication and Value*, Chicago, University of Chicago Press, 1952.

La Palombara, Joseph G., *Politics within Nations*, Englewood Cliffe, N.J. Prentice-Hall, 1974

Laski, Harold Joseph, *The Grammar of Politics*, The Yale University Press, 1938

Lewis, John Royston, *Democracy; the Theory and Practice.* London, Allman, 1966.

Lipsey, Richard G., *An Introduction to Positive Economics*, E. L. B. S. & Weidenfeld and Nicolson,4th Edition, 1975.

Loveday, Robert, Statistics — *A First Course*, Cambridge University Press, 1958.

-       *Statistics — A Second Course*, Cambridge University Press, 2nd Edition 1969.

Macmillan, Harold, *The Middle Way*, New York, St. Martin's Press, 1966 Marcuse, Herbert, *Eros and Civilization,* Boston, the Beacon Press, 1955.

Marx Karl, *Capital, III,* translated from the first German Edition by Ernest Untermann. Chicago, Kerr, 1909.

Marx, Karl & Friedrich Engels, *The Communist Manifesto*, Edited by D. Ryazanoff. New York, Russell & Russell, 1963.

Masters, Roger D, *World Politics as a Primitive Political System*, Published by Princeton University Press.

McKnight, Allan D., et al (editors), *Environmental Pollution Control*. (Technical, Economic & Legal Aspects), London, Allen & Unwin, 1974.

McWhinney & Bradley, *The Freedom of the Air*. A. W. Sijthoff/Lyden, 1968.

M'Gonigle, R. M. & Zacher, M. W., *Pollution, Politics and International Law*. University of Columbia Press, 1979.

Miller, George A., *Psychology – The Science of Mental Life*. U. 8. A., Pelican Books, 1966.

Mills, C. Wright, *The Sociological Imagination*. New York, Oxford University Press, 1959.

Nixon, Richard, *The Real War*. London, Sidgwick & Jackson, 1981.

Nowak, Jolanta (editor), *Environmental Law – International and Comparative Aspects*. The British Institute of International and Comparative Law, 1976.

Oda, Shigeru, *International Control of Sea Resources*. A. W. Sythoff/Leyden, 1963.

-    *The International Law of the Ocean Development: Basic Documents*. Lieden, Sijthoff, 1972.

Ogburn, William F., *Social Change*. New York, Huebsch, 1923.

Okigbo, P. N. C., et al, *Report of the Presidential Commission on Revenue Allocation*. (Federal Republic of Nigeria) 1980.

Onwubiko, K. B. C., *History of West Africa. Book One: 1000 AD to 1800*, Africana Educational Publishers Co. Aba, Nigeria, 1967.

-    *History of West Africa. Book Two: 1800 – Present Day*. Africana Educational Publishers, Onitsha, Nigeria, 1973.

Onwuejeogwu, M. Angulu, *The Social Anthropology of Africa; - an Introduction*. London, Heinemann, 1975.

Parson, Talcott, *Theories of Society*. New York, Free Press, 1961.

Paxton, John, *World Legislatures*. London, The Macmillan Press Ltd., 1974.

Pentony, Devere E. (editor), *Soviet Behaviour in World Affairs: Communist Foreign Policies*. San Francisco, Chandler Publishing Co., 1962.

Pitkin, Hanna Fenichel, *The Concept of Representation*. Berkely, University of Calif. Press, 1967.

Plato, *The Republic*. translated by A. D. Lindsay. London, Melbourne, etc. S. M. Dent & Sons, 1976.

Redmond, P. W. D., *General Principles of English Law*. Plymouth, Macdonald & Evans, 1964.

Reijnen, Gibsbertha C. M., *Utilization of Outer Space and International Law*. Amsterdam, Elsevier, 1981.

Reisman, David et al, *The Lonely Crowd*. New Haven: Yale University Press, 1950, (Reprinted, Doubleday Anchor Books, 1953).

Russell, Bertrand, *History of Western Philosophy*. London, Unwin Paperbacks, 1979.

Sabine, George H. & Thomas L. Thorson, *A History of Political Theory*. Hinsdale Illinois, Dryden Press, 4th edition, 1973.

Schatz, Sayre P., *Nigerian Capitalism*. Berkely, University of California Press, 1978.

Schoehbaum, David, *Hitler's Social Revolution: Class and status in Nazi Germany 1933 —1939*. New York, Double day, 1966.

Sen, Chanakya, *Against the Cold War*. Bombay, Asia Publishing House, 1962.

Shinn, Robert A., *The International Politics of Marine Pollution Control*. New York, Praeger, 1974.

Shirer, William Lawrence, *The Rise and Fall of the Third Reich —A History of Nazi Germany*. New York, Simon and Schuster, 1960.

Smith, Adam, *The Wealth of Nations Vol. II*, edited by Edwin Cannan, Strand, Methuen & Co. Ltd., 1961.

Solzhenitsyn, Alexander, *The Gulag Archipelago I*. Translated from the Russian by Thomas P. Whitney, Britain, Fontana, 6th Impression, 1979.

- *The Gulag Archipelago 3*. Translated from the Russian by H. T. Willetts, Britain, Fontana, 1978.

- *The First Circle*. Translated from the Russian by Michael Guybon, Britain, Fontana, 1970.

- *One Day in the Life of Ivan Denisovich*. Translated by Max Hayward and Ronald Hingley. New York, Bantam Books, 1963.

- *The Love-Girl and the Innocent*. Translated by Nicholas Bethell and David Burg. New York, Bantam Books, 1969.

Spiegel, Murray R., *Theory and Problems of Statistics*. Schaum's Outline Series, New York, etc., McGraw-Hill Book, Co., 1972.

Spufford, Peter, *Origins of the English Parliament*. London, Longmans, 1967.

Stride, G. T. & Caroline Ifeka, *Peoples and Empires of West Africa. (West Africa in History 1000 – 1800)*, Lagos, Nigeria, Thomas Nelson Ltd., 1971.

Tang, Peter, S. H., *Communist China Today*, Vol. 2. New York, Atlantic Book, 1958.

Teclaff, L. A. & Albert E. Utton (editors), *International Environmental Law*. New York, Praeger, 1974.

The Constitution of the Federal Republic of Nigeria. A Daily Times (Lagos) Publication, 1979.

Trevor-Roper, Hugh Redwald, *The Last Days of Hitler*. London. Macmillan, 1962.

Veblen, Thorstein, *The Theory of the Leisure Class*. New York, Random House, 1931.

Whittick, Arnold.   (editor), *Encyclopaedia of Urban Planning*. New York, etc., McGraw-Hill Book Co., 1974

Whyte, William H., *The Organisation Man*. New York, Simon and Schuster, 1956.

Wilson, Logan & William Kolb, *Sociological Analysis*. New York, Harcourt, Brace, 1949.

Wolin, S. & Slusser, R. M. (editors), *The Soviet Secret Police*. Connecticut, Greenwood Press, 1974.

Young, Roland, *Approaches to the Study of Politics*. Evanston ILL., North-western University Press, 1958.

Young, Roland Arnold, *The British Parliament*. Evanston, North-western University Press, 1962.

1999 Constitution of the Federal Republic of Nigeria, Published by the Federal Government Press, Lagos, Nigeria

Local Newspaper Articles and Reports

Adeyeye, Dayo, 'Leaders and the ideological question'. Lagos, *The Punch*, July 9, 1984.

Adinuba, C. Don, 'The Judiciary also deserves a Purge'. Lagos, *National Concord*, May 25, 1984.

Africa's Population Alert. Lagos, *National Concord*, August 8, 1984.

Ajobaju, Jeph (reporter), 'Accountant exposes untaxed N3b. Income'. Lagos, *The Guardian*, October 1, 1984.

Alao, Abayomi, 'Russia Going Capitalist?' Lagos, *Times International Magazine*, December 8, 1986.

Awa, Eme (Professor), 'Federal Character: Bane or Boon?' Lagos, *Sunday Times*, October24, 1982.

Balogun, Kolawole, 'The State System has come to stay'. Lagos, *The Guardian*, September 18, 1984.

Bamigbade, Tunde, 'Time to phase out traditional rule'. Lagos, *National Concord*, May 25, 1984.

Dike, Enwere, 'The Dilemma of Choice of Technology'. Lagos, *The Guardian*, August 10, 1987.

Enahoro, Anthony (Chief), 'Towards a Democratic Nigeria'. Lagos, *The Guardian*, May 22; 23 and 29, 1986.

Igiebor, Nosa et al., 'Democrat Gorbachev Vs. Soviet

Communism'. Lagos, *Newswatch Magazine*, March 2, 1987.

Ikpenwa, Tobias M., 'Nigeria in Ideological Crisis'. Enugu, *Satellite*, July 7, 1983.

Where do we go from here?' Enugu, *Satellite*, July 8, 1983.

Iwere, Ted, 'Who's Press Council', Lagos, *The Guardian,* June 21, 1984.

Izeze, Eluem Emeka, 'The Tottering World of the UN'., Lagos, *The Guardian*, December 7 and 10, 1984.

Jika, Nkem, 'Curbing Unemployment in our Polity'. Lagos, *Sunday Concord*, August 5, 1984.

'Quota System Negates National Growth'. Lagos, *National Concord*, October 3, 1984.

Kale, Oladele O., 'Prospects of Free Health in Nigeria'. Lagos, *The Guardian*, June20 and 21, 1984.

McGill, Peter, 'Japan's Employment System Plagued by High Technology'. Kaduna, *New Nigerian*, September 24, 1983.

Mpinga, James, 'Stripping of Earth's Ozone Layers'. Lagos, *Daily Times*, December 21, 1984.

National Concord Opinion, 'Judicial Reforms'. Lagos, *National Concord*, April13, 1985.

'The Amended Revenue Allocation Formula'. Lagos, *National Concord*, February 4, 1985

NBA Panel's Report on Courts Congestion. Lagos, *The Guardian*, June 7 – 10, 1985.

Nigeria, 50 others sign law of the Sea Treaty. Lagos, *Vanguard*. December 13, 1984.

Nnoli, Okwudiba (Professor), 'Musical Chairs, and Cheers for the Music'. Lagos, *The Guardian*, May 30 and 31, 1984.

Nwabueze, Ben. (Professor), 'Viable Political Order for Nigeria'. Lagos, *The Guardian*, March 21; 22 and 27, 1986.

Nwolise, O. B. C., 'Apartheid as neo-Nazism'. Lagos, *The Guardian*, January 8 and 9, 1985.

Nwosuh, Chika and Obu Udeozor, 'About Checking Out: the truths Andrew hasn't told'. Lagos, *The Guardian*, December 28, 1984.

Obasi, Nnamdi, 'Issues before the Mexico Population Conference'. Lagos, *National Concord*, August 8,1984.

Odum, Fidel, 'The System as a Culprit'. Lagos, *National Concord*, March 22, 1984.

Odusile, Waheed (reporter), 'Prison Congestion Blamed on Police'. Lagos, *National Concord*, March 5, 1985.

Ofeimum, Odia, 'Labour Over-Priced?' Lagos, *The Guardian*, November 22, 1985. 1984.

Ogunbiyi, Yemi (Reporter/Interviewer), 'Awo Speaks', Lagos, *The Guardian*, March 6 and 7, 1985.

Olisa, Michael, 'Way Out of Electoral Malpractices'. Lagos, *National Concord*, April 13, 1985.

Olusanya, G. 0. (Professor), 'Nigeria needs an Ideology'. *National Concord*, February 4, 1985.

Onabule, Duro. (reporter/interviewer), 'Face to Face with Zik'. Lagos, *Sunday Times*, November 20 and 27, 1977

Oyedijo, Adesayo, 'The many evils of corruption'. Lagos, *National Concord*, December 28, 1982.

Russia on the Economic Map of the World. Enugu, Sunday, *Satellite*, September 23, 1984.

Saro-Wiwa, Ken, 'On Federal Character'. Lagos, *The Guardian*, January 22, 1985

Sero, A., 'U.S. Election as "A Contest of Moneybags"'. Lagos, *National Concord*, August 8, 1984.

Uko Ndaeyo (reporter), 'Federal Character Comes Under Attack at Management Dialogue'. Lagos, *The Guardian*, June 27, 1984.

Umaru, Richard, 'What role for traditional rulers?' Lagos, *The Guardian*, September 18, 1984.

Umeakuesie, Ifeanyichukwu, 'Futile search for Ideology'. Lagos, *National Concord*, February 25, 1983.

Umozurike, Oji, 'The State-of-Origin Conundrum'. Lagos, Police. Lagos, *National Concord*, March 5, 1985. *The Guardian*, December 10 and 11. 1984.

UNIDO Cautions Africa. Lagos, *Daily Times*, August 6, Wachukwu, Alozie (Dr.), 'The Presidential System as a Democratised Monarchy'. Enugu, *Satellite*, June 24, 1983.

Wilson, Roger, 'Antarctic minerals and the Third World'. Lagos, *Daily Times*, April 6, 1983

Woodruff, John, 'China to expand Private Economy'. Lagos, *Daily Times*, February 2, 1983.

Mao Tse-Tung, 22
Maoist, 20
Marahrens, Bishop, 32
Marchais, 12
Marx, Karl, 4, 5, ,6, 7, 8, 9, 10,
13, 59, 151 Marxism, 9, 10
Marxist Theory, 5, 10
McGill, Peter, 142
Mediterranean, 216, 224, 236
Mendelssohn, 33
Mercantilism, 37
Middle Class Repression, 4
Middle East, 221
Middlemen, 145, 148
Miller, George A., 42
Mobocracy, 169
Modern Societies, 61, 77, 90, 97, 145
Moi, Arap, 217
Monarch, 161, 162, 163
Monarchy, 4, 161, 162, 163, 164, 165,166, 169, 286
Monopolies, 38
Monopoly, 45, 61, 136, 157, 192, 240, 243

Mpinga, James, 236
Multi-party System, 53, 167, 290
Mussolini, Benito, 25, 26
National Assembly, 279
National Judicial Service
Commission, 285
N a t i o n a l P o p u l a t i o n Commission, 285
National Presidential Council,
286
Nationalism, 183, 184, 185, 186, 188, 189, 190, 193
Nationalization, 43, 44 45, 47, 48, 136, 139
National-will, 249, 253, 254
Nation-States, 100, 172, 185,
189, 193, 201, 218, 243, 280
Natural Disasters, 232
Nazi Party, 9
Nazi, 9, 25, 32, 33, 34
New Economic Policy, 16
New Nigerian, 142
New Society, 7, 9